D0217577

DISRUPTIVE FIXATION

PRINCETON STUDIES IN CULTURE AND TECHNOLOGY
Tom Boellstorff and Bill Maurer, series editors

This series presents innovative work that extends classic ethnographic methods and questions into areas of pressing interest in technology and economics. It explores the varied ways new technologies combine with older technologies and cultural understandings to shape novel forms of subjectivity, embodiment, knowledge, place, and community. By doing so, the series demonstrates the relevance of anthropological inquiry to emerging forms of digital culture in the broadest sense.

Sounding the Limits of Life: Essays in the Anthropology of Biology and Beyond
by Stefan Helmreich, with contributions
from Sophia Roosth and Michele Friedner

Digital Keywords: A Vocabulary of Information Society and Culture
edited by Benjamin Peters

Democracy's Infrastructure: Material Politics and Popular Illegality in South Africa
by Antina von Schnitzler

Everyday Sectarianism in Urban Lebanon: Infrastructures, Public Services, and Power
by Joanne Randa Nucho

Disruptive Fixation: School Reform and the Pitfalls of Techno-Idealism
by Christo Sims

DISRUPTIVE FIXATION

School Reform and the Pitfalls of Techno-Idealism

Christo Sims

PRINCETON UNIVERSITY PRESS

Princeton and Oxford

Copyright © 2017 by Princeton University Press
Published by Princeton University Press, 41 William Street, Princeton,
    New Jersey 08540
In the United Kingdom: Princeton University Press, 6 Oxford Street, Woodstock,
    Oxfordshire OX20 1TR

Excerpts from *Waiting for Godot* by Samuel Beckett, are copyright © 1954 by Grove Press, Inc.
    Copyright © renewed 1982 by Samuel Beckett. Used by permission of Grove/Atlantic, Inc. Any
    third party use of this material, outside of this publication, is prohibited.

press.princeton.edu

page iv: jacket art credit line still to come

All Rights Reserved

Library of Congress Cataloging-in-Publication Data

Names: Sims, Christo, 1978–author.
Title: Disruptive fixation : school reform and the pitfalls of techno-idealism / Christo Sims.
Description: Princeton : Princeton University Press, [2017] | Series: Princeton studies in culture
    and technology | Includes bibliographical references and index.
Identifiers: LCCN 2016021583 | ISBN 9780691163987 (hardcover : acid-free paper) |
    ISBN 9780691163994 (pbk. : acid-free paper)
Subjects: LCSH: Educational change—New York (State)—New York. | Educational technology—New
    York (State)—New York. | Educational anthropology—New York (State)—New York. | Community
    and school—New York (State)—New York. | Social change—New York (State)—New York.
Classification: LCC LA339.N5 S55 2017 | DDC 370.9747—dc23 LC record available at
    https://lccn.loc.gov/2016021583

British Library Cataloging-in-Publication Data is available

This book has been composed in Janson Text

Printed on acid-free paper. ∞

Printed in the United States of America

10 9 8 7 6 5 4 3 2 1

For my parents

Let us not waste our time in idle discourse!
(Pause. Vehemently.) Let us do something, while
we have the chance! It is not every day that we are
needed. Not indeed that we personally are
needed. Others would meet the case equally well,
if not better. To all mankind they were addressed,
those cries for help still ringing in our ears! But at
this place, at this moment of time, all mankind is
us, whether we like it or not. Let us make the
most of it, before it is too late! Let us represent
worthily for once the foul brood to which a cruel
fate consigned us! What do you say? *(Estragon
says nothing.)* It is true that when with folded
arms we weigh the pros and cons we are no less a
credit to our species. The tiger bounds to the help
of his congeners without the least reflexion, or
else he slinks away into the depths of the thickets.
But that is not the question. What are we doing
here, *that* is the question. And we are blessed in
this, that we happen to know the answer. Yes, in
the immense confusion one thing alone is clear.
We are waiting for Godot to come—

—Samuel Beckett, *Waiting for Godot*

Contents

———

Acknowledgments

First and foremost I would like to thank my research participants, for without their generosity, trust, and openness, this project would not have happened. The designers, backers, and educators of the reform project that this book takes as its focus provided me with nearly unfettered access as they attempted to launch an ambitious and highly visible new intervention. Attempting to re-design social systems is a messy process, and doing so in the public eye takes extra courage. Those whose jobs involved trying to bring this new project into being were far more generous and open with me than they needed to be. While I have taken a critical perspective on the modes of intervention of which they (and I) were a part, I hope the project's designers, backers, and educators know that I respect what they were trying to accomplish and that I have no doubts about the sincerity of their philanthropic intentions nor about their dedication to trying to help others. If anything, I hope the book helps convince more people that it is both unrealistic and unfair to place the responsibility for actualizing broader social ideals on the shoulders of so few.

I am also grateful for the generosity of the parents and guardians that participated in the study. Many invited me into their homes and a few became real friends. I have yet to have children of my own, but if and when I do, I will keep these families fondly in mind as I try to navigate the inevitable—and often impossible—dilemmas inherent in processes of child rearing. I also want to offer an especially heartfelt thanks to the students. Being a middle school student is often a confusing, awkward, and painful experience, even for the so-called popular kids. In going to middle school, students learn to judge and be judged, they learn that just about everything they say or do means more than they thought, and they experience seemingly solid friendships that suddenly evaporate, bodies that no longer look or feel the way they used to, and that everyone is changing and it's not at all clear if and how they should change as well. At the same time, middle school can be exhilarating. There are new people, new places, new outfits, new music, new routines, and new things to try out. I feel lucky and grateful that so many young people allowed me into this awkward and bewildering moment in their lives, that they were willing to share their excitements and agonies, and their moments of pride and joy as well as their moments of embarrassment and sorrow. At the end of the day, getting to know these young people was the best part of doing this project.

Beyond the field, I have been supported by such a wide and generous collection of people that I cannot do justice to all of their contributions. Paul Duguid deserves special thanks since he has done more than anyone to help me develop as a scholar. If it were not for Paul, I would not be where I am today, and there is a good chance I would not have made it through graduate school. Paul is one of those rare scholars who puts far more effort into advising than the profession demands or rewards. As I have spent more time in academia, it has become increasingly clear that Paul's approach to advising is as uncommon as it is exceptional. At Berkeley I was also fortunate to receive generous feedback and support from Jean Lave, Barrie Thorne, Peter Lyman, Anno Saxenian, Jenna Burrell, Dan Perkel, Megan Finn, and Janaki Srinivasan, all of whom I thank fully and sincerely. During this time I also had the good fortune to work on several collaborative research projects, and through these experiences I was lucky to receive generous support and mentorship from more senior scholars, most notably Heather Horst, C. J. Pascoe, Becky Herr-Stephenson, danah boyd, Ingrid Erickson, Diana Rhoten, Richard Arum, and Mimi Ito. During my time in New York City, Christina Dunbar-Hester and Jeffrey Lane provided invaluable intellectual guidance and moral support. At UC San Diego, where I now work, I would like to offer special thanks to Robert Horwitz for reading and providing helpful feedback on a full draft of this manuscript, as well as Fernando Domínguez Rubio for reading sizable portions of the manuscript during an especially challenging period of writing. I am also grateful to Lilly Irani, Chandra Mukerji, Vanesa Ribas, Natalia Roudakova, Kelly Gates, and Angela Booker for reading portions of the manuscript, as well as Mike Cole, Stefan Tanaka, Jay Lemke, and the rest of my colleagues in the Department of Communication for their ongoing encouragement and support. Similarly, I would like to thank the two anonymous reviewers, Tom Boellstorff, Fred Appel, and the rest of the Princeton University Press team for their support and for helping me improve the manuscript and learn the academic book-publishing process more generally.

To my family, I offer thanks for years of encouragement, dedication, and love. The older I get, the more I realize how fortunate I am for having grown up with the family I did. It is a debt that I can only hope to repay by drawing on their example in my relations with others. Finally, to Paloma I offer heart-felt gratitude for her ongoing intellectual and emotional support. Writing a book entails its own fixations, and those who are closest to the author share the tolls that these fixations extract in particularly intimate ways. I am especially indebted to Paloma for helping me sustain an enchantment for writing, and for life more generally, throughout this process.

Preface

—————

The practical privilege in which all scientific activity arises never more subtly governs that activity (insofar as science presupposes not only an epistemological break but also a *social* separation) than when, unrecognized as privilege, it leads to an implicit theory of practice which is the corollary of neglect of the social conditions in which science is possible.

—PIERRE BOURDIEU, *Outline of a Theory of Practice*, 1977, 1.

This is a book about how a technologically cutting-edge philanthropic intervention—in this case, the attempt to redesign the American school for the twenty-first century—ended up mostly remaking the status quo, as well as its problems. The book also examines what perennial cycles of techno-philanthropism manage to accomplish—politically and for whom—even as actual interventions routinely fall far short of their stated aims. It is a book about how enduring yearnings for a promised polity and wishful thinking about recent innovations in media technology come to be entwined anew, mostly survive a barrage of unanticipated setbacks, and help produce effects in the world despite decades upon decades of disappointing results.

To help contextualize what follows, readers should know that this is not the book that I set out to write, nor is it based on the study that I originally thought I was conducting, nor am I the same person that I was when I began working on this project. The book and I have changed over the years alongside not only changes in the subject matter, but also changes in the conditions that have allowed me to conduct and write research. Since the book draws special attention to the role of idealism in cutting-edge phil-anthropic interventions and since it makes the argument that this idealism emerges from and is sustained through situated practices, I also reflect on the role that idealism has played in my own pragmatic work activities, first as a technology designer and now as an academic.

Disruptive Fixation is a revision of *The Cutting Edge of Fun* (2012), my PhD thesis for the School of Information at the University of California,

Berkeley. I came to this project after having worked for three years on a large-scale collaborative research project that ethnographically examined the role of digital media in the everyday lives of children and young people coming of age in the United States. That project was funded by the same philanthropic foundation that provided substantial support for the reform project that this book takes as its focus. I was able to gain access to this reform project, as well as to many of the people who worked to bring it into being, in large part because I had worked on the earlier research project. I got involved in both projects partly because I wanted to learn how to do the craft of ethnography and partly because I wanted to develop a better understanding of how contemporary social divisions were being experienced, made, and changed among young people growing up in the so-called digital age. But, and to the point of this preface, I also got involved in both projects because I was trying to find a professional career path that felt socially beneficial and personally meaningful. In this regard, I believe I had quite a bit in common with many of the designers and reformers who are featured in this book, as well as with many of the academics with whom I continue to work.

Graduate school in general, and these projects in particular, were in many ways attempts to bring together my hopes for a more fair and egalitarian social order with my (admittedly privileged) desire to find a career path that was personally fulfilling, challenging, creative, and respected. Graduate school was not my first attempt to knit together these disparate yearnings. I entered graduate school in 2005 after having worked for five years in the quickly changing profession that nowadays refers to itself as interaction design, user-experience design, or, even more ambitiously, just experience design. I had found my way into this facet of the new economy as a twenty-one-year-old who was quite unsure about what to do after graduating from college. Mostly I knew what I did not want to do. When I graduated from college, many of my classmates were headed toward what I considered to be well-heeled establishment professions: fields like management consulting, finance, and the law. It was against these grooved pathways into elite factions of adult working life that the emerging world of interaction design appeared to offer a more creative, exciting, and socially beneficial route. What is more, I was able to find a position in a company that worked exclusively for not-for-profit organizations. At the time I thought I had found a way to develop a career that was both socially beneficial and cutting edge, and at first I was quite enchanted with my job.

After several years that enchantment began to fade. At the time I attributed my growing disillusionment to the fact that most of the projects on which I had worked were for marketing purposes. Even though we were working for not-for-profit organizations, we were still in the business of selling and manipulating, and, as such, my career seemed to be headed toward the same sorts of establishment professions that I had been trying to avoid.

I did, however, continue to enjoy working on experimental design projects with my colleagues, most of whom were young and tech-savvy graduates of the Rhode Island School of Design. While working on these tech-design projects, we often felt as if we were helping to invent the future, but I worried that we were doing so for the wrong purposes. In an attempt to distance myself from marketing while continuing to develop professional expertise in technology design, I began to think about going to graduate school.

When I enrolled at The School of Information at UC Berkeley, I hoped that graduate school would allow me to learn how to do research, and particularly ethnographic research, for technology design projects that helped people. My experience in the world of tech design had introduced me to the term *ethnography*, and I thought graduate school was a place where I could begin to learn that craft. Within the worlds of professional technology designers, ethnography was often idealized as a way to help correct for the shortcomings of many social engineering and design interventions. From this human-centered design perspective, designer-ethnographers were positioned on the side of users in a collective struggle against the seemingly alienating forces of poorly designed technologies and institutions. Designer-ethnographers, from this perspective, were in the business of helping technology designers, engineers, aid workers, educators, government bureaucrats, health care practitioners, managers, and other knowledge workers develop a better understanding of their users, customers, citizens, students, patients, and so forth. Ethnographically informed design, from this perspective, would help organizations and technologists design products, services, and experiences that were more attuned to their users everyday needs and circumstances. It was this idealization of design-ethnography that largely reenchanted my otherwise pragmatic decision to go to graduate school.

Not long after entering graduate school, I got involved in the first of the two research projects mentioned earlier. I was a master's student at the time and I joined the project still thinking I might return to the world of tech design when I graduated. Initially I did not think much about the philanthropic foundation that sponsored our work nor about what they might be trying to do. As with my earlier forays into technology design, being involved in this project seemed like an opportunity to develop a career that was cutting edge and socially beneficial. The philanthropic foundation that supported the project had a long history of trying to promote social justice agendas, and their new interest in ethnography and technology resonated with the sort of expertise that I was hoping to develop. Equally important, working on the project was a way to get through graduate school without taking on a lot of debt. As with before, my idealism about the philanthropic character of my work was intimately entwined with practical concerns.

As I transitioned into the PhD program, I learned more about the larger philanthropic initiative that was funding our work. For example, I learned that the foundation had grown disillusioned with its previous years of educational grant making and had abruptly redirected its entire educational grant making toward investigating the seemingly unprecedented opportunities for learning that the rise of digital media was making possible. The research project on which I was working was in the vanguard of this new philanthropic direction, and over approximately the next ten years the foundation would spend more than $200 million on various research projects and design interventions focused on digital media and learning. I was employed on various research projects sponsored by this initiative for about eight of those years, and throughout this time I often shared, and helped construct, idealizations like the ones that this book problematizes.

As I increasingly came to see myself as an academic, I assumed that my contribution to this broader initiative was to help to produce academic knowledge that designers and practitioners would then apply in real-world situations and interventions. Such a view was reinforced by the way the foundation organized its grant making, which was split into two main streams, one for research and the other for design. I was funded on the research side, and in several cases designers did try to translate our research into seemingly cutting-edge interventions. But what I did not yet fully understand was that in many ways the relationship between research and design was reversed. Particular commitments about how to make social change had already enframed the sorts of problems and questions that those of us on the research side would pose and seek to answer. In particular, it was always already assumed that some sort of designed educational intervention involving new media technologies would be the way to make beneficial social change. What we could not as easily consider was that perhaps cutting-edge educational interventions, in whatever configuration, were not capable of, and perhaps even detrimental to, realizing the philanthropic goals that the foundation had set for itself.

I came to realize the degree to which my research and I were caught up with these commitments rather slowly. When I first began designing the research project that has grown into this book, I imagined that I would conduct an academic study that contributed to debates about the roles of technological change in processes of social reproduction and change. I had been inspired by classic ethnographic studies of young people's cultural contributions to these processes, and especially Paul Willis' (1977) *Learning to Labor* and Penelope Eckert's (1989) *Jocks and Burnouts*, both of which stressed how the cultural practices of student peer cultures mediated processes of cultural and social reproduction. Impressed by these works, I wanted to see if and how these dynamics might be different in new times and at a school that had been imagined as a replacement for conventional schooling.

With these works in mind, I began fieldwork, diligently trying to build relationships with the students who attended the innovative new school (see appendix). I wanted to understand these young people's cultural worlds on their own terms, figuring that doing so would let me say something about how their cultural practices mediated broader social and historical processes. During this period of my research, my observations of and interactions with the other people and things that also passed through the new school—technology designers, school reformers, teachers, parents, journalists, media artifacts, and so on—felt like interludes from my real focus. I was, if you will, fixated on getting to know the students and their school-based cultural worlds.

But I also kept track of these other actors in my field notes, and as I did I eventually started to ask myself what was bringing them, as well as myself, into and through the experimental reform project. I began to write about this shift when, several months after the school opened, a television crew visited the school. As the crew constructed a shot of students using the school's most awe-inspiring new technology, another visitor to the school, a scholar and designer from South Korea, remarked to me, "This is surreal. The kids aren't just studying the media, they're in the media." When I wrote my field notes that evening I also wrote a memo about the incident. At first I was curious how the students might have felt being "in the media" and, particularly, whether it contributed to a sense that they and the school were unique and special. But then I started writing about what was left out of the TV crew's frame but included within my own. I compared the representations that the TV crew produced to the ones that I was producing in my field notes, the latter of which also included the TV crew. At first I felt rather self-satisfied in having a more expansive perspective than the journalists, but then I had the eerie feeling that someone could just as easily make a representation of the scene that included me representing the television crew representing the students with the technology. It was then that I started to consider that I too might be "in the media," that is, caught in the phenomenon that I thought I was studying.

On one level, this realization was a moment of coming to terms with what I had previously only read about, namely, the politics of ethnographic representations, which have rightly received much critical attention among anthropologists since the 1980s (Clifford and Marcus, eds. 1986). My satisfaction in having a wider frame than the television crew was caught up with the modernist dream of producing unsituated scientific knowledge, a dream that Michel de Certeau (1984, 92) famously characterized as the "lust to be viewpoint and nothing more." But it was also the beginning of my wrestling with what we might call a politics of entanglement. I began to realize that I was not just producing representations of these worlds in the name of ethnography or social science; I was also actively participating in the production and maintenance of the worlds that I was studying, not just by way of my participant-observation research method, but also by way of my being a researcher who had a legitimate place studying a site such as this.

Over time it became increasingly clear to me that my work and I were entangled not only with the philanthropic foundation's commitments about how to make social change, but also with the processes that construct and sustain techno-philanthropism more generally. Over several years I came to see that it was these broader processes, as well as my entanglements with them, that I was trying to understand and navigate. With time I came to see that all the actors that I had initially placed on the margins of my research frame—the school's designers, parents, NGOs, philanthropists and philanthropic foundations, academic researchers including myself, journalists and pundits, politicians and government officials, companies developing and selling supposedly beneficent media and technologies, audiences that consumed accounts celebrating innovative philanthropic interventions, and so forth—were taking part in producing, sustaining, and reconfiguring what I describe in this book as disruptive fixation.

As I tried to better understand and navigate these social and political entanglements, I also began to see that some of my peers in graduate school were facing surprisingly similar dilemmas despite studying what appeared to be quite disparate phenomena. In particular, I kept finding myself with much to talk about with peers who were participating in undertakings that seemed equally cutting edge and philanthropic, ones that brought together scholars, ethnographers, technology designers, NGOs, government agencies, large and small companies, on-the-ground practitioners, and so forth: the world of Information and Communication Technologies for Development, or ICTD. The processes and rhetorics that we were documenting and trying to analyze, while importantly different, bore strong family resemblances, and in some cases they even involved the same people, organizations, artifacts, and rhetorics.

I now see that this familial resemblance, as well as our ability to recognize it, was partly a product of the somewhat ambiguous location that Information Schools inhabited within the academy at the time. On the one hand, the distinctive specializations of Information Schools were not yet well defined. Information, we came to realize, was a term that could refer to just about anything, and, as such, the term—as well as those of us who claimed to specialize in it—routinely traveled across numerous disciplinary divisions. While such amblings were naïve and fret with hazards, they did allow some of us to begin to trace connections across realms of specialization that were typically kept apart. On the other hand, our ambiguous, and frankly fantastic, claim to be experts in information or the digital also attracted the interest of powerful groups and funding sources, such as the National Science Foundation, transnational technology corporations, large philanthropic foundations, and so forth. This combination of an ambiguously defined expertise that was nevertheless supported by established networks of power allowed some of us slowly, and with guidance, to develop critical perspectives on these arrangements from the inside.

And yet, and to return to the theme of this preface, our possibilities for developing and voicing these perspectives have also been structured by the different conditions in and through which each of us is trying to make a living since finishing our PhDs, conditions which tend to foster and sustain their own flavors of fixation. Some of us have found jobs in academic departments that are somewhat protected from the pressure to secure large grants, others are working in industry, state institutions, NGOs, or academic departments that are under intense pressures to secure funding from state, corporate, and philanthropic institutions. In any case, the institutional conditions through which each of us is attempting to make a meaningful career are shaping what we can and will say to whom, as well as how we idealize and sanctify our work.

I raise these points in the preface because while the book that follows focuses primarily on technology designers, reformers, and other "applied" professions, the concept of fixation, as this book develops it, is as much a problem for those of us who make our living as academics as it is for anyone else.[1] The presumed distinction between academic and applied domains of expertise is one such fixation, and like the idealizations that this book examines, it persists and exerts the forces that it does in part because so many of us who enjoy the practical privilege of calling our work academic repeatedly repair and sustain it.

San Diego, California
April, 2016

1

INTRODUCTION

We are familiar with social reformers who promise cutting-edge remedies for entrenched social problems. We are accustomed, for example, to arguments that herald recent breakthroughs in information and communication technologies for their potential to reinvent outmoded educational systems, to develop areas of the world with high rates of poverty, or to knit together the planet in a harmonious way. Perhaps we have heard about how Massively Open Online Courses will radically democratize access to education and hence opportunities, how low-cost computers and cell phones will launch impoverished nations and persons into the digital age, or how the Internet will bring together people across divisions of nation, class, and tribe. Further in the past, some may recall confident claims about how film, radio, television, and then computers would make for a radically more efficient and engaging educational system, how electronic media would bring forth a harmonious global village, or how the printing press would create a whole new democratic world. If we are familiar with claims of this sort, then we should also be aware that philanthropic interventions premised on these arguments have repeatedly fallen short of reformers' lofty aspirations, often dramatically so.[1] If we are aware of this history, then we should not be surprised when a new cutting-edge philanthropic intervention is unable to fulfill the good intentions of those who designed and proselytized it. What is puzzling is how so many of us hope, and even demand, that the next time will be different.

I was on hand when one of these next times was unveiled in the borough of Manhattan, New York City, in the late summer of 2009. After several years of research and design, an expert team of media technology designers, academic specialists, and educational reformers opened the Downtown School for Design, Media, and Technology—henceforth the Downtown School—with a single sixth grade class.[2] The school was a centerpiece in an ambitious new philanthropic initiative that aspired to reinvent educational systems for the twenty-first century. According to the project's designers and philanthropic backers, both the world and children had changed in dramatic ways, but educational institutions had not kept up. We were living in a radically new, interconnected, technologically saturated, and unequal era, the school's designers and backers argued, and inherited educational institutions had become woefully out of date. The Downtown School would help overcome this disconnect by opening the school to the world and meeting students where they presumably lived their lives. It would be a "school for digital kids," as the school's tagline read, and the entire pedagogy would be organized like a game. Instead of the rote and boring activities that were common at conventional schools, students at the Downtown School would spend their days actively and creatively working through complex challenges in designed game worlds. Rather than passively consuming media, technology, and knowledge, students at the Downtown School would learn to be creative makers, remixers, and hackers of technology and culture. Instead of taking on the identity of obedient pupils, students at the Downtown School would role-play the identities of scientists, designers, inventors, programmers, entrepreneurs, and other tech-savvy creative professionals. What is more, the school would offer its services to students from any background. Thus the new school would equitably and engagingly prepare young people for the increasingly interconnected and competitive world and job market of the twenty-first century.

This vision of a school designed for the realities of the twenty-first century garnered enviable support and interest for a new public school. Between 2005 and 2015, one of the most prestigious philanthropic foundations in the United States gave millions of dollars to the nonprofit organization that designed and launched the Downtown School, and it spent more than $200 million on related research projects and interventions focused on digital media and learning. Other powerful philanthropic foundations also generously supported the school and its designers' associated projects. The Chancellor of New York City public schools granted the Downtown School special status as an "innovation zone" school, allowing it to bypass some of the bureaucratic hurdles that encumbered experimentation in more conventional public schools, and the Department of Education gave the school premium space in the heart of one of Manhattan's most renowned cultural districts. Transnational media and technology companies, local universities, and nonprofit organizations donated equipment, space, and services. The Downtown School had more laptops than students, the latest hardware and software for making and hacking media technologies, and one of only two "semi-immersive embodied learning environments" in the world. In addition to teachers, administrators, and staff, the school hosted an in-house team of media-technology designers and curriculum specialists. In short, the school was as well supported as just about any experimental new public school could hope.

Before it opened, many other people were already taking a special interest in the school, and over the next several years the school's fame and influence would spread widely. In the spring and summer before its first year, scores of intrigued parents attended information sessions, many applied, and more than a few were distraught when their child was not admitted. During the school's first few years, local, national, and international news organizations produced and ran hopeful stories about the new school, and the *New York Times Magazine* even featured the Downtown School as the cover story for its yearly education issue. New corporate partners, including one of the largest video game developers in the world, joined the founders' efforts to design game-based learning environments. One of the largest and most powerful philanthropic foundations in the world hired one of the school's founders to locate and fund similar experiments in digital media and learning. Educational reformers from South Korea to Los Angeles visited the school as they worked to launch similar projects back home. Philanthropists, technology designers, policymakers, academics, educational practitioners, and social entrepreneurs hosted the school's designers, educators, and even select students to make presentations about their innovative experiment in locations as varied as Aspen, Austin, and Doha. Members of the United States Congress and officials from the White House invited the school's designers to forums and workshops on the future of education. In all these cases, the Downtown School was celebrated as one of the most innovative and promising attempts to redesign schooling in the first decades of the new millennium, one that swept away antiquated educational conventions and replaced them with an innovative and improvisational culture that was more akin to a Silicon Valley startup than a traditional public school.

Long before I stopped fieldwork in 2012, the Downtown School had become much like the schools that it had been designed to replace, and it was helping to remake many of the problems that it had been designed to remedy. The school's founders and backers had imagined a playful game-based pedagogy in which students, rather than teachers, took the lead, and yet daily life at the school quickly turned into a lot of tightly scripted behavior and familiar relations of power. They had hoped to connect students and the school to the world, and yet in countless areas reformers, educators, and especially involved parents worked to close it off. They aspired to uproot inherited social hierarchies and yet ended up with a system that entrenched more deeply many of those same inequities.

And yet throughout my time in the field, many smart and well-intentioned people continued to portray the Downtown School, as well as the larger initiative of which it was a part, as a cutting-edge and morally just model of social reform that was worthy of emulation. What is more, they often did so with passion, sincerity, and conviction. If history is a guide, these swells of idealism will eventually recede. But history also suggests that other seemingly cutting-edge philanthropic initiatives will take the Downtown School's place, and swells of hopeful optimism will once again come rushing forth. How is it that this idealism, while temporarily tarnished by recurring shortcomings and failures, does not take long to renew? Why does techno-philanthropism seem immune to the lessons of history?[3] How, in other words, do we reconcile recurring "failure" with persistence? These are the central questions that this book explores.

This is a book about how genuine frustrations with the status quo and understandable yearnings for social change are converted, again and again, into seemingly cutting-edge philanthropic interventions that not only fall far short of reformers' aspirations, but that often also help sustain and extend the status quo, as well as its problems. It is a book that addresses how concerns about the putrescence of inherited institutions as well as longings for a promised polity come to be fixated on apparently unprecedented versions of familiar mechanisms for making social change, despite decades upon decades of disappointing results. By examining these processes ethnographically, the book investigates how optimism and idealism for new rounds of techno-philanthropism spring forth and mostly survive encounters that should seemingly deflate them. The book also examines what this perennial rejuvenation of optimism and idealism manages to accomplish, even as enthusiasm for a particular disruptive project or movement eventually recedes.

This book explores these themes by taking a close look at one recent attempt to radically redesign, or "disrupt," education. Educational reform projects are especially common places where philanthropic yearnings repeatedly come together with hopeful idealizations about the transformative powers of recent technological breakthroughs (Cuban 1986; Buckingham 2007), but they are far from the only places where these yearnings and idealizations recurrently conjoin. Some of the most illuminating literature that I read while working on this project focused not just on the perennial character of seemingly cutting-edge educational reforms (Tyack and Cuban 1995; Varenne and McDermott 1998; Lashaw 2008; Labaree 2008; Mehta 2013; Ames 2015), but also on international development programs and humanitarian interventions (Ferguson 1994; Escobar 1995; Li 2007; Fassin 2010), as well as on techno-scientific schemes for social improvement more generally (Latour 1988; Akrich 1992; Bowker and Star 1999; Brown and Duguid 2000; Suchman 2006, 2011; Morozov 2013). Indeed, the problems and processes that this book investigates appear to arise whenever social reformers knit together yearnings for what they see as beneficent social change with seemingly unprecedented techno-political solutions (Scott 1998; Rose 1999; Mitchell 2002).

While the themes that this book explores have broad pertinence, education is also remarkable for the extent to which it is repeatedly targeted for disruption, especially in the United States. This ambiguous distinction is partly because idealizations about education, like the market, are tightly interwoven with the state's and the polity's sense of themselves in the United States. As American educational historians have demonstrated (Tyack and Cuban 1995; Labaree 2008), when social reformers in the United States have yearned for a more idealized polity, they have repeatedly attempted to fix education, and particularly public schools, as a—if not the—means for transforming their longings into reality. This recurring tendency has not only made the school instrumental, but it has also made it difficult to question the institution too profoundly without also questioning the state and the polity. As such, public debates about education reform tend to focus narrowly on how to fix educational structures rather than on asking whether these are the right structures to be fixing in order to bring about hoped-for social outcomes.

This book takes a different approach. The book does not systematically diagnose the shortcomings and successes of this particular attempt to disrupt education, nor does it prescribe better ways to do education reform or technology design. Rather, the book examines a concrete attempt to disrupt education in order to offer an intimate perspective on how more widespread and enduring yearnings come to be interwoven with especially optimistic ideas and feelings about the transformative potential of recent technological breakthroughs.[4] The book also takes a close look at how this braiding recurs and produces concrete effects in the world despite its routine failure to accomplish wished for outcomes.

While the case of the Downtown School is distinctive, it can take us to the heart of some of the most hotly debated questions about technological innovation, social change, and, hence, the social and political ordering of modern life. Wherever new technologies are advanced as a novel means for disrupting the status quo, public discussions tend to be deeply divided between those who are generally, if not enthusiastically, optimistic about these enterprises, and those who are predominantly, if not profoundly, cynical. These seemingly irreconcilable divisions are partly a consequence of the audiences to which each side addresses themselves. Optimists tend to address reformers, technology designers, policymakers, engineers, business people, and activists, and, as such, their discourses tend to be managerial, technocratic, and focused on potentialities. Cynics, by contrast, tend to write for other social and cultural theorists, and, accordingly, their discourses tend to be demystifying and sometimes alarmist. These divisions are also rooted in opposed assumptions about how each side understands the "real" function of the domain that reformers aim to disrupt, as well as quasi-deterministic assumptions about the role that new technologies and techniques will play in these processes. Optimists often take it as a given that liberal institutions are fundamentally beneficent but broken (and, hence, in need of fixing) or lacking (and, hence, in need of enhancement). By contrast, more cynical accounts tend to treat these institutions as instruments that accomplish the (often unstated) interests of entrenched structures of power.

A quick glance at stalemated debates around education reform helps illustrate this dynamic. Optimists of education reform tend to fall into a long and dominant liberal tradition that understands public education as one of the main mechanisms for creating an enlightened, egalitarian, and united polity. According to this liberal perspective, hierarchical social divisions are commensurate with democratic values so long as these inequalities have been accomplished meritocratically. When confronted with systemic inequities in education and society—which conventional sociology of education consistently identifies—a key question for liberal reformers is how to redesign education so as to create equal opportunities for all.[5] And, as we will see, one repeatedly seductive means for trying to fix education so as to fix society is to try to leverage the seemingly unprecedented possibilities of recent innovations in media technology (Cuban 1986; Buckingham 2000, 2007).

Against these dominant perspectives, cynics of educational reform tend to see public education not as a means for realizing an idealized polity, but rather as a mechanism for producing, maintaining, and extending a hierarchical and governable social order. As social reproduction theorists have argued since the 1970s, schools do not so much dismantle inherited structures of power as help reproduce and extend them (Althusser 1971; Bowles and Gintis 1976; Bourdieu and Passeron 1977; Collins 2009).[6] From this perspective, public education is understood as an apparatus of the capitalist state or, more recently, as part of a governmental dispositif that mechanistically produces and differentiates subjects so as to guide them onto the uneven circuits of a capitalist and technocratic social and political order. Similarly, cynics tend to argue that new educational interventions reconfigure and extend these techniques and technologies of control even further, beyond the school and throughout one's lifetime (Deleuze 1992; Rose 1999).

While optimists and cynics typically hold opposing assumptions about the inherent function of educational institutions, they ironically tend to share similar assumptions about the special role that new technologies play in these processes. Both optimists and cynics tend to assign to new techno-scientific breakthroughs a predominant, if not determining, role in their accounts, they just cast these new technologies as heroes and villains, respectively. Optimists tend to see techno-scientific innovations as finally allowing education to make good on its democratic promises, whereas cynics tend to see the deployment of new technologies as reinforcing the reach and power of technocratic modes of control.

Both of these perspectives are important, but both are also unsatisfying theoretically and politically. Both optimists and cynics tend to be hamstrung by functionalist assumptions about the real purpose of educational institutions—or the capitalist state, or development, or techno-science—as well as deterministic assumptions about the role that new technologies and techniques play in these processes. As Paul Willis (1977) astutely pointed out about educational debates in the 1970s and as James Ferguson (1994) echoed in his reading of the development literature in the 1980s, optimists tend to naively accept the official definition of these enterprises and hence overlook the ways in which philanthropically sanctioned interventions are always sites of power relations and politics.[7] By treating development or educational reform as technocratic exercises, optimists depoliticize these endeavors as well as the problems they are designed to solve.

Yet more cynical accounts are often also problematic because they tend to treat designed interventions as mechanistic black boxes. In the case of educational debates, the problem is not that cynics are wrong for trying to debunk the diagnoses, prescriptions, and ideologies of liberal reformers; nor are they wrong for pointing out that educational interventions routinely help produce and legitimate unjust political and social orders. The problem is that cynics tend to rely on ideal types to explain these phenomena, and, as such, they tend to treat the outcomes as a forgone conclusion. From such a perspective, the incredibly heterogeneous ensemble of actors that have to be assembled in order for a philanthropic intervention to come to life are unsatisfactorily portrayed as either conspiring in an elite agenda or blinded by dominant ideologies and rationalities. Empirically, such claims are not satisfactory since ethnographic inquiry has long shown that there is no smooth congruence between the interests and strategies of elite groups and the complicated medley of events that actually transpire in and through the situated practices of a reform endeavor.[8] Additionally, cynics tend to imply that those who are targeted by philanthropic intervention are "cultural dopes," to borrow a phrase from Stuart Hall (1981), interpellated by capitalist ideologies or, more recently, seduced by neoliberal modes of governmentality (Rose 1999). In either case, resistance, acquiescence, and negotiation tend to be overlooked as constitutive forces in the actualization of a philanthropic intervention. What is more, both boosters and cynics tend to attribute to expert-designed interventions powers that they do not in fact have. As Ferguson astutely observed about debates between optimists and cynics of international development programs, "Empirically, 'development' projects in Lesotho do not generally bring about any significant reduction in poverty, but neither do they bring about significant economic transformations. They do not bring about 'development' in either of the two senses identified above, nor are they set up in such a way that they ever could" (1994, 16). As the chapters that follow illustrate, a similar inadequacy characterizes purportedly unprecedented attempts to disrupt education.

TECHNO-PHILANTHROPISM IN PRACTICE

If debates about cutting-edge philanthropic interventions appear to be stuck in a familiar stalemate, then perhaps what is most needed are theoretical and methodological approaches that refuse the assumptions of either camp. For both Willis and Ferguson, the key shift that was needed in order to move beyond this unsatisfactory stalemate was to forgo assumptions about the inherent purposes of planned interventions and to instead look *ethnographically* at how these projects actually worked as well as what they managed to produce, even as they often failed to fulfill their professed aims. Ethnography was needed, these authors argued, so as to hold off the functionalist assumptions that often undergird the work of both optimists and cynics, and interviews were inadequate because researchers could not expect participants in these worlds to report fully or accurately on what transpired.

How can we build on these insights?

Anthropologists Dorothy Holland and Jean Lave (2001, 2009) have developed one powerful mode for conducting such an inquiry, which they refer to as "social practice theory." Rooted in a historical and material conception of social life, Holland and Lave suggest that the starting point for an inquiry into the workings and consequences of a designed intervention should be persons-in-practices, that is, persons being made through their participation in a historically produced world as they simultaneously help make the world what it is through their participation in it.

Such a perspective has important implications for how scholars come to understand the ways in which different actors contribute to continuity and change. From this perspective, participants in a philanthropic intervention actively and creatively help make history through their materially mediated cultural practices and productions, but they do so on an inherited terrain that is highly uneven and with cultural resources that they did not invent. One way that they do so is by participating in socially differentiated and culturally figured worlds that preexist their arrival. Rather than seeing these historical formations as fields, as would be the case in a Bourdieuian problematic, or as complexes or assemblages, as would be the case in many political-economic and poststructural analytics, Holland and her colleagues developed the notion of "figured worlds" (Holland et al. 1998), which has much in common with Lave's notion of "communities of practice" (Lave and Wenger 1991). One of the advantages of these conceptions of historically differentiated domains of praxis is that they help analysts resist the temptation to reduce participants in a philanthropic intervention to either strategic actors pursuing their interests or puppets in broader political-economic and discursive structures. Instead, both notions draw attention to how culture and structure make and remake each other through people's ongoing participation in the situated practices that sustain and change different figured worlds. From this social practice theory perspective, it is through people's participation in historically produced, intersecting, and culturally figured worlds of practice that broader structures of power and privilege are reproduced and changed, even if these effects are not the aim of a world's participants.

Thus, for Holland and Lave the foci and loci of both continuity and change are "local contentious practices," which can be understood as the concrete activities through which history-in-person and history-in-institutionalized-struggles are coproduced (2009, 2–5). The notion of local contentious practice is similar to the concept of friction, as developed by Anna Tsing (2005) to account for how global connections are historically made and animated, as well as Tania Murray Li's (1999, 2007) and Gillian Hart's (2004, 2009) recommendation to attend to how regimes of rule inevitably involve compromises, unexpected contingencies, and contradictions, especially as rationalities of rule are transformed into efforts to enact them. All these scholars encourage analysts to pay attention to the ways power relations and politics are manifest in even the most quotidian realms of social life, and they ask us to notice how everyday struggle, contestation, acquiescence, and negotiation are *constitutive forces* in designed interventions and, hence, in processes of structural production and change. They also encourage scholars to attend to the slippages, fissures, and contradictions that characterize any social reform endeavor, for it is in these openings that alternative possibilities for more far-reaching changes can in part be found.

Another key advantage of examining disruptive philanthropic interventions through the lens of social practice theory is that doing so provides guidance for understanding how those who participate in an intervention often contribute to the maintenance and expansion of the very structures that they aim to dislodge and dismantle. Holland and her colleagues give particular emphasis to the importance of collective imaginings in social life, what they call the "as if" character of figured worlds. According to this perspective, the experts who design and attempt to implement a cutting-edge philanthropic intervention coordinate their thoughts, emotions, and activity in part through collectively realized fictions, dreams, myths, and even fantasies. For example, Holland and her colleagues note how participants in the figured world of heterosexual dating and romance on college campuses in the United States act *as if* women have to worry about whether they are attractive to men and how participants in some figured worlds within academia act *as if* books are so important that they spend years writing them, even though few people may actually read them, let alone understand what their authors had hoped to convey (Holland et al. 1998, 49).

Paying attention to the *as if* character of social life is especially important when studying the figured worlds of the people who design and carry out seemingly disruptive philanthropic interventions because most participants in these worlds act *as if* what they are doing is both novel and beneficent for others—or at least that their collective efforts could be so with more tweaks and adjustments. In the case of seemingly unprecedented educational interventions, designers and reformers coordinate their activity, thoughts, and feelings *as if* they are disrupting inherited institutional arrangements so as to help remedy social problems, such as opportunity gaps and social divisions. By and large, the people that inhabit these worlds are not cynical, nor have they simply been interpellated by a dominant group's ideology. In many cases, experts participate in these worlds not only sincerely, but often also passionately (Lashaw 2008, 2010).

To say that the figured worlds of the people who design and implement a cutting-edge philanthropic intervention are produced in part through the realization of collective fictions is not to say that these fictions are just ideology, instances of false consciousness, or some other (presumably wrong) mental content that is simply in need of enlightened debunking (Mosco 2004, 22–31).[9] Nor are these fictions just culture, in the conventional sense of internalized schemes of norms, values, beliefs, and so forth. Rather, these *as if* imaginings exist and operate as *lived fictions* for participants in a figured world. These fictions exist only so long as they are repeatedly and collectively realized in and through reformers' coordinated material practices. They have to be constantly remade, maintained, and repaired in order to survive. Reformers' embodied skills, ensembles of discursive and material artifacts, and configured environments structure—and are structured by—these lived fictions. From such a perspective, skills, artifacts, and environments are not simply means that facilitate, support, or mediate what really matters (e.g., experts' philanthropic plans and intentions); rather, they are mediums through which reformers' practices, and their fictions, take the forms that they do. What is more, by coordinating activity in part through these lived fictions, participants in a philanthropic intervention produce social relations and other effects that are not imaginary.[10] All social reality, from this perspective, entails the ongoing production and maintenance of collectively lived fictions.

Without the continuous production and maintenance of these collectively lived imaginings, the figured worlds of the experts who design and enact disruptive philanthropic interventions, as they are currently organized, would fall apart. Recognizing as much draws our attention away from various forms of top-down determinism and toward the concrete work by which various actors' lived fictions are sustained, repaired, and renovated in practice. Such work is especially important in the figured worlds of experts who design and implement cutting-edge philanthropic interventions because their efforts are constantly under assault, both from within their figured world—as different factions jockey for resources, status, and approaches while also struggling to get a grip on problems they do not have the power to solve—and from various outsiders who criticize specific reformers and projects for failing to make good on their promises. When seen in this light, the endurance of these figured worlds is a rather stunning feat that raises important anthropological and political questions. Any explanation of how designers, reformers, and other experts contribute to the construction, maintenance, and extension of broader regimes of rule needs to account for how their collectively lived fictions are maintained, repaired, and renovated despite round after round of often disappointing setbacks.

DISRUPTIVE FIXATION

The chapters that follow investigate the cyclical processes by which swells of optimism and idealism for seemingly disruptive philanthropic interventions often produce a countercurrent, or undertow, that paradoxically helps lock social processes into enduring and regressive forms while also, and ironically, renewing faith in the promise of more rounds of cutting-edge interventions. As shorthand, I call this recurring, yet ultimately contingent, cycle disruptive fixation.

To sketch the movements and rhythms of this cyclical process, it is helpful to consider the polysemous character of the term *fixation*. In common contemporary usage, the term fixation often refers to a seemingly unhealthy psychological, cognitive, or cathectic attachment, much like an obsession or an idée fixe. Fixation, in this sense, has to do with directing intense emotional, cognitive, and perceptive energies towards something in particular while excluding awareness of and concern for just about everything else. When people use the term in this way they often do so pejoratively and with the implication that whomever is fixated needs to get over their obsession. In a related, but less pejorative, sense, the term fixation can also mean directing one's gaze towards a particular object. Like the more pejorative use of the term, this sense of the term fixation also implies a narrowness of view, yet such intense focus is not necessarily considered a bad thing, and indeed one could argue that any form of craftwork involves countless instances of fixing one's attention rather narrowly and intensely (see appendix).

Both of these uses of the term *fixation* refer to subjective phenomena, and both are fairly recent inventions. But there is also a much older, less psychological, and less pejorative use of fixation. With roots in alchemic practices, fixation can also refer to processes that transform volatile energies and forces into something more settled and stable. In this sense, fixation refers to material processes of trying to make order from apparent disorder, of trying to get a grip on forces that appear to be unwieldy and out of control. It is from this notion of fixation that we now typically use the phrase *to fix*.

While these different senses of fixation are often used independently, in cases of techno-philanthropism they are perhaps more helpfully understood as mutually constitutive. When we consider the different notions of fixation together, our attention is drawn to how attempts to design and enact seemingly cutting-edge philanthropic interventions tend to produce fixation, in both senses of the term. Some of these fixations are akin to the lived fictions that Holland and her colleagues identified as constitutive of all figured worlds. So, for example, the people who design a cutting-edge educational intervention act *as if* their intervention is both innovative and capable of uprooting entrenched social problems, like bureaucratic rigidity, inequality of opportunity, and social division. These collectively realized fixations are not problematic in themselves because they help coordinate activity, emotion, and thought, but they can become problematic under conditions in which specialists are tasked to fix problems that they do not have the power to solve. Under such conditions, attempts to disrupt the status quo can paradoxically remake and extend the regimes of rule that reformers aim to dismantle, while also, and ironically, renewing confidence in the philanthropic potential of similarly inadequate remedies.

How does this happen?

Fixation, in the sense of tunnel vision, occurs through the processes by which concerns about the status quo and yearnings for social change— what the anthropologist Tania Murray Li (2007) refers to as the "will to improve"—are translated into concrete programs of expert designed intervention. These fixations allow reformers to imagine and design interventions that they can foreseeably implement and to argue for their project's moral relevance to themselves and potential supporters. But they also produce blind spots and distortions of just about everything that cannot be easily measured with their diagnostic tools or manipulated with their proposed remedies. Critically, part of what this tunnel vision often excludes are political-economic relations, which is why James Ferguson (1994) famously characterized the development industry as an "anti-politics machine."

As Li (2007) helped explicate, this tunnel vision occurs through two key and interrelated processes that allow yearnings for beneficent social change to be translated into designed interventions. The first is problematization and the second is what Li, drawing on Rose (1999) and Mitchell (2002), calls "rendering technical."[11] Problematization refers to the processes by which reformers specify problems that need to be fixed or improved. So, for example, the founders of the Downtown School problematized many aspects of conventional approaches to schooling—its severing of the school from the rest of the world, its reliance on top-down and tightly scripted pedagogic activities, its disregard for students' out-of-school lives and interests, and so forth—all of which, according to these problematizations, prevented schooling from fulfilling its liberal-democratic promises.

Rendering technical refers to the ways by which experts imagine and conceptualize the worlds into which they plan to intervene as both intelligible with, and amenable to, the instruments they have on hand or are designing. To make these worlds intelligible and seemingly fixable with the tools in hand, reformers render the worlds into which they plan to intervene as made up of bounded systems of objective relations that their diagnostic instruments can accurately measure and their designed interventions can foreseeably manage and transform. In this sense, rendering technical is akin to Scott's (1998) famous analysis of "state simplifications," Mitchell's (2002) and Callon's (1998) notion of "enframing," and Suchman's (2006), Brown and Duguid's (2000), and Dourish's (2007) respective analyses of the reductive idealizations used by technology designers. Critically, the solutions, or fixes, that reformers have on hand or are designing are intimately linked to experts' processes of specifying problems. The fixes that experts have on hand shape the problems that they construct, and new technologies and techniques for intervening lead reformers to construct new problems. So, for example, social reformers have long rendered more general problems, such as inequality and social division, as educational problems, such as achievement gaps, the latter of which experts can measure and potentially remedy with new educational interventions. More recently, reformers who have been inspired by the educational potential of new digital technologies have rendered structural social divisions as "digital divides" and "participation gaps" (Jenkins et al. 2006). The implication of such diagnoses is that new educational interventions centered on digital media can ameliorate, if not fix, larger problems, such as inequality of opportunity. In all cases, the entwined processes of problematization and rendering technical entail tunnel vision because much of what reformers cannot manipulate with their fixes, and particularly political-economic relations, is left out of the picture.

While professional experts do much of the work of specifying problems and solutions, their fixations are not simply products of their own making.

These experts' power is "fragile" (Mukerji 1989) and "compromised" (Li 1999) in part because they rely on the support of more powerful outsiders in order to follow up on their insights and to promote their work. As Howard Becker (1963, 147–63) observed in his analysis of morally charged social reform movements, powerful people who are generally not experts in the worlds they seek to philanthropically transform tend to play an especially influential role in social reform enterprises. Because Becker was concerned with the construction of various forms of deviance, he called these powerful reformers "moral entrepreneurs," which I will modify slightly as entrepreneurial reformers, given this book's focus on calls for innovation and disruption.[12] While entrepreneurial reformers have historically arisen from numerous worlds, many contemporary entrepreneurial reformers in the United States have amassed their power in the business world, particularly in the financial and high-tech sectors. At the Downtown School, the most influential of these entrepreneurial reformers accrued their wealth, power, and expertise in high-tech industries, and, as such, they were especially optimistic about the philanthropic potential of new media technologies and the innovative work cultures of high-tech designers (chapter 2).

As Becker observed, moral entrepreneurs are often fervent and confident about what they perceive to be wrong with the world, and they are often equally zealous about what a fixed version of that world would look like. Yet they generally are not motivated simply by self-interest or an attempt to dominate others. While their visions of social transformation often entail trying to change how other people live their lives, often in ways that more closely approximate the reformer's own self-image, entrepreneurial reformers tend to see their efforts in philanthropic terms: they believe that the transformations they seek will lead to a better way of life for others. Given these philanthropic aspirations, education reform is one of the figured worlds that entrepreneurial reformers routinely descend upon when they seek to make social change, and international development is another. For example, the entrepreneurial reformers who helped sponsor the Downtown School wanted to provide everyone with a chance to participate in what they saw as the exciting and rewarding work of the new economy, as well as in the public and civic possibilities of a global connected age more generally.

Reformers' fixations are also shaped by the more general conditions of a given historical conjuncture. Calls for techno-philanthropism tend to proliferate and exert an especially strong moral and normative force when seemingly intractable political and economic problems—such as poverty, entrenched social divisions, shrinking economic opportunities, and so forth—threaten the hegemony of a reigning political-economic order, a phenomenon that Stuart Hall (1987), citing Gramsci, referred to as a "crisis of authority." In these moments, discontent with established authorities and institutions, such as schools, tends to spread, and these general feelings of discontent provide openings for entrepreneurial reformers to articulate calls for disruptive interventions. As chapter 2 explores, the Downtown School was imagined and launched during one of these crises of authority in the United States.

While entrepreneurial reformers play a significant role in a cycle of disruptive fixation, their visions of change are not smoothly converted into concrete programs of intervention. As Becker observed, entrepreneurial reformers do not tend to have deep expertise in the worlds that they seek to transform, nor do they often have time for, or interest in, working out the specificities of an intervention (Becker 1963, 150–52). As such, they call upon and often offer to support various professional experts. For example, the entrepreneurial reformers who helped sponsor the Downtown School recruited especially well-regarded technology designers, scholars of learning and technology, and educational reformers to their cause. These experts were amenable to the entrepreneurial reformers' calls for disruption not only because they were in a compromised position, as discussed earlier, but also because they tended to share much of the entrepreneurial reformers' visions for a better future. Additionally, these experts had strong ideas and feelings about the right and wrong ways to remake education, and these ideas and feelings mostly resonated with the entrepreneurial reformers' more general sense of how education should change. For example, both the entrepreneurial reformers and the professional experts that committed themselves to the Downtown School were proponents of educational interventions that promoted student agency, creativity, and improvisation, and all were also critical of what they saw as overly scripted and top-down approaches to instruction, the latter of which had become increasingly dominant in the United States in the prior decades (chapter 2). Because of these divisions within the figured worlds that specialize in reform, experts can associate their problematizations of other experts' approaches to reform with outsiders' more general calls for disruptive change, especially when the former's approach to reform is currently not dominant. In this way, one reform project or movement's shortcomings become fodder for other reformers' practices of problematization. While these practices of problematization entail partial insights into the limits of recent approaches to reform, they leave intact the lived fiction that a redesigned institutional apparatus can finally fulfill the philanthropic ideals with which it is routinely tasked.

In the chapters that follow, I primarily use the term *fixation* to refer to the collectively realized forms of tunnel vision that occur through the interrelated processes of problematization and rendering technical. Fixations, in this sense, are the lived fictions through which participants in a disruptive philanthropic intervention plan and imagine their project as well as the worlds into which they plan to intervene. A good deal of the book—chapters 3–6—focuses on what these collective fixations, once realized, do as well as how they fare in practice. Because fixations narrowly "enframe" (Callon 1998) how reformers imagine the world, once a project is launched, factors and forces that were excluded during processes of problematization and rendering technical overflow the project and threaten its stability. Despite years of careful preparation, once the Downtown School was launched, it suddenly felt as if the project was a ship caught in an especially tumultuous tempest, bombarded from all sides by unanticipated forces that showed no signs of letting up and, if anything, appeared to be multiplying. Technology did not work, students did not respond to the gamelike pedagogy as anticipated, cutting-edge after-school programs struggled to attract a diversity of students, privileged parents put increasing pressure on school leaders, contentious racialized class struggles reared their head, and so on.[13]

Thus, for the people who design a new intervention the most important initial consequence of fixation is urgent and even existential crisis. At the Downtown School, reformers began to worry that their project could suddenly and embarrassingly collapse on the second day of school, and these seeds of concern grew into a full-blown crisis within a few months of the school's opening. In theory, these crises are moments when reformers could perhaps break out of their fixations; reformers could, for example, attempt to trace the sources of the destabilizing forces that they are encountering so as to better understand the worlds into which they are intervening, and some reformers do begin to reexamine aspects of their fixations in these more extensive ways. But the predominant tendency is not so much to question fixations as to engage in a different and more pragmatic form of fixation: reformers attempt to quickly stabilize the project against the unanticipated forces that are unsettling it. As mentioned before, at the Downtown School many reformers worried that the project could embarrassingly collapse, and under such conditions the dominant response was to look for stabilizing resources wherever they could.

Ironically, many of the ready-to-hand stabilizing resources and techniques come from the traditional versions of the institution that the reformers hope to disrupt. In a process that DiMaggio and Powell (1983) have described as "mimetic isomorphism," reformers at the Downtown School tended to borrow and affix canonical and often quasi-Tayloristic techniques for producing order and discipline in schools, many of which Foucault (1977) chronicled. However, and in a departure from DiMaggio and Powell's classic analysis, reformers also tried to stabilize the project by forging alliances with powerful locals, in this case with privileged parents, even though these locals in no way represented the interests of all the people that the intervention had been philanthropically sanctioned to help and often exerted isomorphic pressures that were at odds with reformers' disruptive aspirations. These powerful outsiders became influential insiders in part by stoking reformers' fears of collapse while also, and simultaneously, offering stability in exchange for concessions and power sharing. While these partnerships helped temporarily stabilize the Downtown School and hence ease reformers' anxieties about an embarrassing collapse, they also turned much of daily life at the school into the sorts of tightly scripted activities that reformers had hoped to relax, and they helped remake many of the same social divisions that reformers had hoped to mend.

REPAIRING IDEALISM

One of the curiosities about the dynamics I have been sketching is that many of the people who committed themselves to the Downtown School continued to act *as if* they were taking part in a disruptive philanthropic endeavor even as they helped make the project more and more conventional and more and more conventionally problematic from the standpoint of substantive social change. Their idealism for the project seemed impressively immune to the forces that repeatedly thwarted their efforts. This resilient idealism not only helped keep the project going, but it also helped sustain and spread the project's reputation as an innovative model of reform that could and should be emulated. The resilience of this idealism in the face countless setbacks is a rather amazing cultural accomplishment as well as an important anthropological and political puzzle.

I address this puzzle in more detail in the conclusion, but a few key themes should be introduced now since they play an important role in the following chapters. I have already suggested that philanthropically sanctified fixations occur though processes of problematization and rendering technical and that these fixations exert an especially strong moral and normative force during a more general crisis of authority. These processes are particularly prevalent during the design phases of a philanthropic intervention, and they help explain why reformers face a torrent of unanticipated forces once they attempt to realize their designs in practice. But processes of problematization and rendering technical do not adequately account for how many participants in a disruptive intervention manage to repair their idealism even as they witness the shortcomings of their efforts firsthand and even as they help make their projects more isomorphic to that which they aim to disrupt. To account for how seemingly futile cycles of disruptive fixation persist, we need to consider how the lived fictions that help organize and morally sanctify a cutting-edge philanthropic

intervention are not just produced but also maintained, repaired, and rationalized in the face of corrosive forces.

In part, many of the people who committed themselves to the Downtown School were able to more or less maintain their idealism for the
project because they were able to overlook and downplay many of the
practices that contradicted and undermined their professed values and
aspirations. Reformers recognized that their introduction of stabilizing resources was a move toward the sorts of organizational forms and
processes that they had hoped to disrupt, but they also often discounted
and underestimated the extent to which they were remaking and extending these forms and processes. One likely reason that they were able to
do so is again made evident by DiMaggio and Powell's (1983) notion of
mimetic isomorphism. Because the stabilizing resources that reformers
deployed were so common in the figured worlds of professional educators and educational reformers, they were often taken for granted among
experienced educators and reformers, especially after they had been introduced. Additionally, a spatialized division of labor, as well as asymmet-
rical relations of power across these divisions, tended to separate those
who designed, managed, and most forcefully promoted the intervention,
some of whom were relative newcomers to education reform, from those
who made the intervention run on a daily basis. While the former held
power over the latter, the former were also often absent from the messy
business of keeping the school running day after day. Because of this spatialized division of labor, the intervention's designers and boosters could
remain especially idealistic about the project while the more regressive
features of the project became part of the taken-for-granted background
of executors' everyday routines. Additionally, neoliberal rhetorics about
consumer choice appeared to have helped some reformers dissociate the
intervention from some of its divisive effects, and popular tropes from
the world of technology design—such as "fail forward"—likely helped
temper feelings of dismay among those who were more familiar with the
project's recurring setbacks.

Yet the maintenance of idealism depends on more than just practices that
overlook, downplay, excuse, and rationalize actions and policies that appear to undermine and contradict a philanthropic intervention's professed
ideals. The maintenance of idealism also depends on the periodic orchestration, documentation, circulation, and ritualistic celebration of practices
that appear to fulfill the intervention's innovative philanthropic promise.
These practices, which I call *sanctioned counterpractices*, played a relatively
minor role in the day-to-day routines of the intervention, and their role diminished as practitioners attempted to stabilize their project against forces
that were not anticipated by their fixations. Yet sanctioned counterpractices
played an outsized role in sustaining idealisms for the project, especially for

reformers, for outsiders upon whose support these experts depended, and for the factions of the local population that found ways to use the intervention's resources to enhance their power. Sanctioned counterpractices were front and center when reformers told stories about the Downtown School to themselves and various supporters and potential allies, including parents, funding agencies, other reformers and practitioners, governmental officials, corporate partners, academics, journalists, and even the general public. At the Downtown School, showcases, festivals, assemblies, ceremonies, publicity materials, wall decorations, Web sites, conference talks, e-mail updates, social media posts, and tours for guests all regularly featured and celebrated the school's sanctioned counterpractices, which focused on student engagement and agency, often with the aid of new media technologies. By contrast, the school's more canonical practices were almost never featured in these ritualized self-representations, and they were sometimes even purposefully erased. As representations of these sanctioned counterpractices were staged and circulated, they not only helped affirm the intervention's novel philanthropic character in the eyes of allies upon whose support the project depended, they also helped repair reformers' sense that their project was a cutting-edge and morally just intervention that could and should be generalized.

Of course, these selectively cheerful self-presentations are hardly surprising. As Howard Becker (1998, 90–93) bluntly put it, organizations often tell lies about themselves to outsiders. Yet it seems to me that it would be a mistake to interpret the outsize attention that insiders give to sanctioned counterpractices as merely an attempt to conceal what they are really up to. At the Downtown School, the ritualistic staging, documentation, circulation, and valorization of sanctioned counterpractices over everyday routines did not so much conceal reformers' real intentions as help reformers and their supporters realize the collective experience of having good intentions and being cutting edge. One consequence of putting sanctioned counterpractices front and center was that it helped reformers secure wider support and legitimacy for their intervention, but it did so only because many reformers appeared to sincerely believe that they were participating in a project that was both innovative and philanthropic and also because many others apparently wanted to believe the same. The staging of sanctioned counterpractices exerted a strong moral and normative force not because reformers set out to dupe potential supporters but because sanctioned counterpractices appeared to verify both insiders' and outsiders' idealistic and hopeful yearnings. By sharing representations of sanctioned counterpractices with broader communities and networks, many reformers and sympathizers for the project helped convince each other that now was a moment when substantive and beneficent change was actually possible.

While the staging and celebration of sanctioned counterpractices helped repair idealism and thus helped secure broader support for the project, the valorization of sanctioned counterpractices also produced side effects that ironically thwarted reformers' aspirations. Sanctioned counterpractices are unique from other institutionally sanctioned practices in that, on the one hand, people in positions of authority recognize and value them positively, while, on the other hand, they have not yet been standardized, codified, and normalized as best practices across a figured world. As such, subordinates who are best positioned to coadapt with authorities' changing understandings of sanctioned nonconformity gain institutional recognition and rewards without authorities in the project or successfully adapting subordinates' tending to see those adaptations as socially and culturally moored.[14] But since sanctioned counterpractices tend to be modeled after the practices of currently successful individuals and groups—in this case, professionals who worked in the so-called creative class—those most inclined and able to adapt to these constantly changing ways of being acceptably unconventional—which is often read as being creative—also tend to be those who are most socially proximate to the model groups and their practices. As such, the subordinates who are best positioned to adapt to authorities' changing understandings of permissible nonconformity tend to be those who are already privileged—in the case of the Downtown School, boys from households with creative professional parents, most of whom were also white. And it is not simply that persons and groups that are more socially distant from the exalted model groups are often disadvantaged or disinclined to coadapt with changing sanctioned counterpractices, although that is often true, but also—and as Willis (1977) evocatively demonstrated—authorities tend to have trouble recognizing, understanding, and valuing the counterpractices of persons whose communities and networks are not well represented in the exalted model groups. As such, at the Downtown School many persons from nondominant groups either felt that they were not well matched for the cutting-edge school or they tried to comport themselves to celebrated models of sanctioned nonconformity but from significantly disadvantaged positions. In either case, the staging and valorization of sanctioned counterpractices helped obfuscate isomorphic tendencies as it helped legitimate the further entrenchment of privilege.

The following chapters are organized to move back and forth between how experts' collectively lived fixations come to life through processes of problematization and rendering technical, how those fixations cause trouble for reformers once a disruptive philanthropic intervention is launched, and yet how many people manage to mostly repair and maintain their idealism even as they help make the intervention more and more conventional and more and more conventionally problematic. Chapter 2 situates the emergence of the Downtown School within historical cycles of purportedly disruptive educational reform in the United States. It examines how reformers' inability to remedy the social and political problems with which education has repeatedly and increasingly been tasked—which reformers also recurrently promise to fix—help produce conditions in which both crises in education and calls for disruptive remedies can recurrently spring forth. Against this historical backdrop, the chapter also explores how particular fixations occurred as the Downtown School's designers and reformers responded to calls for disruption by engaging in processes of problematization and rendering technical.

Chapters 3–6 explore what these fixations did as well as how they fared once the project was launched. Each of these chapters examines how forces that were excluded by reformers' fixations overflowed the project once it was launched. They also explore how reformers and designers tended to respond to these turbulent forces by engaging in a more pragmatic form of fixation: they quickly reached for stabilizing resources even though doing so undermined and contradicted their disruptive and philanthropic aspirations. Each of these chapters emphasizes how reformers' handling of forces that were excluded by processes of problematization and rendering technical played a constitutive role in making the project what it was. The first in this series of chapters, chapter 3, focuses on how fixation limited and distorted the ways that reformers imagined space. The chapter contrasts reformers' imaginings of connected but circumscribed "learning environments" with the ways that parents and caregivers helped construct and connect socially differentiated spaces for their children. Chapter 4 examines reformers' fixations about pedagogic activity and begins to empirically develop the notion of sanctioned counterpractices. The chapter details and analyzes the surprising disparity between the limited role of sanctioned counterpractices in the project's everyday routines and yet their prominence in ritualized self-presentations of the project. Chapter 5 compares how reformers imagined subjects that would be amenable to and fixable with their intervention with the ways that students negotiated identification and difference with each other at school and online. Chapter 6 compares reformers' fixations about the relationships that they would form with the "local community"—in this case parents—with how powerful factions of that imagined community grabbed onto the project and steered it toward their own ends. The conclusion, chapter 7, addresses what cycles of disruptive fixation manage to accomplish, politically and for whom, even as philanthropic interventions routinely fail to realize their ideals. The appendix offers a reflection on how the ethnographic approach that guided this investigation tends to produce its own fixations.

Before turning to these chapters, I would like to caution against several conclusions that a more careful reading will hopefully disabuse. Since much of what follows focuses on the limitations of idealistic attempts to design social change, the book could be read as a sort of Burkean tale cautioning against any attempt at radical change. Yet the focus of the book is not on the follies of trying to make radical change in general. Rather, the book focuses on the problems than can ensue when people rely on particular approaches for doing so. Disruptive fixation appears to be quite pervasive and enduring, but it is also a historically specific phenomenon that has to be constantly remade. It is a particular mode of converting understandable frustrations with the status quo and genuine yearnings for change into concrete interventions, and other modes are both possible and preferable. Part of what I hope to show is that many self-professed disruptive and philanthropic approaches to structural social change are in fact quite conservative, both in terms of their methods as well as their consequences. As such, I hope the book helps open up conversations and imaginings about other ways in which differently positioned actors can contribute to political and social change.

Similarly, the book is not arguing that currently existing educational systems cannot be improved or that technology designers should play no role in philanthropic undertakings. Educational institutions and digital technologies are inextricable aspects of contemporary life for many people, and thus their design and organization will continue to have important political and social consequences. The book does not so much argue that cutting-edge philanthropic interventions should play no role in efforts for social change as try to show how they often play a limiting and even counterproductive role, especially when they are deployed to fix problems that they do not have the power to solve. Relieving technology designers, educators, and philanthropically oriented social reformers of this burden could open promising opportunities for contributions from each, but doing so will also require raising difficult, and often uncomfortable, questions about contemporary political-economic relations, gender and sexuality, race and racialization, the feasibility of large-scale democracy, expertise, what sorts of changes differently positioned people want, and what different roles differently positioned persons and technologies can play in theses efforts. Finally, in examining how designed interventions often seem to fail, the book could be read as making an argument in favor of neoliberal or market-based solutions as a supposedly preferable alternative to top-down planning. However, and as the following chapters show, it was in part because of neoliberal rhetorics and policies—especially about consumer choice and the virtues of entrepreneurial citizenship—that the school's designers not only fell short of their stated aims but also contributed to remaking that which they had hoped to disrupt. Neoliberal rationalities and policies do not escape the problems that this book addresses; rather, they often make reformers accountable to even more centralized, and often thinner, accountability metrics while also shifting the responsibility for (not) uprooting structural problems downward onto idealistic reformers and citizens. If the book makes a contribution, I hope it helps direct concerns toward recognition that it is not just schools, the state, neoliberalism, or technology, but also our fixations that we have to think of working on.

2

CYCLES OF DISRUPTIVE FIXATION

In the fall of 2009 I watched an eleven-year-old boy sit at a desk with a large laptop computer. The desk faced a blank wall in a long and empty hallway. I was standing with about six other adults who were watching the student demonstrate a software program that allowed him to design video games. A television production crew for an ABC News affiliate was between the boy and me. The Downtown School had opened in lower Manhattan only two months earlier, but it was already attracting broad interest and many enthusiastic endorsements. In the school's first year a steady stream of distinguished guests toured the school: scholars and designers from around the world, the president of one of the most respected philanthropic foundations in the United States, the chancellor of New York City's public schools, executives from international media and technology conglomerates, and journalists from PBS, the BBC, and the *New York Times Magazine*, among many others.

Over the previous several years, a world-renowned media technology designer, one of the world's most prominent learning theorists, several professional educational reformers—two of whom held PhDs—and several other technology designers and educational experts had imagined and designed what they hoped would be a radical new model of schooling for the twenty-first century. Their work was sponsored, promoted, and legitimated by multiple powerful backers, including high-ranking officials and board members from several major philanthropic foundations, transnational technology and media corporations, and numerous prominent news outlets, as the preceding vignette begins to illustrate. All these parties seemed to agree that conventional approaches to education, and particularly public schooling, were badly broken. According to the project's designers and supporters, these inherited systems were failing to fulfill their democratic ideals, and, what is more, they were gravely out of touch with the dynamic, technologically saturated, and vastly interconnected world and job market of the twenty-first century.

By contrast, the design team for the Downtown School had created an imaginative, bold, and thoughtful alternative, a redesigned school for new times. Changes in media technology, the school's designers and backers argued, now made it possible for students to be active makers, rather than passive consumers, of media, technology, and knowledge. Video games in particular and innovations in digital media more generally provided inspiration and resources for redesigning the school. Instead of memorizing information and collectively enacting adult-scripted activities, students at the Downtown School would be active, creative, and enterprising learners in designed game worlds. Instead of memorizing knowledge and acquiring skills for a presumed future use, students at the Downtown School would learn how to improvise and work though complex problems as they faced them in situ. Such an approach, the school's designers and backers argued, would allow students to become lifelong, technically sophisticated, and flexible learners, innovators, and problem solvers. They would learn how to adapt to rapidly changing circumstances as well as how to draw on and develop different realms of expertise. They would learn how to identify and solve problems that were not yet known, and they would develop the capacity to work cooperatively with others. Thus the school would help students develop into the types of citizens and workers that many people have suggested the twenty-first century world and economy demand.

What is more, the school's designers and backers planned to offer this new model of schooling to an uncharacteristically diverse cohort of students for an urban public school, one that more closely approximated the cosmopolitan, and yet highly uneven, character of New York City and other large global cities (Sassen 2001). The school would open with a single sixth grade class of seventy-five students and planned to add an additional class each year until the inaugural class reached twelfth grade. In its first year, about half the students came from households where at least one parent held a graduate degree and worked in a professional field, and most were dual-income households. The parents of these students tended to work in the cultural industries that cluster in New York City—fields such as academia, design, art, television, film, new media, publishing, nonprofits, and advertising—whereas others worked in professional fields such as medicine, law, and psychology. Most of these families lived in upscale bohemian neighborhoods in the lower part of the borough of Manhattan—neighborhoods such as Tribeca, SoHo, Chelsea, and Greenwich Village—and many of the children of these families had spent significant portions of their lives outside the United States for their parents' work or on extended vacations. Several had at least one foreign-born parent, and a few had lived years, if not most of their lives, in Europe and Asia. Almost all these students identified as white or Asian American on official Department of Education forms.[1] As shorthand, I refer to these families as *privileged* in this book, although, and as is true with any such classification, the jobs, incomes, and cultural and social capital of these families varied, as did their views and political commitments.[2]

Contrasting sharply with these families were families that also tended to have numerous overseas connections but that inhabited far less-privileged social class conditions. About forty percent of the student body qualified for free or reduced-price lunch, which is used among educational researchers in the United States as a common measure of lower-income status, and many of these students had parents or caregivers with some or no college education. Most were employed in comparatively low-paying manual and service work or were currently unemployed. These families lived in a greater diversity of neighborhoods, many of which were located outside the Downtown School's official school district boundary, but despite these disadvantages they had found creative ways to gain access to the well-resourced new school (chapter 3). As shorthand, I refer to these families and students as *less privileged*, although, and as with my use of privileged, the same qualifications about heterogeneity within this category apply. Many of the school's less-privileged students also had numerous ties abroad, and some had spent significant time outside the United States but in very different transnational networks than their more-privileged peers. A good portion of these students had parents or grandparents who were born in Puerto Rico, the Dominican Republic, and other Caribbean countries; others had parents or grandparents from Central and South America as well as West Africa. The rest were from families that the Department of Education classified as black or African American. Many kept in touch with relatives overseas as well as across the United States. Most schools in global cities like New York do not accommodate students from such diverse backgrounds, but the designers and backers of the Downtown School were not aiming to create another typical urban school.

Back in the hallway, the camerawomen lifted her face from the view-finder and moved her tripod closer to the boy at the computer. The video production team had staged the shot in the hallway to avoid the diverting clutter of the classroom, but now another production crew, this one for a nationally televised public affairs series, had entered the back-ground of their shot. For the next several hours the two television crews danced around each other as they gathered footage for their stories. At one point, the school's principal and two student tour guides entered a classroom with a group of prospective families in tow. As a camera crew maneuvered to capture footage of one of the student tour guides dem-onstrating the school's most cutting-edge technology—a "semi-immer-sive embodied learning environment," the tour guide said—one of the prospective students let out an elongated "Cooool." When these stories ran, they presented the school as profoundly unlike traditional schools, a highly imaginative and cutting-edge attempt to redesign schooling for the twenty-first century.

As educational historians David Tyack and Larry Cuban (1995) convincingly demonstrated, social reformers in the United States have long translated their concerns with the status quo and their yearnings for an idealized democratic polity into urgent demands for education reform. As Tyack and Cuban (1995, 2) wrote, "Repeatedly, Americans have followed a common pattern in devising educational prescriptions for specific social or economic ills. Once they had discovered a problem, they labeled it and taught a course on the subject." This recurring tendency to translate social, political, and economic concerns into educational problems and solutions has led to a situation in which public education has been asked to solve many problems that are far beyond its reach (Tyack 1974; Tyack and Cuban 1995). These unrealistic expectations are woven throughout the lived fictions that help reformers imagine, design, and sanctify their interventions as cutting edge and philanthropic, and they play a fundamental role in producing the fixations that this book examines. As Tyack and Cuban document, the outsized expectations that are routinely attached to educational interventions leads to cycles of wishful thinking followed, eventually, by periods of disillusionment as seemingly cutting-edge philanthropic interventions fall far short of their professed aims. Because of these inevitable shortcomings, state educational systems are commonly judged as in a perpetual state of crisis, and yet these crises ironically help legitimate even more rounds of overly optimistic educational reforms (Arendt 1961; Tyack and Cuban 1995).

Cuban (1986; 1996; 2001) also documented how these recurring swells of wishful thinking are often invigorated by optimism for the seemingly unprecedented educational possibilities of the new media technologies of the moment, a yearning that tends to dovetail with hopeful feelings about the democratizing character of new technologies (Marx 1964; Nye 1994; Buckingham 2000, 2007; Mosco 2004). Consider, for example, the following quote from Thomas Edison in 1922, as quoted in Cuban (1986, 2):

> I believe that the motion picture is destined to revolutionize our educational system and that in a few years it will supplant largely, if not entirely, the use of textbooks. . . . The education of the future, as I see it, will be conducted through the medium of the motion picture.

Similarly confident predictions of educational disruption accompanied the introduction of radio, television, and the personal computer. For example, more than sixty years after Edison made his claim, Seymour Papert—a prominent computer scientist, mathematician, and learning theorist from MIT—confidently declared, "There won't be schools in the future. The computer will blow up the school."[3] Such recurring hopes even antecede the development of electronic media. As the historian Paul Duguid (2015) observed, similar sentiments occurred to eighteenth-century liberal reformers, such as the prominent Anglican essayist Vicesimus Knox, who in 1781 questioned the usefulness of universities in an age of books:

> [T]he principal cause of establishing universities in an age when both books and instructors were scarce, no longer subsists. Let them therefore be reformed, and rendered really useful to the community, or let them be deserted.[4]

None of these anticipated disruptions have come true, and yet well over 200 years after Knox, nearly 100 years after Edison, and more than 30 years after Papert, we still routinely hear echoes of their confident idealism. In books, articles, and speeches with titles such as *Disrupting Class: How Disruptive Innovation Will Change the Way the World Learns* (Christensen, Horn, and Johnson 2008), and *The End of College: Creating the Future of Learning and the University of Everywhere* (Carey 2015), contemporary advocates of techno-philanthropism assure us that now video games, personalized learning software, online learning platforms such as MOOCs, big data, or virtual reality will disrupt the educational status quo.

This recurring tendency to translate social and political concerns into educational problems and to then wish hoped-for educational, and hence social, transformations onto the latest innovations in media technologies is especially evident in moments that Stuart Hall (1986) has characterized as crises of authority for societies that aspire to liberal-democratic ideals. Liberal-democratic polities have long characterized themselves as new and qualitatively different models of society, ones dedicated to individual freedom and meritocratic distinction rather than social oppression and entrenched hierarchies. And liberal reformers have long seen education as a, if not the, main mechanism for actualizing these ideals, particularly the ideal of meritocracy. When the gap between these idealized versions of a democratic polity and reality becomes especially wide, educational systems often catch much of the public outrage, leading to the perennial crises in education as a political issue and perpetual reforms that promise to disrupt education in order to fix society.

At the historical moment when the Downtown School was being designed and launched, the gap between idealized versions of the United States and many people's lived realities was becoming increasingly clear. While evidence of increasing economic inequalities and a weakening position on the global stage had been mounting since the 1970s, the extent of the United State's challenges became increasingly apparent after the turn of the millennium. Design for the Downtown School began in 2006, with economic inequality at levels not seen since the 1920s, the middle class hollowing out, China, India, and other new geopolitical powers on the ascent, and rates of relative economic mobility falling behind those of many other wealthy countries.[5] The year before the Downtown School opened, financial markets collapsed and globalized capitalism nearly imploded. None of these developments squared with the long-held ideal that the United States was a shining example of meritocratic opportunity that other nations and people emulate.

Yet in these troubled and precarious times, many influential people saw high-tech industries and highly skilled technologists as casting a hopeful light. Over roughly the same period that economic opportunities were shrinking, impressive things were happening in the nation's high-tech sector. Countless social commentators and reformers pointed to Silicon Valley and other high-tech centers as hubs of "disruptive innovation," a phrase coined by business management scholar Clayton Christensen (1997). According to their supporters, these hubs of innovation offered models for social reform, especially of state institutions that were unable to fulfill their social ideals. Commentators and reformers celebrated cases in which tech-savvy people from around the world had used various online platforms to create exciting new collectives organized around shared interests (Gee 2003; Ito 2008), cultural productions (Benkler 2006; Jenkins et al. 2006), and causes (Shirky 2008). In otherwise gloomy times, these success stories appeared to many as beacons of a more prosperous, participatory, and harmonious future, one that more closely resembled long-standing, but never realized, idealizations of the liberal-democratic experiment. Yet these success stories were also exceptional, making the question of their generalization problematic. For many, and especially those who rightly worried that the opportunities of the "connected age" (Ito et al. 2013), the "networked society" (Castells 1996), or the "knowledge economy" (Powell and Snellman 2004) would not spread automatically or evenly, the answer lay in urgently reforming education lest much of society get left behind.

Using planning for the Downtown School as an example, this chapter examines the processes and conditions through which enduring yearnings for a fair and united polity as well as hopeful feelings about the philanthropic potential of cutting-edge technologies come to be linked anew. While such linkages are pervasive and recurring, they are not simply diffused from the top down by capitalists, state officials, or other powerful actors, even though powerful actors do play an important role in perpetuating cycles of what I am referring to as disruptive fixation. Rather, for a cycle of disruptive fixation to start anew, these enduring yearnings and hopeful feelings have to be collectively remade and maintained as part of the lived fictions that help coordinate thought, activity, and emotion among the various actors that take part in philanthropic reform endeavor. This chapter examines how these lived fictions came to life among the specialists who imagined and designed the Downtown School. It explores how the school's sponsors and designers came to feel and act *as if* they were creating something unprecedented and powerfully philanthropic as they gave new life to a long and cyclical process that repeatedly produces disappointing results. The chapter first establishes that the ongoing tendency to translate social, political, and economic concerns and yearnings into technological-educational problems and solutions is both widespread and enduring. It then turns to the specific case of the Downtown School to show how the reformers' designs for a disruptive new model of schooling were imagined and constructed during a particular crisis of authority in the United States, and in part as a critical response to the perceived failings of the approaches to education that had been dominant in the United States since the 1980s, which themselves had been imagined and deployed partly as a critical response to the perceived failings of approaches to education that were popular during the 1960s and 1970s. Throughout, the chapter draws attention to how particular fixations occur as part of reformers' processes of problematization and rendering technical (Li 2007). The following chapters explore what these fixations do, as well as how they fare, once a seemingly disruptive philanthropic intervention is launched.

TRANSLATING THE POLITICAL-ECONOMIC INTO THE TECHNICAL

While writing this book I attended an interdisciplinary workshop on mitigating social inequality and promoting social mobility that brought together numerous experts from the University of California, San Diego, where I work. Two of the four invited panelists were economists. The first economist joked that economists could not agree on anything, but the one thing that they could agree on was how to address increasing inequality and the lack of social mobility in the United States. "There are three things we should do," the first economist said, "education, education, and education." He then went on to show several graphs indicating the tight correlation between income inequality and levels of educational attainment. The economist elaborated that there was a "skills gap," especially in science, technology, engineering, and math (STEM) fields, and, as such, the way to remedy problematic inequality and lack of mobility was through educational reforms that cultivated these skills. The second economist agreed with the first economist but added an additional prescription, "We need to learn how to produce more Tiger Moms," she said, in a not-entirely joking reference to the provocative book by Yale law professor Amy Chua (2011).

I include this anecdote from San Diego because the economists' diagnoses and prescriptions echoed themes that I encountered on my very first day of conducting fieldwork for this project. Two weeks before the Downtown School was scheduled to open, the school's designers and educators hosted an event for incoming parents and students to get to know each other. Most of the evening consisted of mingling, eating food, and students playing various get-to-know-you games in a large auditorium at a local university. Educators and the school's designers also interspersed short presentations, and the event culminated with a screening of a YouTube video that was projected on a large screen. One of the educators introduced the video as "capturing what the Downtown School is all about." The video consisted of a series of seemingly factual textual assertions accompanied with animated information graphics, all set to the song, "Right Here, Right Now," by the electronic musician Fatboy Slim. The statements, which I have shortened, were as follows:

> We are currently preparing students for jobs that don't yet exist, using technologies that haven't been invented, in order to solve problems we don't even know are problems yet.
> . . .
> We are living in exponential times.
> There are 31 billion searches on Google every month.
> In 2006, this number was 2.7 billion.
> To whom were these questions addressed B.G.? (Before Google)
> . . .
> During the course of this presentation 67 babies were born in the US.
> 274 babies were born in China.
> 395 babies were born in India.
> And 694,000 songs were downloaded illegally.
> So what does it all mean?

Despite the very different venues and presentation formats, the similarity between the economists' presentations for other academics in San Diego and the video that educational reformers played for parents and students in New York City illustrates how commonsensical certain assumptions had become. One such assumption was diagnostic: the reason that the United States, and many other nations, had such historically high levels of inequality was because technological change and globalized economic relations—both of which were often assumed to be generally beneficial and outside the realm of politics—had made the skills of many people outdated and not as valuable. Another assumption was prescriptive: the belief that cutting-edge educational interventions were the way to remedy these problems and, in particular, the belief that all citizens should be molded into the sorts of creative, tech-savvy, and entrepreneurial subjects that had done comparatively well in recent decades. Both episodes also fused political and economic concerns with nationalist—and particularly orientalist (Said 1978)—anxieties.

During the period of this study, these were not fringe views in the United States, nor were they aligned with a particular political party or ideology. Rather, they had come to be seen by many people as both centrist and realist. For example, such views were, and remain, pervasive in the widespread push for science, technology, engineering and math in US education, as well as calls for educational interventions cultivating people's capacities for innovation. Similar diagnoses and prescriptions were exemplified by Richard Florida's (2002) extolment of the creative class, the widespread valorization of the new economy, and the increased interest by educational researchers and management scholars on how to foster creativity and entrepreneurialism.[6] Similar assumptions undergirded economists' theories of skill-biased technological change, digital inequality scholars' focus on the skills gaps and the participation gap, and the proselytizing of design and design thinking as twenty-first century literacies. Nor were these assumptions limited to just idiosyncratic places like California or even the United States. For example, while arising under different circumstances, Irani (2015) documented resonant discourses among professional designers in Delhi, India, as did Lindtner (2014) among Do-It-Yourself makers in China, Takhteyev (2012) among software developers in Rio de Janeiro, Ames (2015) among ed-tech reformers in Paraguay, and Lindtner, Hertz, and Dourish (2014) among "makers" in Europe, North America, South America, and Asia.[7]

While these sorts of arguments have sprung forth in many places and with abundance in recent decades, they also give new articulation to a much more enduring tradition. The urgent demand to disrupt education so as to fix society has recurred again and again in the United States, and these recurring demands repeatedly position citizens as in an educational race against two competitors: citizens of other nations and technological change. Consider the following three quotes:

> Whether we like it or not, we are beginning to see that we are pitted against the world in a gigantic battle of brains and skill, with the markets of the world, work for our people, and internal peace and contentment as the prizes at stake.

> Our Nation is at risk. Our once unchallenged preeminence in commerce, industry, science, and technological innovation is being overtaken by competitors throughout the world. . . . [T]he educational foundations of our society are presently being

eroded by a rising tide of mediocrity that threatens our very future as a Nation and a people. What was unimaginable a generation ago has begun to occur—others are matching and surpassing our educational attainments.

Thanks to globalization, driven by modern communications and other advances, workers in virtually every sector must now face competitors who live just a mouse-click away in Ireland, Finland, China, India, or dozens of other nations whose economies are growing. . . . An educated, innovative, motivated workforce—human capital—is the most precious resource of any country in this new, flat world. Yet there is widespread concern about our K–12 science and mathematics education system, the foundation of that human capital in today's global economy.

The first statement, which is quoted from Tyack and Cuban (1995), was made by Ellwood P. Cubberley, the former dean of Stanford University's School of Education, in 1909. The second comes from *A Nation at Risk: The Imperative for Educational Reform*, the influential report published in the United States by a special presidential committee on education in 1983. The third comes from a 2005 report by another blue ribbon committee assembled by the National Academies, this one titled *Rising above the Gathering Storm: Energizing and Employing America for a Brighter Economic Future*. While spanning nearly 100 years, Cubberley's remarks from 1909, the *Nation at Risk* report from 1983, and more recent assessments such as the 2005 *Gathering Storm* document prescribe urgent educational reforms with nearly identical justifications. Times may have changed, but reformers' anxieties, diagnoses, and prescriptions remained remarkably consistent.

As we saw in the last chapter, these arguments and the assumptions they entail endure and exert significant pressure in part because they appeal to long-standing idealizations about the supposed function of educational systems in a democratic polity, as well as entrenched assumptions about the salient, if not determining, role that new technologies play in processes of historical change.[8] But these arguments also endure because each new articulation sutures educational-technological problems and solutions to anxieties and yearnings that are rooted in the real political, economic, and social conditions of the moment. The United States did face high levels of economic inequality and increasing international economic competition in the early years of the twentieth century when Cubberley made his remarks. When the report *A Nation at Risk* was written, Japan, Germany, and other international powers were exerting increasing economic pressures on the United States. In the decades leading up to the publication of the report *Rising above the Gathering Storm*, economic and political conditions had changed in ways that made many people's lives more precarious. Recent technological changes have been dramatic, and many consequences of those ongoing changes remain unclear. Workers do often compete in an increasingly competitive and global labor market. The American Dream's promise of equal opportunity for all does increasingly appear as a comforting myth, and so forth.

All these historical factors contribute to what Stuart Hall characterized as a political crisis of authority, and it is in these crises of authority that urgent demands for disruptive philanthropic interventions, particularly cutting-edge educational interventions, often foment. And yet, despite many commentators' recurring insistence otherwise, it is far from clear that educational crises play a prominent role in producing the conditions that give rise to a more general crisis of authority. Similarly, it is equally unclear that educational interventions, in whatever form, can fix these broader problems, even if they are buttressed by the seemingly unprecedented possibilities of recent technological breakthroughs.[9]

Consider, for example, the commonsensical arguments that have been made in recent years in favor of STEM-based educational reforms. Countless social commenters, policymakers, and educational reformers have repeatedly insisted that the jobs of the future are STEM related and thus that *all students* needed to develop STEM expertise. To quote the White House under the Obama administration, "To prepare Americans for the jobs of the future and help restore middle-class security, we have to out-educate the world. . . . The Obama Administration stands committed to providing *students at every level* with the skills they need to excel in the high-paid, highly rewarding fields of science, technology, engineering, and math" (emphasis added).[10] Now take a look at table 2.1, which shows the US Bureau of Labor Statistics' (BLS) 2014 projections of the occupational fields that are expected to experience the most job growth between 2012 and 2022.

According to the state's official projections, the vast majority of occupations that are expected to experience the most job growth between 2012 and 2022 have little to do with STEM fields, and many of the occupations that are seemingly related to STEM, such as nursing assistants, do not currently require advanced formal education in STEM fields. According to the BLS, none of the top ten fastest-growing occupations currently requires a bachelor's degree, and only one, registered nurses, expects an associate's degree. As such, when advocates for STEM-focused educational reforms talk about training everyone for the jobs of the future, the jobs they appear to have in mind are a particularly narrow and well-paying subset of the projected future division of labor. Put differently, STEM-focused educational interventions will do little to benefit the many people whose futures will not include working in what the Obama administration described as

Table 2.1. Occupations with the Most Projected Job Growth between 2012–2022.

Bureau of Labor Statistics, United States Department of Labor

	Occupation	2012 median annual wage (dollars)
1.	Personal care aides	19,910
2.	Registered nurses	65,470
3.	Retail salespersons	21,110
4.	Home health aides	20,820
5.	Combined food preparation and serving workers, including fast food	18,260
6.	Nursing assistants	24,420
7.	Secretaries and administrative assistants, except legal, medical, and executive	32,410
8.	Customer service representatives	30,580
9.	Janitors and cleaners, except maids and housekeeping cleaners	22,320
10.	Construction laborers	29,990
11.	General and operations managers	95,440
12.	Laborers and freight, stock, and material movers, hand	23,890
13.	Carpenters	39,940
14.	Bookkeeping, accounting, and auditing clerks	35,170
15.	Heavy and tractor-trailer truck drivers	38,200
16.	Medical secretaries	31,350
17.	Childcare workers	19,510
18.	Office clerks, general	27,470
19.	Maids and housekeeping cleaners	19,570
20.	Licensed practical and licensed vocational nurses	41,540

Table 2.1. *Continued*

	Occupation	2012 median annual wage (dollars)
21.	First-line supervisors of office and administrative support workers	49,330
22.	Elementary school teachers, except special education	53,400
23.	Accountants and auditors	63,550
24.	Medical assistants	29,370
25.	Cooks, restaurant	22,030
26.	Software developers, applications	90,060
27.	Landscaping and groundskeeping workers	23,570
28.	Receptionists and information clerks	25,990
29.	Management analysts	78,600
30.	Sales representatives, wholesale and manufacturing, except technical and scientific products	54,230

See "Table 1.4 Occupations with most job growth, 2012 and projected 2022," *Bureau of Labor Statistics, United States Department of Labor*, accessed May 20th, 2014, http://www.bls.gov/emp/ep_table_104.htm.

the "high-paid, highly rewarding fields of science, technology, engineering, and math."

A similar idealism can be found in arguments that translate national political economic problems, such as rising inequality and stagnated wages, into the technical problem/solution of educational attainment. For example, until recently many mainstream economists argued that growing inequality since the 1970s was in large part a product of "skill-biased technological change" (Goldin and Katz 2008). According to these influential arguments, the globalization of markets and advances in technology were rewarding some people while hurting others. To remedy this disparity while simultaneously promoting national economic competitiveness, reformers of various political persuasions agreed with the economists at UC San Diego: what was needed was more and better "education, education, education." And yet, between 1960 and 2010 there was an impressive increase in both the percentage of the United States population that

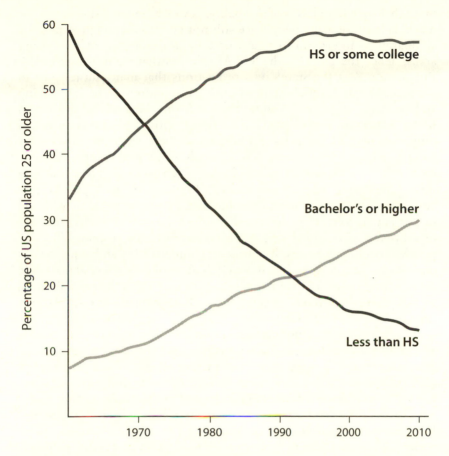

Figure 2.1. Percent of U.S. Population Age 25 and over by Educational Attainment

Source: United States Census Bureau, "Current Population Survey on Educational Attainment."

graduated from high school and a four-year college and, consequently, a steep decline in the proportion of the population that had not completed high school (figure 2.1). If we forget about the rising inequality and stagnating wages that also occurred during this period, figure 2.1 appears to tell an educational success story.

Advocates for educational disruption would likely counter that while it is true that a higher proportion of citizens are more educated than at any time in the United States' history, the reason that the United

States has such high levels of inequality, as well as income stagnation for many, is because many people are still not educated enough, especially compared to international rivals, or they are educated in the wrong areas, hence the push for the STEM reforms that we just examined.[11] But if we accept the state's own projections that many future jobs in the United States, let alone the world, will continue to be low paying and in many ways undesirable, then reforms focused on more and better education cannot provide everyone with a middle-class life, if only they play by the rules. Rather, and at best, such reforms appear to offer additional means by which people can try to compete against each other for access to relatively few high-paid, highly rewarding fields. According to this meritocratic logic, those who go through educational systems as prescribed but end up unemployed or working in low-paying jobs either deserve their lot in life or they were casualties of a broken educational system. In either case, the responsibility for political-economic issues, like widening inequalities and a hollowed-out middle class, is placed on individuals and educational systems, while more contentious political issues—such as taxation and redistribution, or the power of workers in relation to global capital—are left largely unexamined and unchallenged.

This translation of political and economic issues into educational-technological problems and solutions is accomplished through a more general cultural process that the anthropologist Tania Murray Li (2007), who studied development interventions in Indonesia, charac-terized as problematization and rendering technical. According to Li, who drew heavily on Ferguson (1994) and Mitchell (2002), particu-lar means of philanthropic intervention—education reform, develop-ment programs, technology design—lead experts to render political-economic and social problems—such as economic inequality, lack of mobility, or poverty—*as if* they were technical problems that experts could foreseeably remedy with the means that they have available or are developing. It is through these processes of problematization and ren-dering technical that reformers' particular lived fixations arise, and it is because of these fixations that many factors are excluded from view. As we will see, these fixations allow reformers to act *as if* they are designing a cutting-edge intervention that can realize broader social and philan-thropic ideals, but these same fixations also limit their ability to do so. Paradoxically, the routine failure that often accompanies such interven-tions does not lead the figured worlds that specialize in cutting-edge philanthropic interventions to collapse; rather, failure and contestation play a key role in sustaining these worlds, and hence in generating new rounds of disruptive fixation.

FAILURE AS A REGENERATIVE FORCE

While processes of problematization and rendering technical appear to be common and enduring features of techno-philanthropism, the particular fixations that arise through these processes are varied, historically contingent, and frequently contested. Much like the scientists studied by Latour (1987) or the members of art worlds studied by Becker (2008), participants in the figured worlds that specialize in cutting-edge philanthropic interventions assemble changing alliances and divisions as they engage in different controversies that are often related to which diagnoses and prescriptions should prevail. These controversies exist in part because experts hold different theories about the worlds into which they plan to intervene, as well as different theories about how an intervention should be designed and implemented. Reformers also hold different idealizations of the world that they would like to help create. Often, the diagnoses and proposed solutions of one faction of experts dismays experts from other factions and vice versa.[12] And yet the figured worlds of reformers do not endure despite all these controversies but, rather, in part because of them. The recurring inability of well-intended philanthropic interventions to make good on their promises sustains conditions in which powerful people who are typically not expert reformers—such as the entrepreneurial reformers discussed in the introduction, as well as policymakers and journalists—can make urgent calls for disruptive philanthropic intervention. At the same time, factions of experts within a figured world, who depend on such powerful outsiders in order to follow through on and publicize their insights, try to align themselves with these powerful outsiders. They do so in part by problematizing existing social systems while also promising to imagine and design seemingly innovative remedies. Factions of experts that are not currently in a hegemonic position within their figured world are especially apt to forge such alliances, and the design and launch of the Downtown School is a case in point.

As noted earlier, the founders of the Downtown School received substantial support from powerful philanthropic foundations as well as considerable attention from major media organizations. While these actors had diverse interests, perspectives, and concerns, they found common ground in problematizing the existing educational system while also idealizing the philanthropic possibilities of cutting-edge technologies and techno-cultures. The philanthropic foundation that gave the most financial support for the Downtown School did so after deciding to make what they saw as a significant shift in their educational grant making. After more than ten years and tens of millions of dollars invested in trying to improve the management of urban schools, the foundation announced that it was disillusioned with these reform efforts and planned to make a dramatic shift. The foundation would now direct its entire educational grant making toward projects that explored and attempted to build upon the seemingly unprecedented opportunities for learning that new digital media technologies appeared to be making possible. This shift was urged and orchestrated to a large degree by a member of the foundation's board of directors who had amassed considerable power and status. This shift was urged and orchestrated to a large degree by a member of the foundation's board of directors who had amassed considerable power and status at the intersection of the business world and high-tech research and design. By shaping the direction of the foundation's educational grant making, this and other entrepreneurial reformers aimed to create an entire new field of expertise focused on digital media and learning, and to some extent they have succeeded. The Downtown School was one of the first, and biggest, designed interventions of this new philanthropic initiative.

The designers of the Downtown School shared these entrepreneurial reformers' dissatisfaction with existing educational systems in the United States, and they too were optimistic about the exciting opportunities for learning that new digital technologies, and particularly video games, appeared to offer. Some of these experts were fairly new to the world of education reform and had been recruited to bring fresh ideas and energy based on their expertise in technology design, and particularly video games. These relative newcomers, in turn, seemed to be attracted to the project in large part because it allowed them to apply their technical and design expertise toward a philanthropic undertaking: reimagining institutions, as they put it, for the twenty-first century. The rest of the design team consisted of more experienced educational reformers and learning theorists. These more experienced educational reformers mostly welcomed the new voices and ideas from the worlds of technology design, particularly voices that appeared to fit well with their more specialized commitments to particular approaches to pedagogy, approaches that had been marginalized by the dominant educational reforms of recent decades.[13] Routinely, these more-experienced educational reformers problematized the pedagogic approaches that were currently dominant, which they often referred to as "the testing regime." According to these experts, the testing regime was not only ineffective and outdated, but it also failed students and families on *moral grounds*. At the same time, digital media's apparent capacities to engage and connect young people—with technology, with each other, and with the world—appeared to offer unprecedented ways to remedy these shortcomings. Because fixations arise through expert's processes of problematization and rendering technical, it is important that we take a brief detour into the specifics of the debates and struggles in which these more experienced reformers were engaged. As we will see, past reformers help lay the conditions for a new round of disruptive fixation, both in terms of what these previous reforms had failed to accomplish and in terms of what they did manage to put in place, even as they fell short of their professed aims.

From the 1980s and continuing into the second decade of the new millennium, the dominant approach to education reform in the United States had been a move toward, on the one hand, ratcheting up collective discipline, centralized accountability, and standardization in core and strategic areas such as STEM and, on the other hand, trying to create marketlike conditions that would spur innovation and competition within educational bureaucracies. These two dominant strands of reform have often reinforced each other, and they exemplify the more general shift toward neoliberal rationalities and policies that have dominated many aspects of public and private life in the United States since the 1970s (Sennett 2006). In keeping with the important role that processes of problematization play in cyclical rounds of disruptive fixation, the educational reforms that became dominant during the 1980s gained traction and influence in part by problematizing many of the educational reforms that had become popular during the 1960s and early 1970s (Ravitch 2000). What is more, many of the reforms that had gained momentum during the 1960s and early 1970s had themselves emerged alongside the more general challenges to establishment institutions, including schools, that erupted in the mid-1960s (Tyack 1974). Once again professing an urgent educational crisis, the educational reformers who started to become dominant during the 1980s problematized reforms from the 1960s and 1970s for not only for failing to achieve their democratic goals, but also for eroding the rigor, quality, and international competitiveness of the United State's educational system and, hence, the nation more generally.[14]

The report *A Nation at Risk* quoted earlier succinctly expresses the twin moves of problematization and rendering technical that began to come to dominance during the 1980s. The report, and many similar analyses, translated both personal and nationalist anxieties stemming from the economic crisis of the 1970s and early 1980s into an urgent crisis in education, which the authors primarily problematized in terms of rising mediocrity in the US K–12 schooling system. Blending polemical and technical registers, these reformers claimed that the quality of K–12 schooling had eroded in large part because previous reformers had weakened expectations for students to master standardized knowledge in canonical academic domains such as English, math, science, and history. The report also suggested a clear connection between the economic crisis, technological change, and threats of foreign competition—all of which were widely visible to the public in their lives and in the media—and an educational crisis, which was not easily visible to those outside of educational worlds. According to these problematizations, one of the reasons the United States no longer enjoyed the widely shared growth of the post–World War II period was because the education system had become undisciplined and out of step with changes in technology and globalizing economic relations. As a consequence, many US workers were no longer competitive.

This translation of social, economic, and political challenges into problems of an undisciplined educational system also entailed particular solutions: schools should raise standards for all students in the "Five New Basics" and administer annual standardized testing in order to measure what students had learned. Alongside these calls for greater accountability were prescriptions to leverage market principles to reform state institutions. Doing so, advocates argued, would promote competition among public schools, a move that was rationalized as empowering families by offering them choices much like the ones they had for consuming goods and services in capitalist markets. Without having to compete with other schools to attract families, critics argued, public schools lacked incentives to improve, or even maintain, quality and efficiency. Once again, a more general political crisis of authority was translated into an educational crisis, and this problematization was intimately tied to an available technocratic solution: large public bureaucracies should be broken up and individual schools should compete against each other in order to attract students and families. Additionally, public schools should provide objective evidence of their results, often in the form of test scores. Families would supposedly be empowered by having more consumer sovereignty, and standardized tests would provide managers, educators, and families with purportedly objective evidence with which they could evaluate school quality.[15]

As many critics have pointed out, neoliberal reformers deployed similar diagnoses and prescriptions in many other domains, particularly with respect to state institutions. Often these diagnoses and prescriptions have been rendered in more innocuous terms, such as the "autonomy for accountability exchange" (O'Day et al., eds. 2011) and the "pragmatist solution" (Sabel 2005). While these prescriptions have not been fully realized, the dominant trend in state-driven educational reform in the United States since the 1980s has been (1) an attempt to centralize control over educational agendas; while (2) decentralizing responsibility for how those agendas should be carried out to local school officials and families; (3) implementing marketlike conditions that promote choice for families and competition among schools and students; (4) relying on standardized metrics that would supposedly make educational outcomes intelligible to centralized authorities as well as families; and (5) deploying new information technologies that would facilitate the capture, aggregation, and flow of metrics about performance upward to managers as well as outward to consumers.

New York City has been a pioneer of this approach to education reform.[16] While the *No Child Left Behind Act of 2001* (NCLB) extended high-stakes standardized testing to all states, similar changes antedated NCLB in New York State. What is more, New York City Mayor Michael Bloomberg and his Chancellor for the Department of Education, Joel Klein, instituted the vision of "autonomy for accountability" even further with their "Children First" initiative, which launched in 2003. Bloomberg and Klein's initiative attempted to hollow out what they saw as an irresponsive and bloated public bureaucracy, which annually serves more than one million students. They did so by disbanding the publicly elected Board of Education as well as thirty-two community school boards while centralizing administrative control over the city's public schools in the Mayor's office. At the same time, they granted more power over budgets, pedagogy, and hiring to local school principals. Instead of reporting to superintendents that oversaw districts, school leaders could now choose from several School Support Organizations that were intended to provide support services rather than bureaucratic dictates. As a trade-off for these increases in autonomy, however, school leaders had to generate supposedly objective evidence of educational outcomes, primarily through students' standardized test scores. Schools that failed to meet performance targets were restructured or closed.[17]

In keeping with this institutional reorganization, New York City has been at the forefront of promoting marketlike school choice for families, in part, but not exclusively, by increasing the number of charter schools. While there is a long and complex history of reformers in the United States pushing to make public schooling more like idealizations of markets, primarily through vouchers and charter schools, the movement gained new traction during the 1980s and 1990s (Cookson 1994). In New York City, market-inspired reformers found a somewhat surprising ally in the "small-schools movement," which had problematized large middle and high schools for letting many students fall through the cracks. As a remedy, these reformers called for the creation of numerous small schools in which students, educators, and staff would presumably get to know each other more intimately. The small-schools movement began to take off in New York City in the early 1990s with grants from the Annenberg and Diamond foundations and then expanded significantly once administrative control was centralized under Mayor Bloomberg. Considerable grants from the Gates Foundation, the Open Society Institute, and the Carnegie Foundation accelerated the small-schools movement in New York City during the 2000s. While advocates of small schools often focus on the advantages of smaller learning environments, the shift from several large schools to many small schools was also amenable to reformers who wanted educational systems to behave more like their idealizations of markets, which is presumably one of the reasons that the small-schools movement caught on.

These structural-organizational reforms have dramatically reconfigured the landscape of New York City's public schools. Large, often neighborhood-based high schools have increasingly been replaced with numerous small, non-neighborhood-based, middle and high schools to which families apply. In doing so, the reforms have rapidly increased the number of schools and, theoretically, the choices available to families. For example, in 1992 New York City had 99 public high schools and by 2009 it had nearly 400.[18] NCLB policies have helped advance a similar reform agenda at the national level.[19] Teachers unions, some families, and some states have resisted these changes, but by and large reform movements that began in the 1980s have succeeded in instituting standardized accountability mechanisms and, to a lesser degree, marketlike competition as school choice.

These changes in the organizational configuration of urban public school systems have been accompanied by a concentration of the curriculum in specific areas that many policymakers and educational experts deem important to national economic competiveness and future job opportunities for all students. As with many of the recent organizational reforms, the focus on STEM domains is not new, and support for STEM-focused reforms crosses entrenched political divisions in ways that support for most policies do not. The report *Rising Above the Gathering Storm* from 2005 is a paradigmatic example of this genre of problematization and rendering technical. Like the report *A Nation at Risk* from the 1980s, an esteemed committee of experts wrote the report *Rising above the Gathering Storm* in the mid-2000s, and like the report from the 1980s, the authors of the new report warned of losing an educational competition between the United States and foreign adversaries, usually by showing US students, on average, underperforming many of their international peers on standardized tests in STEM fields. The message of this nationalist rhetoric was clear: US students were falling further and further behind their international rivals on standardized measures, especially for math and science, and this inferiority threatened the nation's supremacy as well as citizens' future employment chances. The document both problematized recent techno-scientific developments as an important cause of political-economic problems—for example, "thanks to globalization, driven by modern communications and other advances"—and rendered techno-scientific educational interventions as the solution—for example, that all students need to excel at STEM.

While these tendencies in the world of US education reform remain dominant even at the time of writing, aspects of their shortcomings were already becoming evident by the time that the founders of the Downtown School began their effort to redesign educational systems for the twenty-first century. As with past educational reform efforts, the dominant reforms of the 1980s, 1990s and early 2000s do not appear to have accomplished many hoped-for results. Despite decades of reforms like those chronicled here, the more general political crisis of authority remains alive and well in the United States, especially after the financial collapse of 2008. Despite more people being more educated to purportedly higher standards in strategic areas, wealth inequalities continued to widen and income growth for many remained stagnant.[20] Additionally, families and policymakers on both the left and the right have increasingly resisted the push toward centralized curricula and standardized accountability metrics.[21] Finally, the push toward standardization, collective discipline, and STEM has sat somewhat uneasily with the increasing calls for educational institutions to unleash the country's creative talent. The latter concern has led some STEM advocates to extend their prescriptions to include educational initiatives focused on innovation and entrepreneurship, an expansion that has knit techno-science, design, and now even art education evermore closely with business and industry.[22] The linking together of STEM education with polysemous concepts like design, innovation, and entrepreneurship is part of the longer-term trend toward public-private partnerships and the rising influence of business and management discourses in efforts to reform state institutions. This public-private braiding is a consequence of a more-general bipartisan shift toward relying on market ideals and subsidizing the private sector to fix economic and social problems. But as disappointments with the dominant educational reforms of the last several decades have gathered momentum, new calls for disruption have also arisen.

DESIGNING A "PROGRESSIVE" ALTERNATIVE

Much as "back to the basics" reformers of the 1980s rendered their proposed technical remedies in part by problematizing the shortcomings of earlier "progressive" educational reformers, so a new generation of progressive pedagogic reformers have advocated for educational disruption in part by problematizing the shortcomings of recent educational reforms focused on standardization. The planners and supporters of the Downtown School were at the forefront of these new efforts. According to the designers of the school, as well as many of the entrepreneurial reformers with whom they allied, test-driven educational reforms had facilitated pedagogic approaches that were badly out of synch with the dynamic, interconnected, and technologically saturated worlds that students inhabited, as well as with the esteemed professional worlds that students were hoped to join. What is more, the more tech-savvy of these progressive pedagogic reformers problematized the dominant educational reforms of recent decades for failing to take advantage of the unprecedented opportunities for learning that new technologies seemed to make possible. Such problematizations of the dominant educational reforms of recent decades, as well as a focus on the seemingly groundbreaking educational opportunities of the new media technologies of the moment, helped establish the Downtown School as a credible alternative to recent test-centric reforms.

What these processes of problematization and rendering technical partially occluded, however, was that the founders of the Downtown School were giving new life to an approach to education reform that has a rather long history. While it is an oversimplification to group a diverse history of educational reform projects under the term *progressive*, there are common patterns that help give the term analytic usefulness (for a review, see Labaree 2004). For one, progressive pedagogic reformers' processes of problematization are first and foremost focused on the identification of pedagogical shortcomings in traditional models of schooling. Since the days of social reformers like John Dewey, progressive pedagogic reformers have problematized the theories of teaching and learning that justify the pedagogic practices of traditional schooling. Traditional approaches to teaching and learning, progressive pedagogic reformers have repeatedly argued, start with an established body of curricular content and see teachers and educational media as mechanisms for transmitting this content to students. In a traditional school, teaching and learning are thus framed from the point of view of the teacher or, more accurately, educators and administrators who work at different levels of educational bureaucracies, while students are wrongly conceptualized as passive receptacles of existing social norms and cultural content. Traditional models of teaching and learning, progressive pedagogic reformers have argued, focus too much on ends rather than means, and they thus turn schools into instrumental factories where students are expected to efficiently memorize abstract facts and rote procedures just so they can pass tests and win credentials. Further, these abstract facts and tightly scripted activities have little meaning for students because they are separated from the concrete social and cultural experiences of students' out-of-school lives. Thus, supporters of progressive pedagogic approaches to education problematize more traditional pedagogic approaches for being boring and instrumentalist while concluding that it is no wonder that many students are not more motivated to participate in schooling.

These recurring patterns of problematization are also linked to recurring patterns of rendering technical. As a remedy to the problems they have identified with more traditional approaches to pedagogy, progressive pedagogic reformers have repeatedly advocated for approaches to education that they see as student centered, and many have repeatedly imagined that the new media technologies of the moment offer unparalleled opportunities for actualizing such a model. Originally influenced by romantic notions of the child from the nineteenth century, student-centered pedagogic philosophies tend to emphasize caring for the whole child, with his or her inherent creative capacities and unique interests, needs, and domains of cultural familiarity. Instead of conceptualizing learning as the passive reception of established knowledge and culture, progressive pedagogic reformers have repeatedly emphasized the importance of learners' active involvement in processes of learning and in the production of culture more generally. From this perspective, educators should not be authoritative gatekeepers to knowledge but facilitators who help and support student-driven learning processes. To quote John Dewey's famous maxim, people "learn by doing," not by memorizing abstract facts and rules that they then apply, or transfer, to other situations. Finally, by claiming to take a student-centered view, the progressive pedagogic tradition has tended to align itself with the needs and interests of the disadvantaged. Progressive reformers have helped bolster social justice agendas in public schools in part by foregrounding the ways in which entrenched axes of inequality—race, gender, sexuality, ethnicity, class, ability, and so forth—operate through schooling to further disadvantage nondominant groups.

All these commitments appear to resist the instrumentalizing and distorting effects of rendering technical. Yet when such commitments are brought to life in an actual reform project, we see that processes of rendering technical are not limited to educational reformers of a particular pedagogic or political persuasion. Like the reformers against whom they contradistinguish themselves, progressive pedagogic reformers tend to organize their diagnostic and design activities *as if* a reformed educational system could finally make good on its democratic ideals. Additionally, educational reformers who advocate for progressive approaches to teaching and learning have repeatedly placed their hopes on the new media technologies of the moment (Buckingham 2007). In doing so, even reformers who aim to design student-centered interventions end up participating in the processes of problematization and rendering technical that help regenerate cycles of disruptive fixation within the world of education.

While many of those involved in designing and launching the Downtown School knew that many previous progressive reform projects had not accomplished their goals and while the broader institutional and political-economic context seemed poised to thwart their aims, through processes of problematization and rendering technical they came to collectively imagine that this time could be different. They largely did so by attributing unprecedented opportunities for learning by doing to the new media technologies of the moment, as well as history-making powers to techno-scientific change more generally. By elevating the transformative power of both new technologies, which they knew well, and tech-savvy professionals, which some of them were, the founders of the Downtown School rendered the worlds into which they planned to intervene as especially amenable to their techniques and areas of specialized knowledge. At the same time, they problematized more conventional approaches to schooling for failing to solve the social problems with which they had been tasked and for being out of synch with a changed world, as these reformers imagined it.

In terms of the tight coupling between a proposed technical remedy and the ways reformers render the world as especially amenable to that remedy, the school's designers routinely evoked popular claims that associated recent technological changes with a new historical era: the digital age, the information age, the networked society, the connected age and so forth. This new era, which changes in technology had helped bring about, demanded new types of citizens and workers, the school's designers and backers claimed, and thus we urgently needed to change the ways we conceived of and built educational systems. As the designers of the intervention wrote in what they described as the "seminal document" of their design process, their new educational intervention would "respond to the needs of kids growing up in a digital, information rich, globally complex era prizing creativity, innovation, and resourcefulness."[23] This rendering of the world justified the particular educational remedy that they were designing as it problematized the more conventional educational reforms that focused on rote learning and standardized testing.

Moreover, the school's designers rendered the imagined targets of their intervention as especially amenable to the prescriptions they were designing. Like progressive-pedagogic reformers before them, the founders of the Downtown School saw themselves as designing a student-centered educational intervention. Such imaginings were bolstered by stereotypes of young people that were particularly popular at the time, namely, those that primarily conceptualized young people in terms of a naturalized, omnipresent, and enthusiastic relationship with digital media, particularly video games.[24] As the school's founders wrote in a document that described their design process:

> Today we live in the presence of a generation of kids who have known no time untouched by the promise and pitfalls of digital technology. . . . [T]oday's kids are crafting learning identities—hybrid identities–for themselves that seemingly reject previously distinct modes of being. . . . The phrase that best explains this change comes from Mikey, a student, who in talking about games said, "It's what we do." The "we" he was referring to are kids these days, the young people of his generation.

The school's founders emphasized this technophilic generational identity prominently on the school's Web site, in its promotional fliers, and even in the school's tagline: "a school for digital kids." In keeping with the progressive pedagogic tradition, the school's founders and supporters collectively imagined that the school's embrace of digital media and games made their reform student centered because children were presumably members of the digital generation. In this vein, the school's educators and founders frequently suggested that they had designed the school "with kids themselves in mind," and that they had "leveraged what kids are really interested in today, social networking, video games" and other digital media. Not only would educators supposedly focus on these themes during the school day, but all the school's initial extracurricular and enrichment programs would focus on making, remixing, and hacking new media technologies, valorized techno-cultural practices that young people presumably already took part in and enjoyed.

The school's designers also imagined that they could design new technologies that allowed the school to connect with students' lives outside of school. In doing so, they once again imagined students and parents' out-of-school lives primarily in terms that were amenable to the information and communication technologies they had on hand or were developing. For one, the school's founders designed and deployed a variety of digital tools for communicating with parents. These included a homework Web site, a weekly e-mail from the principal, and fairly regular e-mail exchanges between teachers and some parents. Additionally, and with the help of technology designers and the financial backing of philanthropic foundations, the school's founders helped design and build a Web site modeled after popular social media sites like Facebook and YouTube but limited to students, educators, and officials who were part of the various educational interventions that the foundation was sponsoring. The Web site was designed so that students and educators at these various sites could share media with each other, especially their own media productions, give feedback on each other's creations, and communicate with each other more generally, regardless of where they happened to be physically located. The Web site was imagined as an omnipresent space—much like the now popular metaphor of the cloud, although that metaphor had yet to catch on—that would accompany students as they navigated different physical spaces in and outside of school. For example, in a presentation at a conference for fellow educational reformers, one of the school's founders gave indication of how the school's design team had imagined a typical day in the life of a student at the Downtown School: shortly after waking up, the designer suggested, this archetypical student would log onto the school's proprietary Web site to chat with fellow students about an aspect of an educator-assigned challenge that they had yet to solve; at school he or she would continue to work doggedly on this and other assigned projects with her teammates; and, finally, after the school day was over, the student would once again log onto the proprietary Web site to hang out with classmates as they did their homework, shared and commented on each other's work, and generally had fun. As we will see, such imaginings did not anticipate that many students might resist or reject this version of schooling that had been designed with kids themselves in mind (chapters 4 and 5).

In addition to imagining that digital media and games would allow educators to connect to students' out-of-school interests and lives, the school's founders hoped that their cutting-edge intervention would meaningfully prepare students for the information-rich and globally connected adult worlds they would eventually join. Again, the aspiration to connect schooling to the real world is a recurring theme among school reformers who have repeatedly championed the seemingly unprecedented opportunities of the new media of the moment (Cuban 1986). Whereas previous generations of reformers had hoped that radio, motion pictures, television, and the personal computer would finally bring the real world into the school, the founders of the Downtown School attached this enduring yearning to the Internet and games.[25] The reformers' version of these long-held aspirations was particularly shaped by the scholarship of contemporary learning theorist James Paul Gee and Gee's former colleague David Shaffer. Both Gee (2003) and Shaffer (2006) had written influential books on the educational potential of video games, and Gee served as an advisor for the school. Gee was also funded by one of the same philanthropic foundations that had funded the design of the Downtown School, and he was one of the leading voices of this foundation's broader initiative focused on exploring and designing the seemingly unprecedented opportunities for learning that new media technologies now made possible. According to Gee, Shaffer, and the school's founders, well-designed video games were inherently engaging because they created worlds that allowed players to engage in continuously meaningful exploration and problem solving at a level calibrated to their current ability and knowledge. As Gee wrote, well-designed games are *"richly designed problem spaces"* and "context here then means a *goal-driven problem space"* (2008, 26 [emphasis in original]). In making their arguments in support of games and in keeping with the progressive pedagogic reform tradition, Gee, Shaffer, and the school's founders repeatedly contradistinguished a game-based model of pedagogy with the pedagogic model that took place at conventional schools, the latter of which, they argued, asked students to obediently and passively internalize cultural knowledge and follow rote scripts. A gamelike model of pedagogy, by contrast, would allow students to actively and creatively take on, or role-play, the identities of characters in designed game worlds. As Shaffer, Squire, and Gee (2005, 4) wrote,

[Video games] let players think, talk, and act—they let players *inhabit*—roles otherwise inaccessible to them. A 16 year old in Korea playing *Lineage* can become an international financier. . . . A *Deus Ex* player can experience life as government special agent.

What is more, the school's designers imagined that by playing and designing games, students would cultivate generalizable skills that could be applied in worlds beyond the school. In this vein, the school's founders routinely argued that "systems thinking" and "design thinking" were key bridging skills between the school and the real world. Echoing cybernetic arguments from the middle of the twentieth century, the school's founders argued in their design documents that the school would focus on

Connecting student learning to the demands of the twenty-first century and on supporting young people in their learning across digital networks, peer communities, content, careers, and media. The school is being designed to help students bridge old and new literacies through learning about the world as a set of interconnected systems.

In this version of rendering technical, school-based games, which the reformers could design and attempt to control, and the broader world, which they could not design or control, were analogously structured. Both were, at root, abstract systems, and thus games could be designed as simulations of the systems that organized the world beyond the school. As such, games appeared to provide an almost perfect media technology for overcoming the spatial and conceptual chasms that divided designed educational spaces from the esteemed worlds for which students were presumably being prepared: educational games could be designed as immersive, and yet simplified, simulacra of real-world professional worlds. According to this view, by exploring and solving simulated problems in designed game worlds, students/players would take on the identities of scientists, engineers, and practitioners in "other valued communities of practice" (Shaffer, Squire, and Gee 2005, 19). Echoing this sentiment, the school's recruitment materials claimed, "the school focuses on learning to 'be' rather than learning 'about.' Students take on identities of mathematicians, scientists, writers, historians, and designers." Through the challenging yet pleasurable process of playing these educational games, students would acquire the real-world knowledge, skills, values, and ways of thinking and acting of practitioners who inhabited these esteemed communities of practice.[26] More abstractly, students would develop presumably flexible and hence transferable skills such as "design thinking," "systems thinking," and, most abstractly, "twenty-first century competencies."

This new model of schooling, the school's designers argued, would not only provide students with a hands-on and engaging way to connect schooling to worlds outside the school, but it would also align the school with the more general, and often state-driven, mandates for STEM-focused educational reforms, and, in particular, the call to produce a generation of tech-savvy makers, innovators, and entrepreneurs. As the school's designers wrote in their planning document, "Design and innovation are two big ideas for the school." The designers of the school often made such claims as they problematized the pedagogic models associated with the dominant reforms of recent decades. Creativity and innovation, they argued, were best fostered by an approach to pedagogy that emphasized giving students the freedom to make decisions and explore solutions, both individually and in small groups, not by making students memorize known ways of solving known problems.

Giving a new articulation to the progressive pedagogic tradition's commitment to project-based learning, the founders also emphasized how contemporary new media technologies were especially well suited for collective cultural productions. Drawing on both popular and academic analyses (Papert 1993; Benkler 2006; Jenkins et al. 2006; Lessig 2008; and Resnick et al. 2009), the school's designers routinely emphasized that new digital tools and infrastructures now made it possible for anyone to become a designer and a maker, rather than just a passive consumer, of media, technology, and knowledge. But to do so people needed to have the right tools and competencies, which educational interventions like theirs could provide. The Downtown School's designers planned to cultivate makers, designers, and innovators in several ways. First, all students would take a media arts course, which in the first year focused on game design, as one of their required classes. Second, the school's designers planned to weave media and technology production activities throughout all classes, including those where the curriculum was defined by state standards. Third, the regular class schedule would be suspended during the last week of each trimester so that students could work in small teams on a single project. I will call this period at the end of each trimester "Level Up" in reference to the school designers' view that these sessions were a culmination of the term's curricular focus, as well as an opportunity to transition to the next, more complicated, challenge. Finally, and as already mentioned, the Downtown School would offer a suite of after-school programs that focused exclusively on making, designing, remixing, and hacking media technologies.

By arranging the pedagogy to be gamelike and by focusing on the creation, rather than the consumption, of media technology, the school's founders not only imagined that students would learn in ways that were more meaningful, active, creative, and engaging than conventional pedagogic models, but they also imagined that their remedy would uproot entrenched inequities in ways that conventional schools had not. As such, and like educational reformers more generally, the Downtown School's designers rendered their particular philanthropic intervention as an urgent *moral imperative*. As one of the school's designers stated in a press release when the school was launched,

> In an age when low-income urban kids continue to drop out of school at alarming rates, yet research is consistently showing the high levels of engagement youth are exhibiting in various media platforms, it is incumbent upon educators to take notice and indeed to redirect teaching methods to meet the needs and interests of students.

In sum, while processes of problematization and rendering technical helped the founders of the Downtown School imagine, design, and advocate for an alternative educational intervention to those that were dominant at the time, these processes also gave new life to a recurring pattern in which reformers advocate for seemingly innovative and disruptive educational interventions premised on recent advances in media technology. The founders of the Downtown School drew inspiration and interpretive frameworks from the progressive pedagogic reform tradition as well as from contemporary rhetorics about the transformative powers of gaming and digital media more generally. And yet, while the reformers explicitly differentiated, and in part justified, their remedy by problematizing the shortcomings of other recent educational reforms, the design and launch of their alternative was also made possible by what previous reformers had managed to put in place. In particular, the STEM mandate, and its expansion to include innovation and entrepreneurialism, school choice, and the autonomy portion of the autonomy for accountability exchange had produced conditions that allowed a remedy like the Downtown School to be imagined and deployed. That these opportunities would entail unwanted and uncontrollable pressures down the road did not appear to have diminished these reformers' optimism.

CONCLUSION

When contrasted with one another and viewed over decades or longer, educational reform experts can appear forever at odds with each other—and yet similar. Reformers who favor more traditional approaches to pedagogy and canonical knowledge routinely criticize progressive pedagogic reformers for weakening standards and failing to deliver promised outcomes. Progressive pedagogic reformers similarly criticize more conventional reformers for also failing to fulfill the philanthropic promises of education while also turning education and learning into a tedious and instrumental enterprise. Reformers also often disagree about what sorts of citizens'—and hence polity—planned educational interventions should try to produce: some wish for a more collectivist polity, while others wish for a more individualistic polity; some aim to produce creative and self-expressive citizens and workers, whereas others aim to produce citizens and workers that are disciplined and obedient; some imagine a harmoniously connected global world, while others warn of fierce national competitions. And yet, despite these differences, debates about the right approach to education reform share a tendency to match available means to desired outcomes in a way that also calls on us to forget that we have tried this before, repeatedly. And when reformers do recall that we have been down this road before, they often promise that this time will be different by bringing in claims about the unprecedented opportunities of new technologies, by asserting that we are in a fundamentally new historical era, or by professing new expertise that previous reformers presumably lacked, and so forth.

I should note that I am sympathetic to the ways that progressive pedagogic reformers tend to problematize more conventional pedagogic approaches to schooling as well as some of the theories of learning upon which they draw. I am also sympathetic to the social justice outcomes that they seek to advance. The problem is not that they misdiagnose problems with conventional schooling, that they have poor insights about how people learn, or that they desire a more just and collectivist polity. The problem is that processes of problematization and rendering technical translate broader political-economic and structural problems into problems that cutting-edge educational interventions could foreseeably fix. While approaches to reform differ in important and complex ways, together they help perpetuate the assumption that educational disruption can remedy issues of public concern, the latter of which are already abstracted generalizations of the different ways in which differently positioned people are trying to cope with precarious and uneven circumstances. And, if anything, reformers' conflicts and inevitable shortcomings generate conditions that help sustain further rounds of seemingly disruptive interventions. One reform project's inability to fix problems that are beyond its reach becomes part of the ground from which another project's processes of problematization and rendering technical spring forth. Regardless of which particular approach to reform takes root at a given place and moment, the idealization of educational disruption as a, if not the, means to realize more extensive social and political yearnings lives on.

This seemingly perpetual cycle is not animated by the idealism of experts alone. Experts do much of the concrete work of problematization and rendering technical, and, as such, they shoulder much of the emotional, intellectual, and physical burden required to propel a new cycle of disruptive fixation into motion. But these experts do so in response to demands and yearnings that are much more general. Because these experts depend so heavily on the resources of powerful outsiders—who have their own criticisms of the status quo, as well as their own passionate ideas about what beneficent social change would look like—the outsized promises that reformers repeatedly make are in many ways set by people that they can only partially control and influence. State officials, media pundits, and, increasingly, entrepreneurial reformers from the worlds of technology design and finance call upon and offer to support especially ambitious educational disruptions, and their offers to do so often set the stage for inevitable failure. As such, expert reformers are in something of an impossible situation. If they do not respond enthusiastically to the passions of these powerful outsiders then they cannot enact their ideas, yet in responding to these calls they also often have to make promises that they cannot be expected to keep.

As the following chapters examine, the fixations that processes of problematization and rendering technical entail limit reformers' abilities to accomplish their professed aims, and, if anything, they often lead reformers into the paradoxical situation of contributing to the very problems they hope to fix. Like any framing practice, these fixations help make the world intelligible to reformers in ways that are seemingly manageable and transformable with the tools they have in hand or are developing. They help specify objects of knowledge, allow for the diagnosis of ailments that can and should be addressed, and underpin imaginings of a better future. Yet these same fixations produce "tunnel vision" akin to Scott's (1998) analysis of state simplifications, and, as such, they are constantly being "overflown" (Callon 1998), literally from the moment that a cutting-edge philanthropic intervention is launched. The remainder of this book explores the relationship between fixations and overflowing. In doing so, it examines how fixations fare in practice, as well as what they manage to accomplish, even as a philanthropic intervention falls far short of its reformers' good intentions.

SPATIAL FIXATIONS

The Downtown School's new space was beautiful, but one of its doors was creating problems. The second academic year had just begun and the school's reformers and educators had barely finished moving into their new, and hopefully permanent, home. I had heard much about this new space during the previous spring when the school's designers and leaders scheduled a Parent-Teacher Association (PTA) meeting to discuss the proposed move. The school's original location on the east side of Manhattan had been temporary and could not accommodate the school as it grew, so the school's leadership, in partnership with the Department of Education (DOE), had been working diligently to find a new home. What they proposed at the meeting seemed to me, as well as the school's designers, like a big improvement over their temporary location, which consisted of only half a floor in a fairly rundown building from the 1920s that also happened to be around the corner from several methadone clinics.

According to the school's leadership, the Downtown School would get portions of at least two floors in a huge prewar building in one of the city's premier cultural districts on the west side of Manhattan. The new neighborhood was cleaner and wealthier than the current one, and the building included marble-lined hallways, depression-era murals by the Works Progress Administration, cherrywood cabinets, exposed brick walls, an impressive auditorium, and a swimming pool that was soon to be renovated. Additionally, one of the most selective public middle schools in Manhattan was right down the street, and one of the school's university partners was only a few blocks away. What is more, the DOE was promising the school a large part of the building's top floor, which had impressively high ceilings and arched brick windows with views of skyscrapers in midtown. That section of the top floor, which was currently being used as a recreational space by other schools in the building, could be used as an experimental space, a representative from the DOE suggested at the meeting. According to the DOE representative, Joel Klein, the chancellor of New York City's schools, "recognizes that the Downtown School is different . . . that you have a need for space so that you can be innovative." The space on the top floor could be a "play area," one of the proponents of the move suggested, "we can build it out and do whatever we want with it!"

Yet despite these apparent advantages, a formidable bloc of both privileged and less-privileged parents nearly derailed the school's plans to relocate. These parents were concerned, they said, with their children's safety and security. Interestingly, they were not so much concerned with threats from adults outside the school as with students from other schools that shared the same building. As discussed in the last chapter, in the years leading up to the opening of the Downtown School, New York City educational reformers had promoted marketlike school choice in part by closing large schools and replacing them with numerous small schools. Doing so, they claimed, would promote more intimate and cohesive learning environments as well as more choice for parents and families. The problem was that the DOE's material infrastructure could not be reconfigured nearly as easily as its organizational architecture. As such, numerous small schools—with different pedagogic philosophies, selection criteria, and hence student populations—were being placed together in buildings that had previously housed much bigger schools. For example, the proposed new home for the Downtown School also housed several other schools, and these schools primarily educated lower-income students, nearly all of whom were also students of color and some of whom were in high school. It was the spatial proximity of these other students that concerned anxious parents. Several parents expressed unease about the proximity of older students, whereas others worried that students from the other schools would resent the Downtown School's students for their newly renovated space, abundance of high-tech resources, and playful pedagogy. One parent cited reports about gang activity and an incident involving a cell phone being snatched in the neighboring park. No one mentioned racialized class struggles or the school's professed commitments to inclusivity.

In the end, these anxious parents were unable to prevent the school's relocation. Their concerns were partially mollified by building officials, who outlined the various ways they planned to keep students from the different schools separated: There would be a carefully orchestrated schedule of movement, there would be different starting and dismissal times for the Downtown School and the other schools, there would be different doors by which Downtown School students would enter and exit the building, there would be constant radio communication for coordination among security personnel as well as with members of the New York City Police Department, there would be a "safe corridor" to the subway, and there would be prevention and "zero-tolerance" policies; finally, the official promised that "if these [other] kids can't achieve success at their schools, we will redirect them to where they can achieve success." More optimistically, one of the school's designers reminded parents that the Downtown School was all about "teaching kids to think like designers and to take charge of their lives." The designer told parents that she understood their concerns, but she stressed that these were the types of challenges for which they could design solutions.

I remembered these tense discussions when I visited the school's new home and marveled at its recently renovated space on the building's top floor: surprisingly fashionable furniture that could be flexibly assembled into clusters for collaborative group projects, curved and multitoned walls, exposed brick, shiny new floors, and enormously tall windows that framed the Empire State Building in the distance. The new space felt more like the offices of a well-funded tech startup than a typical New York City public school.

As I was taking in the impressive new space I happened to notice a small window in a door that led to a gymnasium that students from the other schools in the building also used. Recalling parents' fears about resentment, I wondered what the students from the other schools in the building thought about the Downtown School's newly renovated space as they passed this window on their way to the gym. I imagined them peering through the narrow window into an educational environment that, while separated by only a few feet from their own, may have seemed worlds apart. While chatting with one of the leaders of the Downtown School later that day, I shared how uplifting their new space felt and asked if students or educators from the other schools in the building had expressed any resentment. "Funny you should mention that," the school leader said, before indicating that there had been some unspecified tensions. The next time I visited the Downtown School, the narrow window in the door that led to the shared gym had been papered over from the inside.

Cycles of disruptive fixation recur in part because of the ways that those who debate and design philanthropic interventions imagine and represent space. Through processes of problematization and rendering technical (Li 2007) and with the support and guidance of entrepreneurial reformers (Becker 1963) and other trustees (Li 2007), expert reformers collectively imagine and represent the worlds into which they plan to intervene as if they were amenable to, and controllable with, the remedies they have available. As part of these processes, experts have long imagined and attempted to construct spaces of enclosure—nations, cities, schools, factories, prisons, hospitals, museums, and so forth—that could be observed, measured, analyzed, and governed in seemingly rational ways (Lefebvre 1991; Foucault 1977; Gupta and Ferguson 1992; Scott 1998; Rose 1999, 31–37;

Ingold 2011, 145–55). For example, educational reformers have long paid particular attention to how artifacts, the built environment, persons, and activities *within* the enclosed space of the school can be best configured in order to effectively, fairly, and efficiently administer pedagogical interventions. Yet by focusing on the design and management of spaces of enclosure, these experts also exclude many aspects of the world that impinge upon, and thus help to produce, their carefully designed environments.

Some contemporary experts are aware that the spatial fixations of previous reformers entailed problematic divisions between the enclosed sites they tried to design and manage and the rest of the world, and many recent innovations in reform can be read, in part, as attempts to the fix the limitations of previous reformers' spatial fixations. For example, in the figured world of educational reform, scholars and reformers in the Learning Sciences, of which some of the founders of the Downtown School were a part, have problematized the boundary between the school and the world as they have attempted to extend the loci and foci of their educational expertise to include both formal (e.g., school) and informal (e.g., nonschool) settings.[1] These reformers now render and imagine the geographic contours of their expertise not as schools but as "learning spaces" or "learning environments."[2] For these reformers, a learning environment can be a classroom with a teacher lecturing to thirty students, an educational game in which students role-play the activities of scientists, or even an online course that enrolls hundreds of thousands of people from around the world. The interconnections of these various learning environments are similarly imagined as forming broader "learning networks," or "learning ecologies," that involve numerous actors—including state, corporate, and nongovernmental organizations—all of which should share societal responsibilities that have historically fallen primarily on schools.

The experts who designed the Downtown School were at the forefront of these recent trends. As we saw in chapter 2, the founders of the Downtown School imagined that they were designing a model of schooling that was connected to the world in ways that conventional schooling was not. By organizing schooling to be gamelike and by incorporating digital media production practices throughout the curriculum, the school's designers imagined that they were creating a learning environment that was connected to students' out-of-school lives and interests as well as to the tech-savvy communities of practice that students would hopefully eventually enter. They also imagined that new information and communication technologies offered unprecedented ways to connect the school to other learning environments, including homes, libraries, various sites for extracurricular activities and numerous online sites—such as YouTube, online fandoms, and Wikipedia—that the school's founders referred to as "global communities." While these possibilities for connection were imagined as groundbreaking, they were in fact a rearticulation of a longstanding yearning: that recent breakthroughs in transport and communication technologies—from railroads to television to the Internet—"annihilated space and time" (Marx 1964; Nye 1994; Mosco 2004) and, hence, could overcome the problems of spatial division and allow for the creation of a united democratic polity.[3]

This chapter explores what the spatial fixations that arose through designers' processes of problematizing and rendering technical excluded, as well as how they fared in practice. It does so by looking at the production, interconnection, and splintering of social spaces not only from the perspective of the experts who attempt to design and connect them, but also from the perspective of the people who navigate these spaces as part of their everyday lives. By examining how parents and caregivers, in particular, helped produce, divide, and connect spaces for their children in New York City, we can see how the designers' more expansive imaginings of open and interconnected learning environments remained narrowly fixated. Because reformers tended to render divisions between the school and the world as if they were problems that new media technologies could largely bridge, they also mostly excluded social and political questions at two important and interrelated levels: at the level of the school's entanglement in, and contribution to, processes that produce and maintain spatialized divisions of age, gender, and racialized social class and at the level of efforts to police the social boundaries of the spaces they helped bring into being. As we will see, these oversights contributed to numerous unforeseen, and often unwanted, consequences for reformers once they launched their intervention into the world, and these consequences helped produce conditions in which reformers and educators tended to remake and reinforce many of the same spatialized social divisions that their intervention had been designed to bridge.

RACIALIZED AND CLASSED GEOGRAPHIES

In New York City, residential real-estate markets mostly determine the sorting of students into different public elementary schools. The New York City DOE prioritizes the assignment of children to public elementary schools based on the property address where the child presumably resides. While DOE officials like to emphasize that there are numerous good schools throughout the city, parents and caregivers perceive substantial differences in school quality and thus seek educational advantages for their children using various real-estate strategies. As I got to know parents, I quickly learned that District Two in Manhattan, the district in which the

Downtown School was located, had the most sought-after public schools in New York City. As one of the school's less-privileged parents, a mother living in Brooklyn, described to me, "District Two schools have the majority of the money. That is why a lot of parents want their kids there." At first I thought the mother was equating school quality with a school's budget, but she went on to clarify that perceptions of quality had a lot to do with the sorts of parents who sent their children to District Two schools. She explained that District Two schools "have parents that are very active, and some of the parents there are freelancers, so they have all of this time on their hands so they can participate in school and do their work on the side as well. A lot of them are very well educated and probably went to college and probably have their master's degree. Compared to the schools here in this district, it is not like that. A lot of the parents are low-income families and not that well educated. That affects the school environment, unfortunately a lot."

Like other parents that I got to know, this mother's judgment about school quality was primarily based on social distinctions, a point that the mother admitted with some regret. As other scholars have also observed (Cucchiara 2013; Lareau and Goyette, eds. 2014; Posey-Maddox 2014), one consequence of these perceived variations in school quality is that families in urban areas, and particularly more-privileged families, often compete quite fiercely and creatively for access to schools with high proportions of privileged families; not surprisingly, privileged families are much better equipped in these contests. As such, struggles over admission to schools tend to further reinforce spatialized social divisions, especially racialized social class divisions and, in some cases, gender divisions.

As I learned more about how parents and caregivers tried to navigate New York City's public schools, I learned that the surest, but also most costly, way for parents to get their children into a District Two elementary school was to live in District Two and particularly in a neighborhood associated with its best schools. Many of these neighborhoods were located in the lower portion of Manhattan. Decades ago, theses neighborhoods—SOHO, Tribeca, the Meatpacking District, the Village, Chelsea—had been fairly run down, and some were still being used for industrial purposes, but as artists and other bohemians moved in and as flows of capital began to return to New York City during the 1980s, these formerly affordable neighborhoods quickly gentrified. By the time the Downtown School opened in 2009, demand for residences in these neighborhoods was among the most competitive in the United States, and exorbitant real estate prices—two-bedroom apartments routinely sold for well over a million dollars—had pushed former renters out of what had become prized inner-city school districts. Ironically, fierce real estate market demand, coupled with state-sponsored redevelopment efforts in lower Manhattan following 9/11, accelerated residential development at a rate that exceeded increases in available seats at the very schools that had helped drive residential demand. These capacity problems led the DOE to occasionally break the taken-for-granted coupling of residential geography with a specific elementary school, and when they did, contentious conflicts erupted between wealthy families and the DOE.[4] One consequence of these fights was that privileged families increasingly demanded that the DOE enforce its residence-based admissions policies more stringently.

Even some of the Downtown School's comparatively privileged families were able to remain in these coveted neighborhoods only because they had lived there for decades. These relative old-timers, who tended to work in the culture industries, often expressed indignation about the influx of more wealthy families into their neighborhoods, although these parents did not tend to volunteer that their own arrival had perhaps helped catalyze the gentrification process. As one parent, a bohemian creative professional, explained to me, "People moved to Tribeca just for the school, then the school got so overcrowded. It was ridiculous. It's kind of nauseating, because it went from some downtown professionals, but a lot of artists and a real mix, to a really bourgeois, Wall Street, professional, high-strung professional people." As the parent told me about the transformation, I shared that a similar change was happening in the neighborhood in Brooklyn where I was living while doing my fieldwork. We agreed that the process seemed to be out of control and that the outcomes were disturbing, even for comparatively privileged persons such as ourselves. "The neighborhood is nauseating," he said, "The amount of money, it's totally changed the character."

This swarming of wealthy professional families into neighborhoods with coveted public elementary schools had much more effect on less-privileged families, some of whom, despite their disadvantages, had still found creative, yet precarious, ways to get their children into District Two elementary schools. One family used a relative's Manhattan address on its application form, another student who lived in one of the other boroughs spent her weeknights at her grandmother's rent-stabilized apartment in Manhattan, where various family members took turns looking after her, another girl stayed at her aunt's apartment, a student from the Bronx had an elementary school teacher who introduced her family to the one of the Downtown School's founders after the teacher and the founder went on a camping trip together, and so on.

Additionally, a large number of the Downtown School's less-privileged parents and caregivers had gotten official permission from the DOE for their children to attend an elementary school in District Two. Known as a variance, once a student enrolled in an elementary school in District Two, he or she was promised a spot in a District Two middle and high school.

As such, enterprising parents who could not afford to live in District Two worked hard to get their children into a District Two school during elementary school. One way to do so was by having their child test into the DOE's gifted and talented program, in part because doing so made the student attractive to some of District Two's elementary schools that wanted a more ethnically and economically diverse student body. A sizable portion of the less-privileged students who attended the Downtown School had tested into the city's gifted and talented program, attended District Two elementary schools, and thus had variances that allowed them stay in District Two for middle and high school, if they chose.

However, I learned from these families that the process of getting a variance was becoming increasingly difficult, thanks to the rapid influx of wealthy families that had moved to District Two over the last decade. As one parent who lived in Brooklyn shared with me, "There were all of these schools in Manhattan that used to feed kids in from Brooklyn. They'd say, 'If you're interested in this type of education, come on.'" She shared how her daughter, who had attended one of those schools probably would not have been accepted if she applied today, "The Mayor says, 'We don't have enough seats. There's been so much development. There are so many people who are paying a million dollars for an apartment and their kid can't go to a school. So these kids have to go back to their borough.'" The parent seemed distraught by the change, even though her daughter had managed to get into a District Two school before the policy changes had taken place. "All of this is to say that because of that, as my daughter grew up through her elementary school, the diversity left. When she started it was very diverse and we were so excited to be there. But then, by the time she was graduating, it was less and less and less minority children in the school. The school took on this whole other culture."

These perspectives, strategies, and tactics make it clear that when residential real estate markets mediate access to public schools, parents and caregivers who are seeking educational opportunities and advantages for their children help produce classed and racialized neighborhoods that, by proxy, produce schools that are segregated along the lines of racialized social class. This process reinforces itself so that a few select neighborhoods and schools in the city have become enclaves of privilege surrounded by neighborhoods and schools that are overwhelming attended by students from lower-income families, most of whom are also persons of color. As researchers at UCLA's Civil Rights Project have observed, New York City now has some of the most segregated public schools in the United Stataes, without even taking into account its network of private schools.[5] And as parents clearly understood, New York City's schools were by no means equal since more privileged parents fundraised, donated resources and time, and brought their high levels of social and cultural capital to the select public schools where they coalesced.

When viewed from this parental perspective, the suturing of elementary schools to residential real estate markets complicates the ways in which educational reformers imagine learning environments as well as the connection of these environments to other settings. When parents' real estate strategies are taken into account, schools cannot simply be rendered as contained environments that, if designed properly, can equally promote a beneficent process called learning. Rather, when viewed from the perspective of parents and caregivers, schools appear as one of the main mechanisms by which classed and racialized social divisions are materialized geographically for children and the adults who raise them. Clearly such tendencies are not in keeping with democratic ideals about equality of opportunity and a united polity.

To their credit, educational reformers often look for ways to disrupt these divisive dynamics. But when they do so they tend to render spatialized social divisions as if they were problems that cutting-edge educational interventions could fix. For example, one way that educational reformers in New York City have tried to combat the contribution of real estate markets to the production of segregated schools is by introducing marketlike reforms that have become known as "the choice system." Such reforms have attempted to decouple the close relationship between access to particular schools and residential real estate markets. While well intended, these reforms do not appear to have uprooted the spatialization of entrenched social divisions, especially racialized class divisions. Instead, they appear to have extended the terrain of racialized class struggles beyond clashes over gentrification and into contests among families over who can gain access to, and wield control over, different educational spaces.

THE GAME OF CHOICE

"It's just crazy doing this. Most districts have zoned schools, we have the choice system," a professional mother said to me as we sat in the backyard of her apartment in downtown Manhattan. She repeated the word *choice* while making air quotes with her hands in apparent derision. As I had come to learn, this mother's sentiments about the choice system were rather common among the privileged families who had children at the Downtown School. Even though the choice system had been justified as a way to empower all families, families who lived in comparatively wealthy neighborhoods felt that the reforms had made processes of accessing desirable schools more precarious and labor intensive.

In New York City, the choice system begins in sixth grade. For middle and high schools, the DOE does not assign families to a particular school based on residential zones. Instead, families can apply to any middle school in their district and any high school in the city. Each school district covers a much larger geographic area than the elementary school zones and hence includes more economically and ethnically diverse households. Families can apply to any of the small, often thematic, middle schools in their district, and if they do not get into any of these small schools, they are offered a spot in one of the few remaining large "zoned" schools.

In some ways, the privileged mother's frustration with the choice system can be read as an affirmation that the choice reforms were working as planned. According to those who had advocated for school choice, offering families options would disrupt bureaucratic inertia, increase the power of families by treating them like consumers, and interrupt the feedback loop between residential real estate segregation and school segregation. Instead of concentrating quality schools in a few wealthy neighborhoods, reformers hoped that public schools from across the city would improve and become more diverse as they competed with each other for students. The privileged mother's frustration with the choice system suggests that this last goal was perhaps working as intended.

Yet the choice reforms had hardly overcome the problem of schooling's contributions to the spatialization of race and class divisions in New York City. While the choice reforms appeared to have interrupted the ability of wealthier families to use their superior purchasing power as a means of acquiring access to the city's best public middle and high schools, and while this disruption had contributed to new forms of angst among wealthier parents, the choice reforms had not managed to overcome the divisional dynamics that produced segregated neighborhoods and schools. Rather, they often reconfigured, expanded, and intensified those very dynamics.

While reformers hoped that the choice system would help erode the spatialization of racialized social class divisions and improve school quality more generally, most of District Two's middle schools remained largely segregated along the lines of social class, race, and ethnicity. Competition for entry into schools with predominantly privileged students was remarkably intense. By and large, professional parents in my study listed the same four or five small and selective District Two public middle schools that they considered desirable and acceptable. These schools had much-higher average test scores than the other middle schools in District Two, which was primarily an artifact of their admissions processes. Most of these selective middle schools used test scores and other criteria such as attendance rates in student admissions, and parents and educators suggested to me that these selection mechanisms were alternative means for producing predominantly segregated schools. Demographically, these "good" schools were largely populated by students who self-identified as white or Asian American on DOE forms, and they had comparatively few students on free or reduced-price lunch—a common measure of lower-income status among American educational researchers. By contrast, most of the rest of the middle schools, which privileged families would not consider, were predominantly populated by students who self-identified as black or Latino(a) on DOE forms and had a much higher percentage of students on free or reduced-price lunch. All these statistics, as well as a school's test scores, were accessible to families on the DOE Web site, which families were expected to consult as part of the choice process.

In an attempt to uproot these spatialized social divisions, the DOE had recently prohibited newly created small schools, including the Downtown School, from using test scores as part of their admissions criteria. But the DOE had also included a large loophole in these new policies. During admissions, administrators at new schools could indicate whether or not they felt an applicant was making an "informed choice," a criterion that schools could largely define and that was thus subject to all sorts of internal and external pressures. The DOE then ran an algorithm that matched family and school preferences, purportedly by using a lottery-based system much like the one used to match medical school graduates with residency programs in the United States, although nobody that I met was exactly sure how the process actually worked.[6] As we will shortly see, this informed-choice loophole became one of the ways that racialized class struggles were spatialized at the Downtown School.

While marketlike school-choice reforms had ratcheted up competition among schools, as their advocates had hoped, they had done so in a way that both intensified and expanded the terrain of divisive struggles among families. Just as professional parents swarmed to certain urban neighborhoods in order to get their children into to what they perceived to be the best public elementary schools, so too have these families flocked to the selective middle and high schools. In doing so, competition among families for educational advantages has expanded to include strategies for attempting to gain a leg up in middle school admissions contests, and these contests appeared to be incredibly nerve wracking. According to many of the privileged parents of students who attended the Downtown School, the selective middle schools in District Two were terribly competitive to get into, with some schools receiving more than 1,200 applicants for approximately 200 seats.[7] Professional parents also shared stories about the nuanced strategies families used in order to improve their chances of gaining access to one of these coveted schools, including test-preparation services, cultivating personal contacts with school officials, and aggressively appealing DOE rejection decisions. Much like the early admissions' processes for selective United States colleges, several popular middle schools were rumored to accept only students who had the highest marks on their exams and who also listed that school as their top choice on the DOE application.[8] If their child was not admitted to one of these coveted schools, parents could attend one of the two large zoned schools that had internal tracks that divided students with higher test scores—referred to as "special progress" students—from everyone else. What these professional parents would not consider were the other small public middle schools, which some referred to as "problem schools" or "magnets for problem kids." And as the vignette from the opening of this chapter illustrates, sometimes these nondesirable schools were located in the same buildings as the schools they coveted.

Without the mediation of residential real estate markets in the processes that sorted students into different schools, at middle school the wealthiest professional families who lived in District Two mostly left the public school system for private schools—which cost more than $30,000 a year—or they moved to expensive suburbs. As one professional mother told me, "At middle school, rich people peel off for private, totally. They're out." The transition to the choice system at middle school thus produced a rupture in the geographic trajectories of children from professional families, and this rupture was largely rooted in differences in professional families' economic and cultural capital (Bourdieu 1986). Whereas economically and culturally privileged families often shared neighborhoods and elementary schools, at middle school professional families—who would be considered economic elites by national standards, but not necessarily by New York City standards—entered the choice system without their even more economically privileged professional counterparts. The professional parents that stayed in the public system for middle school, and thus had to navigate the choice system, often worked in culture industries—such as academia, publishing, the arts, media production, design, and advertising—although some also worked as doctors, accountants, and other professional occupations. Unless their children had high test scores, these families had little chance of being admitted to one of District Two's selective middle schools, and even if their children did test well, their odds of being accepted were by no means guaranteed.

Less-privileged families, which generally did not have good local options in their neighborhoods, did not express nearly the same sense of anxiety and injustice with the choice system, but they also did not suggest that the choice system had finally presented them with ample and equitable opportunities. The most selective schools tended to enroll students on free or reduced-priced lunch at much lower rates than their distribution in the general student population, and the lower-income students that they did admit had already distinguished themselves academically from other lower-income students. Privileged and less-privileged parents alike emphasized that it took an exorbitant amount of work in order to do well in the choice system, and even then acceptance to one of the selective schools was highly uncertain.

To navigate the choice system, families were expected to attend numerous open houses at prospective middle schools in the fall of their child's fifth grade year, rank their top choices, and then wait for several months until they heard from the DOE about their match. On numerous occasions professional parents compared the process of getting into middle school to the college admission's process, and several suggested that both the process and the behavior it incited were crazy. Several of these parents also shared that they or their friends felt distraught, even devastated, when their eleven-year-old child did not match at their preferred school, a letdown that was even more distressing when friends and families from their elementary schools did get accepted.

It was partially into these competitive worlds of trying to be a parent in New York City—with their precarious, emotionally charged, and high-stakes educational contests—that the planners of the Downtown School intervened. While the reformers who planned the Downtown School imagined an innovative learning environment that would appeal to and benefit students from all backgrounds and while they worked hard to make sure that economically and ethnically diverse families could access their new school, during reformers' processes of problematization and rendering technical they did not come close to anticipating the aggressive role that parents—whom they could not fully know or control—would play in turning their disruptive intervention into a mechanism that produced and maintained problematic social divisions. During the very months when the school's designers were excitingly preparing to finally open the school, the seeds of these divisive forces were already being sown.

CHOOSING A CUTTING-EDGE ALTERNATIVE

While not yet proven, factions of professional parents, especially creative professional parents with boys, were intrigued when they learned that a new school would be opening in District Two. According to these parents, the Downtown School sounded like a promising alternative to the uncertainties and intense competitive pressures of the choice system, in large part because they had heard that the school would not be part of the regular choice system in its first year. Some had been told by school leaders that if they attended an open house they would likely be admitted. What is more, and like the school's designers and backers, the intrigued parents who worked in the culture industries tended to associate the Downtown School with progress and the future while simultaneously associating traditional schools with outmoded and ineffective conventions. In the context of marketlike school choice, these sorts of socially formed consumer tastes (Bourdieu 1984) played a key role in remaking and reinforcing spatialized divisions of gender, race, and class.

"When we went around to all the tours, I was thinking, 'Where is the school that's going to prepare these kids for the future?' They're all sort of conventional," a creative professional father shared as we discussed the school in his family's loft apartment downtown. "To me," the father continued, "when they opened their mouth at the Downtown School, when they did the open house, it sounded like they were addressing the future. I had been asking, 'Where is the school going to be? There's got to be a middle school somewhere.' And this was the one. I said, 'Oh, this is it, this is the school.'"

The professional parents who sent their children to the Downtown School did not often elaborate how the school's professed innovations would prepare their children for the future. Instead, they tended to distinguish the school in terms of what it was not, namely, a conventional school driven by normative developmental targets, tightly scripted routes for moving toward those targets, and standardized assessments for differentiating students' progress along those routes. All these factors contributed to the intense and disciplined competitions that many of these families hoped to escape.

"When I say progressive, it wasn't about test scores," a creative professional mother shared, "it was about getting these kids to learn and be creative. That's what I consider progressive. So the Downtown School was a good match." As with other realms of consumption, a preference for a seemingly progressive school was integral to how these parents imagined themselves in relation to others. What is more, and perhaps more so than just about any other consumptive act, the act of choosing a particular style of school was integral to how parents imagined the different sorts of persons that their children would become. "A lot of people have an idea of where they want to be in life," the same mother continued, "where they're going to send their kids, and go to medical school and everything. The Downtown School wasn't on that trajectory. The Downtown School was definitely a school that you went to because you really thought, 'Wow, this must be cool.'"

This mother's sense that progressive schools were a good match for her son begins to illustrate how market logics and a sense of choice can help ease tensions that are generated by having little choice but to participate in competitive and individualizing social systems. On the one hand, the mother's problematization of conventional schooling suggests that she understood the limitations of how educational systems sort children into labor market and status hierarchies, especially the tendency of these systems to produce excessive competition and individualistic behavior. On the other hand, she made these critiques in part to justify her family's choice of an alternative within those same systems. I will return to this theme throughout the book, especially in my discussion of what I call sanctioned counterpractices, but it is worth emphasizing now that a seemingly disruptive version of schooling was attractive to both creative professional parents and the school's designers because it seemed to offer a way to ease dissatisfactions that were being generated by their ensnarement in competitive, domineering, and highly precarious structures, but it did so while leaving the sources of those discontents largely intact.

What is more, while parents typically justified, and likely understood, these choices as an attempt to locate services and resources that were well suited for their children, such institutional matchmaking also produced social distinctions. As scholars have long known, when parenting practices involve navigating consumer markets, which they inevitably do, it is often through acts of consumption that parents attempt to resolve the various tensions inherent in trying to be a good parent, as they understand it, and these tensions are both structured by, and structuring of, more entrenched axes of difference (Seiter 1993; Cook 2004). As parents are increasingly treated like consumers of educational services and not just as consumers of neighborhoods that act as proxies for those services, they face similar issues and dilemmas as they do when trying to make parenting decisions through other consumer markets. In the preceding quote, the mother justified her choice of the Downtown School on the basis of what she considered her son's distinctive needs, preferences, and sensibilities. But like her definition of progressive schools, the traits that made the school well suited for her son were often distinguished from traits that were figured as well suited for other kids and families. In the preceding quote, the mother contradistinguished her family's preference for a progressive school against families who guided their children down what she perceived to be congested educational pathways that ended in medical school and, presumably, other high-status but conventional and competitive pathways into adulthood. In valorizing this contradistinction as creative and cool, the mother helped transform her family's experiences of competition and uncertainty—which pervaded her and her husband's professional lives, as well as their efforts to raise their children—into a distinguishing virtue.

This valorization of risk and uncertainty is not an individual trait; rather, it is collectively learned through participation in particular cultural environments and, especially, in certain occupational worlds. As Ross (2003) and Neff (2012) demonstrated, this sort of valorization of risk and uncertainty is a common characteristic of the occupational cultures of which these parents were a part, and it appears as if these parents extended similar sensibilities to the ways they collectively navigated a competitive and uncertain educational system. Indeed, similar orientations toward risk and uncertainty helped assemble the band of professional parents that were willing to enroll their children at the untested Downtown School, and their doing so further reinforced their self-images as creative and unconventional risk takers.

"We all got together," a creative professional mother shared, referring to how this collection of professional parents began to assemble into a coalition before the school even opened. "It was crazy, because it's a brand new school. It was really the risk takers that took it. We're totally risk takers, we just didn't care. It wasn't like we want to send him to medical school."

"Jump off a bridge? Where is it? I'll jump," her husband added laughing.

"I could see that even though [the school's founders] were talking about very strange things that I didn't really comprehend—I don't know, game design and all this stuff that I didn't really comprehend—in the end I just thought they sound like very rational people, they sound smart, and whatever they were saying to me sounded right. It wasn't like they were saying things that were really off the wall. And I think because I'm a creative person, I understood what they were saying. That's why I just said, 'I trust my kids with this school.'"

This sense of distinction from those who pursued supposedly uncreative, non-risk-taking, and well-worn, but highly competitive, educational routes into comparatively stable and high-paying occupations—such as medical doctors—was sometimes also racialized by white professional parents who drew on Orientalized stereotypes.[9] For example, when one of the white professional mothers described to me some of the selective, but more conventional, District Two middle and high schools, she shared, "But honestly, and I know I'm being recorded, but it's going to be a lot more Asian kids."

I told her that she could always tell me not to quote parts of our discussion.

"It doesn't matter," she replied. "Everybody knows that. At Hunter, and that's true at Stuyvesant too. The Asian kids are going to do the best testing."

In another conversation, a more reflexive white professional mother suggested that a lot of the white professional parents in District Two, and especially mothers, anxiously compared themselves to stereotypes about Asian American parents, a perturbation that typically entailed a judgment against supposedly Asian styles of parenting and especially mothering. Later in my study, the same parent noted to me that the publication of Amy Chua's (2011) polemical book, *Battle Hymn of the Tiger Mother*—which champions a set of parenting practices that are largely at odds with progressive pedagogic philosophies—exacerbated these anxieties. As we saw in the last chapter, a similarly anxious economic orientalism has pervaded recent public debates about a US educational crises, and injunctions such as "we need to learn how to produce more Tiger Moms" understandably offend parents who do not identify with these stereotypes or the parenting practices they index.

While creative professional parents tended to see their choice of the Downtown School as an expression of their distinctively risk-taking dispositions, it is worth pausing to consider how they understood and attempted to mitigate the risks involved. Importantly, while professional parents tended to portray themselves as risk takers because the school was brand new, they rarely expressed much concern about the school's seemingly singular pedagogic innovation: the attempt to turn the entire pedagogy into a game. Instead, and in keeping with the ways that parents of various class backgrounds differentiated schools, privileged parents consistently expressed palpable angst about who else might attend the school. As one professional father said to me on the first day of school, "The big unknown is the other students," before noting that the school had not had time to implement selection criteria, which I later learned was not true. Professional parents were careful about how they described these unknown other students, but it soon became clear that they were primarily concerned about lower-income students of color. In private, some privileged parents were more direct and conceded that professional parents were worried about "the underperforming minority students," which was ironic given that seventy percent of the students in New York City's public school system were classified as black and Latino/a in the DOE's demographic surveys. More typically, these parents coded racialized class divisions in ostensibly objective, and hence culturally neutral, terms such as "performance," "students with low test scores," "students who can't read," or "not good students," all of which they often also associated with "behavior problems."

"You want to go to school with kids who can read," another professional mother told me when we chatted at her home. "Because kids who can read in general are going to be a higher level at school, and there are going to be less behavior problems. Because in general the behavior problems correlate with kids who are not good students." Similar concerns were pervasive among the professional parents. As one of the school's founders said to me in an interview, "Rumors started to spread that we were accepting kids who nobody else wanted." I had heard similar rumors from privileged parents, and several professional parents even suggested that the DOE was "dumping" unwanted students on the new school. Not only did these coding practices mask more contentious lines of division, such as race and class, but they were also as inaccurate as they were essentializing and condescending. In fact, many of the less-privileged students who had been accepted into the Downtown School had high scores on standardized tests, and few had been automatically placed into, let alone "dumped" on, the school by the DOE. Professional parents also frequently coded contentious race and class divisions using less-contentious, but thinly veiled, geographical categories, most often labels for neighborhoods and boroughs that were outside District Two. This geographic coding was especially powerful because it accurately identified where a lot of the less-privileged families lived as it implicitly implied that families who lived in these neighborhoods were not supposed to be at the Downtown School.

To mitigate this sense of risk—while simultaneously propagating the collective sense that they were risk takers—in the spring and summer before the school opened, privileged parents assembled a coalition mostly of other professional families who agreed to attend the school en masse. This coalition was informal yet was assembled in part so that its members could wield greater power as they interfaced with a formal institution. While the school's founders did not know it at the time, this coalition had formed several months before the school opened, when one of the professional mothers contacted the guidance counselor at her child's elite public elementary school in Greenwich Village. She did so in order to find out which other parents from the school were considering the Downtown School. She also contacted guidance counselors at other elite public elementary schools that were located in wealthy Manhattan neighborhoods and asked for a similar list of parents who were considering the Downtown School. She then contacted these parents, started an e-mail thread, and eventually invited the prospective parents and children to meet each other at her family's home. Many of the professional parents who ended up sending their children to the Downtown School attended this meeting, where they agreed to attend the new school so long as a sizable number of other professional families attended with them. About a month after the school opened, members of this coalition held all the Parent Teacher Association's leadership positions, and they went on to shape the school in significant ways, as we will see in chapter 6.[10]

A very different portrait of choice, risk, and spatialized social divisions emerges when we consider how parents and caregivers from less-privileged backgrounds came to choose the Downtown School. Unlike professional families, these families did not tend to differentiate between five or six good District Two middle schools and all the rest, nor did they tend to express a strong preference for a school with a progressive pedagogic philosophy or present themselves to me as pioneers or cutting-edge risk takers. Instead, they often said that they sent their children to the Downtown School in order to mitigate the limited opportunities and heightened risks that they associated with their neighborhoods.

"I realized pretty soon that there are only so many good schools for the amount of kids that want to get into them," a father from the Bronx whose daughter attended the Downtown School shared with me as we sat in the kitchen of his home. "And basically, we didn't have much of a choice, being that we live in this neighborhood." Like the mother from Brooklyn, this father also differentiated school quality primarily in terms of the social composition of its families. "So that's another big factor for why I chose the Downtown School," he added, "because it's down there, and I know that kids are going to come from different backgrounds, different everything, different economic situations. And I wanted her to have that in her life."

As previously noted, a good portion of the school's students who came from less-privileged backgrounds lived outside of District Two, and these parents and caregivers tended to see District Two as the main choice to fight for in their children's education. In a different perspective on choice, one mother from the Bronx told me, "It doesn't have to be the middle school of your choice. . . . If you are in District Two, basically there are no bad middle schools in District Two." Parents and caregivers who lived outside of District Two routinely suggested similar sentiments when they explained why they had chosen the Downtown School. As one aunt who looked after her niece told me, "I did not want to put her in the school that everyone was going to. Only because some of those kids—and I'm not judging anyone—but some of those kids come from rough backgrounds." In another case, a less-privileged mother chose the Downtown School not because it was flush with technology and had a gamelike pedagogy but instead because the school her son had initially been accepted to required him to commute by foot past a public housing complex that had a history of conflicts with kids from their housing complex. "I didn't want to risk it," she told me, once again showing the variability in how families conceived of the risks associated with the spatialization of different learning environments.

When less-privileged families explained their rationale for seeking a spot in a District Two school, they also revealed how these strategies, while impressive as individual cases, would be difficult to expand into a more general political strategy and, as such, were beset with dilemmas about one's relations to families in their neighborhoods who did not or could not attend a District Two middle school. As privileged parents from District Two increasingly patrolled school borders, only a few lucky outsiders were allowed into District Two elementary and middle schools. As such, competition for these limited spots could fuel jealousy, resentment, and division among less-privileged families in their local neighborhoods, communities, and networks. Some less-privileged families seemed quite torn about these dilemmas, as evinced in the preceding quote in which the aunt included the caveat, "I'm not judging anyone," as she explained her decision to send her niece to the Downtown School, and many of the less-privileged families had strong ties to their local neighborhoods. Yet these parents and caregivers also often worried that the economic and social conditions of their neighborhoods could limit their children's potential, a concern that often intersected with ethnic and racial distinctions.

"This has been, for a long time, like a working class neighborhood of Puerto Ricans mostly," a father from the Bronx who had immigrated from South America explained. "I don't have a problem with the idea of working, doing things, labor. I like it. And that's so far what I get to do. But when people are," he paused, seemingly searching for the right word, "I call them doormen. They are living the life, sleeping, not being aware of things because they have too many, too much noise around them. I know that happens in every level, but more so in the working class because they explore less, I guess. So that I don't like. I don't like the fact of the economic situation rules your growth."

Less-privileged parents and caregivers also attempted to resolve this dilemma in part by justifying their acceptance to a District Two school in terms of a mixture of good luck and hard work, both of which were true. "My family and I, we kind of lucked up on the District Two," a mother from outside of District Two explained. But she had also done a tremendous amount of work trying to get her children seats in a District Two school. All her children had tested into the city's gifted and talented program, and yet the DOE still tried to place them at a local school, which the mother thought was inadequate. "I had to get a little muscle into it, a little bite, and I had to pull. My baby had to take the test over to get her seat and all these different things. But hey, that's what we have to do. And so when everybody asks me that question, 'Well, how did you get your children into that school?' I say, 'Excuse me, I worked to get them there.'"

There are several important themes that these varied expressions of choice, risk, and dilemma help reveal. The first is that nearly all parents were dissatisfied with, and in some cases even exasperated by, their educational choices. Some privileged families were concerned, if not distraught, with having to subject their children to highly competitive educational races and admissions contests, especially when their children were still so young, and less-privileged families were often concerned about the quality of schools, as well as other perceived risks in their neighborhoods. Second, in distinguishing the Downtown School from conventional schools, parents not only revealed dissatisfaction with the precarious conditions in which they were trying to rear their children, they also suggested a partial critical understanding of how educational systems contributed to this distressing precariousness. While these partial insights and inclinations were perhaps opportunities for deeper critical reflection, broader solidarity, and amplified political clout, the tendency for privileged and less-privileged families alike was to seek alternative ways of improving their family's chances within the very processes that produced competition and spatialized social division. Third, in making judgments about preferred learning environments within these systems, a key, and arguably primary, criterion of differentiation was the social background of the children and young people that attended these environments, a distinction that was often rooted in racialized class divisions but expressed in less politically contentious terms. Fourth, the increased emphasis on treating families as consumers of public educational resources not only amplified racialized class struggles in admissions contests, but it also made the process of choosing a school yet another occasion for negotiating intersecting dimensions of social identification and division.[11] As schools tried to differentiate themselves and as families tried to find a good fit for their children, the resulting matches often remade, and even exacerbated, the most deeply entrenched social divisions. For example, in its first year the Downtown School attracted boys at approximately a three-to-two ratio, an early indication that the school's disruptive new model might include inherited, but unexamined, cultural biases.[12]

The important lesson to be taken from this exposition is that outsiders' calls for disrupting education, as well as reformers' attempts to imagine and design cutting-edge learning spaces that will fulfill these calls, tend to overlook the often contentious social and political processes by which parents and caregivers help produce learning environments as social spaces. When educational reformers engage in processes of rendering technical, they imagine learning environments as if they were apolitical and culturally neutral spaces that experts can design, manipulate, and ideally replicate; the task for the reformer is to adjust the configuration of elements within and across learning environments—their activities, temporalities, artifacts, spatial arrangements, interconnections, admissions policies, and so forth—in order to create effective and fair mechanisms for transforming children from any background into idealized citizens and workers. It is precisely the possibility of this generalizability that allows reformers to specify learning environments as objects that they can design, manipulate, and connect. Yet these spatial fixations do not anticipate all the other actors who take part in the production of social spaces by way of their spatialized practices (Lefebvre 1991). When we look at how parents and caregivers face learning environments, we see that these are not just spaces of opportunity and affinity but also spaces of division, that is, mechanisms that spatially divide young people from adults and each other.[13] Parents' competitive and divisive contributions to the production of learning environments stand in stark contrast to reformers' imaginings of spaces of open and connected learning. Reformers' fixations about space do not incorporate these forces, in large part because the remedies that they have available cannot rectify the political and social conditions that produce such competitive and divisive dynamics, nor do they have the power to fully control parents, especially in the context of the choice system. As we will see, reformers are similarly hamstrung in their ability to construct learning networks that inclusively connect various sites of learning to each other. In order to elaborate these limitations, it is again helpful to look at how what contemporary experts call learning environments are connected to one another not just by reformers and educators but also by parents. As with parents' divisive competitions over access to and control over schools, reformers' spatial fixations mostly overlook and distort the ways in which parents and caregivers help produce and connect these nonschool spaces.

IMAGINING AND PRODUCING CONNECTED SPACE

As numerous scholars have observed (Holloway and Pimlott-Wilson 2014; Snellman et al. 2014), children and young people in wealthy countries like the United States, and especially children and young people from more middle-class families, spend an increasing proportion of their out-of-school lives in spaces that are ostensibly for children and young people but that are designed and managed by non-kin adults.[14] While these environments are not typically focused on formal schooling, scholars such as Annette Lareau (2003) have made important and influential arguments about how patterns of engagement in these spaces are rooted in class-based parenting strategies and are thus consequential, but often unexamined, sites in processes of social reproduction.[15] While Lareau was mostly critical of what she saw as a middle-class parenting strategy, which she referred to as "concerted cultivation," concerns about uneven participation in these nonschool activities have increasingly animated calls to extend the foci and loci of educational interventions beyond the settings of classrooms and schools. The founders of the Downtown School were at the forefront of attempts to do so by leveraging the seemingly unprecedented opportunities for connection that recent breakthroughs in information technologies appeared to offer. And yet, as the historian Larry Cuban (1986) has demonstrated, this desire to connect the school to the world has been a recurring longing of techno-reformers since at least the early 1900s.

It is important to recognize that this longing for a more extensive approach to educational intervention is appealing to reformers in large part because it seems to provide a way to finally overcome the spatial limitations of conventional schooling. As such, this imagining of seemingly disruptive remedies entails partial insights into the shortcomings of existing institutions, and these critical insights, coupled with invocations to new technological breakthroughs, help reformers convince themselves and others that their philanthropic intervention will be different from the disappointments of the past.

For the planners and allies of the Downtown School, new digital technologies seemed to offer a powerful new way to overcome the spatial limitations of conventional schooling because (1) new media technologies seemingly supported the proliferation of countless new learning environments that could match a diversity of different student interests, hence escaping the fierce competitions for access to physical schools, as discussed in the previous section; (2) new information and communication technologies seemed to provide a means for connecting learners to these environments, no matter where the learners happened to be located, hence overcoming the problem of geographically entrenched social division; and (3) these same technologies appeared to provide a means for connecting both learners to each other and learning environments to one another, hence transcending the problems of both enclosed educational silos and inherited, and hence unchosen, social division (for a more detailed articulation of this vision, see Ito et al. 2013).

One of the ways that the founders of the Downtown School designed their project in keeping with this more extensive imagining of connected educational spaces was by designing a suite of after-school programs that would allow students from different backgrounds to discover and develop their diverse interests with new media technologies. All the Downtown School's initial afterschool programs focused on practices that scholars have celebrated as "geeking out" (Ito et al. 2010) with media technologies, including comics, animations, game design, hacking toys, a marketing campaign for a new video game, electronically enhanced fashion items, fan-fiction, and so forth.[16] The hope was that these afterschool programs would lead students to participate in various online and offline worlds that were organized around their diverse interests.

During the years when the Downtown School was being designed, all these media practices, as well as the online spaces that they helped produce, had been championed by new media enthusiasts as uplifting examples of ordinary people's creativity, diversity, and agency in an otherwise corporate political-economy and normative social order (Benkler 2006; Lessig 2008; Shirky 2008). Examples of these "participatory cultures" (Jenkins et al. 2006) or "affinity groups" (Gee 2003), which primarily formed online, included Harry Potter fandoms, online gaming communities, fan-fiction sites, anime subtitling communities, virtual worlds, and so on. According to advocates, these emerging collectives were creating promising new spaces for learning. Unlike schools and locally-sited extracurricular activities, these online learning spaces cut across geographic borders and could theoretically be accessed by anyone with a good Internet connection. Additionally, advocates argued that these learning spaces had low barriers to entry, age-heterogeneous membership, and numerous opportunities for participation and, hence, learning. Finally, social relations within these learning spaces were primarily seen as supportive and cohesive, rather than competitive and divisive. The only real problem was that committed participation in these emerging learning spaces (e.g., geeking out) was uncommon, leading their supporters to warn of an emerging "participation gap" (Jenkins et al. 2006) that should be remediated through expert-designed educational interventions. If educational reformers could use schools and other sites of designed intervention to connect students to these emerging online learning environments, then they could also potentially overcome the spatial limitations that have consistently thwarted past educational reformers.

Such a vision of connecting learning environments directly influenced the founders of the Downtown School. In their planning documents, the school's designers indexed this spatial reach by referring to these online spaces as "global communities." In addition to sponsoring numerous after-school opportunities for students to geek out, the founders of the school helped build and implement a Web site that would allow members of the Downtown School to share and discuss their media productions and interests even when they were not collocated. As mentioned earlier, the Web site was funded by one of the philanthropic foundations that had sponsored the design of the Downtown School, and it was initially imagined as an online social network that would help constitute and connect various online learning spaces to each other as well as to various locally situated learning spaces, such as the Downtown School. The long-term plan was that young people from around the United States, if not the world, would eventually use the site to connect with each other around their particular interests in media technology. Importantly, and ironically given reformers' calls for openness and interconnection, both the after-school programs and the internal social network site were designed as enclosed environments, and only people who had been accepted to affiliated programs were permitted inside.

While the school's designers anticipated attracting broad, diverse, and enthusiastic participation in these interest-driven learning environments, it quickly became apparent that most students' interests lay elsewhere. Only a small faction of students regularly attended the school's after-school programs, almost all the regular participants were boys, and most of them had creative professional parents. Only one girl, whom I'll call Nita, regularly attended the school's after-school programs. Similarly, the school's private online social network site was a flop. Hardly any students used the site except when they were required to do so as part of a class assignment, and the handful that did use the site voluntarily were primarily students who also attended the school's media-focused after-school programs. The initial launch of the Web site was hamstrung by technical bugs, but even as technology designers smoothed out these problems, student participation remained tepid and eventually fizzled out.

To understand how seemingly innovative learning environments and networks ended up catering to a narrow, and primarily privileged, group of students, it is again helpful to look at the interconnection of learning environments not just from the point of view of those who call for and attempt to design and connect them but also from the perspective of parents and caregivers (this chapter) as well as students (chapter 5). As we will see, both of these perspectives largely escaped outsiders' calls for educational disruption as well as reformers' attempts to respond to these calls through processes of problematization and rendering technical. For one, while all the students had fairly extensive histories with digital media outside of school and while some even had experience with media and technology production, most students did not fulfill designers' stereotypes about a digital generation. Instead, these students spent much of their nonschool time in a variety of organized activities in New York City that did not focus on design, new media, STEM, STEAM, making, hacking, or other recently valorized tech practices. In contrast to some important and well-received arguments (Lareau 2003), I did not find a strong class-based difference in parents' attempts to locate extracurricular environments, but I did find that less-privileged families were significantly disadvantaged in their attempts to do so and that class differences shaped families' preferences. According to parents, New York City had a diverse and eclectic assortment of very good extracurricular options to choose from, but most were private and very pricey. Privileged families navigated, and hence helped connect, an eclectic diversity of spaces for their children, including numerous private classes, lessons, and tutoring for learning musical instruments, foreign languages, academic enrichment, horseback riding, ice skating, tennis, dance, martial arts, parkour, skiing and snowboarding, surfing, swimming, religious classes, and working out. Participation in these nonschool activities was also highly gendered, in large part, I believe, because of the salience of these activities in students' identity negotiations with peers at school, where pressures to participate in gendered peer groups were especially strong (chapter 5).

While privileged children had a fair degree of influence over selecting their extracurricular and leisure activities, privileged parents still played an important, but not always acknowledged, role. Like their choice of schools, the question of who else participated in these learning environments tended to be a key criterion for parents, regardless of their class condition. Just as privileged parents had networked with other privileged parents before applying to the Downtown School, privileged parents also often coordinated with other privileged parents to arrange collocated social activities for their children, to chaperone collective outings, and to enroll their children in the same after-school programs. When their children were younger, these privileged parents attempted to coordinate with other parents to arrange collocated play dates, and as their children aged, they extended these spatialized coordination practices to collective outings and organized after-school involvements. These practices of trying to facilitate and manage their children's peer relations through the coordination of col-located activities were especially common among parents, and especially mothers, of the privileged female students, suggesting that even parents who self-identified as progressive about gender issues continued to play a prominent role in remaking gender divisions among young people and that child-rearing responsibilities continue to be unevenly gendered in many families.[17]

According to the privileged parents who spoke with me about the topic, their efforts to shape their children's collocated participation in out-of-school activities were both pragmatic and strategic. Pragmatically, these parents took turns chaperoning each other's children as they shuttled them between homes, school, after-school activities, and others settings in the city. Their ability to do so was supported by having some flexibility about when and where they did their professional work as well as their ability to hire help. One professional mother, who often worked from home, had a routine of letting a handful of girls from the Downtown School hang out at her apartment on Wednesdays, a day when school let out early. Another professional mother sponsored a weekly ice-skating trip by paying a chap-erone to accompany a group of select girls to and from the rink. While this mother presented the ice-skating service as open to "whoever wants to go," in practice primarily privileged girls from one clique attended, in part be-cause ice skating was expensive. She offered this service in part so that her child would have something fun to do after school, but she also suggested that it was a way to facilitate her daughter's peer relations at school.

"Pretty early in the year I realized that I needed to help facilitate her social life more than I anticipated doing," the mother shared. Again reveal-ing how the classed social boundaries of residential neighborhoods threat-ened to break down once children reached middle school, she continued, "In elementary school, we walked to school and walked home, and it was easy, and she had friends in the neighborhood. Coming together for all of District Two, where the kids are from all over the place, it's much harder to manage socializing, and my daughter was a little more lost socially in this place." As neighborhood boundaries no longer did much of the work of producing spatialized social division, her tactics changed: "So I orga-nized: my babysitter picks them up on Fridays and takes whoever wants to go skating. So usually like ten kids go skating every Friday, it's fantastic." The ice skating was indicative of a more general attempt to manage her daughter's friendships, and it appeared to be paying off at school. "A lot of the girls' moms coordinate stuff," she continued, "A lot of the girls eat lunch together. And that definitely helped them feel more comfortable at school. So that's one of the things they do, that's just a social activity, but it's definitely a nice thing for them, that they have a social thing with other kids at school."

Once again we can see how parents played an active role in producing the actual, as opposed to imagined, social spaces and networks that their children navigated. Moreover, by attempting to shape their children's participation in various social spaces outside of school—which parents could more easily control and access—they also attempted to manage their children's peer relations within the school, a space that parents could not as easily access. As this mother rightly recognized, students' participation in various out-of-school spaces often played a significant role shaping the ways that their children helped produce spatialized social divisions within the school (chapter 5).

Less-privileged parents and caregivers also tried to manage their children's spatial trajectories and peer relations outside of school, and like privileged parents they often sought diverse options in an effort to find those that appealed to their children's interests and talents. But because of these families' economic circumstances, they had far fewer designed learning environments that they could access, and competition for affordable and high-quality options was often extremely intense. One mother from the Bronx shared with me how she would get up before dawn on a winter morning in order to wait in line for hours all in an attempt to enroll her daughter in an affordable and high-quality summer program offered by New York City's Parks Department. Even then, she was not always successful. "They start accepting applications in February," she explained, "and they start accepting applications at 9:00 in the morning. They only have 40 spots so I left my house at 4:30 a.m. last year. Do you hear me? 4:30 a.m. When I got there, I was number 55. I was like, 'Oh, my God. I can't believe it.' But I took the number." February in New York City is often bitterly cold, and I was trying to imagine waiting outside in the early morning for four and half hours, especially when the whole effort could be futile. "You stay on the line because if you don't have all your paperwork and you don't have the stuff, they won't take your application," she continued. "You have to have everything. So there were a few people that didn't have their stuff or whatever. This is what you have to do. This year I left at 4:00. I was like number 30 or something like that." The mother's efforts were admirable and impressive, but like less-privileged families' attempts to gain access to District Two schools, her strategy could not be generalized as a political strategy, and it too created competitive resentments. "People were there from the neighborhood, and, you know, they feel like, 'This belongs to us. We are in the neighborhood so we should have first choice.'" The competitive pressures and stress that such conditions encouraged were palpable and intense. "If you want your kid in something nice," she continued, "these are the things that you have to do. If you can't really afford some of this stuff, you have to beat the crowd."

Not only does this mother's story illustrate that there are not enough good services to go around, hence creating divisive and competitive relations among families seeking to access affordable programs for their children, but it also shows how residential geography is often viewed as a form of entitlement. In other words, just as we saw competitive and divisive class struggles in families' attempts to gain access to schools, so we see similar dynamics in families' attempts to structure their children's access to nonschool spaces.

In part because of the high costs associated with accessing private nonschool programs, less-privileged parents also tended to direct their children toward different spaces and networks of extracurricular activities than their more-privileged peers. Many of these students participated in after-school programming offered by other schools or community-based organizations like the Boys and Girls Club, the Make-A-Wish Foundation, or local churches. And as with their more privileged peers, the less-privileged students' participation in leisure and enrichment activities was often gendered. Several of the less-privileged boys were deeply involved in group sports, especially basketball and football, some of which were sponsored by not-for-profit community-based organizations, like the Boys Club, and some of which were offered by private leagues. The Boys Club was significantly more affordable than the private leagues, but even some families with limited economic resources saved up for a private football league. In general, less-privileged girls tended to spend more time in activities that were not managed and directly supervised by adults, in part because there were fewer subsidized activities that were attractive to them and in part because some of these girls participated in gendered forms of labor in the home. Some of these girls hung out at libraries after school, others went to their parents' work, others helped look after younger family members and cousins, and several just went home. Interestingly, and in part because of this relative autonomy from adult-managed practices during the afternoon hours, these girls were also among the most precocious students of social media; yet, ironically, these online spaces were not the ones that the Downtown School's designers imagined and valorized as part of their learning network, and, if anything, they were the topic of didactic lessons about online safety and civility.

In sum, parents and students' did navigate and help connect an eclectic variety of extracurricular spaces that could be characterized as different learning environment and learning networks. But designers' renderings of diverse learning spaces connected by new media technologies hardly approximated the lived spatial connections and related social divisions that parents and students helped construct through and beyond the school.

Reformers' processes of rendering spaces as technical objects that were amenable to their control almost completely excluded the ways in which parents—whom they could not fully control—helped constitute not only the various environments that students traversed but also the social connections and divisions between these spaces. The vast majority of the nonschool spaces that families sought had little to do with digital media or design, and access to these various environments was both structured by and structuring of entrenched social divisions. Designing and subsidizing learning environments played a role in producing these divisions, in part because the enrichment activities that reformers supported in these spaces appealed to some students much more than others. As one lower-income mother with a daughter put it, "I think the Downtown School has a great idea, I just think they should have more outside activities." At her old school her daughter had participated in various performing arts programs—including dance, singing, and theater—and she had become quite good at and enamored with these activities, none of which were supported by the Downtown School. "A kid is not going to be stuck to the computer all day," she shared. "Offer programs, offer dance classes, offer yoga." She also recognized the tight coupling between a learning environment's programmatic emphasis and the production of social division, especially in an era of choice. "It expands the school," she astutely observed, "Other people might want to apply. You might want to have a band, you know? A basketball team. Anything like that. Cheerleading. You know? Things like that."

In subsequent years school officials did expand and diversify the school's after-school offerings, in large part because they were having difficulty getting families with girls to apply to the school. But despite these efforts, the proportion of girls in the student body had fallen to thirty percent by the school's fourth year.

CONCLUSION

When people in positions of power and influence recurrently call for disruptive philanthropic interventions, they often commendably point to problems of spatialized social divisions and the inequitable access to opportunities, educational or otherwise, that often characterize those divides. They also typically invoke new technologies as a means for finally bridging spatialized social divisions and, hence, to help realize the long-held promise of a fair and united polity (Marx 1964; Nye 1994). When such calls descend upon the figured worlds of experts, as they repeatedly do, participants in these worlds engage in processes that problematize spatial divisions as they render the production and interconnection of space as if they were processes that reformers could control with the technical remedies that they are developing. For example, when these remedies center on new media technologies, as they do time and time again, reformers routinely render problems of spatialized social division as if they were problems that the information and communication technologies of the moment could overcome (Cuban 1986; Mosco 2004). Like other fixations, these spatial fixations exclude many factors that contribute to the production, division, and interconnection of space, including the contributions of the intervention's intended beneficiaries (Lefebvre 1991). In the case of the Downtown School, reformers rightly saw that conventional schools had been problematically imagined and constructed as enclosed spaces that separated the school from the world, but they also imagined that recent advances in digital and networked media would let them bridge these divisions. Through processes of problematization and rendering technical reformers' spatial fixations occluded many of the forces that would help produce and connect the spaces that they were designing. Once viewed from the perspective of parents and caregivers, reformers' imagined learning environments and learning networks no longer appear as spaces that experts can craft, connect, and deliver to the world in equitable ways. Rather, they appear as political spaces that help produce social divisions as various parties' attempt to access and control them. As the vignette that opened this chapter illustrates, the attempt to produce and connect special spaces for learning involves the ongoing production and maintenance of spatial divisions, and the construction and management of these divisions mediates the production, and often reproduction, of social divisions. Parents play an important, but often underacknowledged, role in these processes. When parents attempt to gain access to educational spaces for their children, one of the most important criteria that they consider is who else is included in and excluded from the enclosed environment. Parents attempt to make and use spaces as means of social division for many reasons, but they often do so under conditions that encourage divisively competitive dynamics. Widening economic inequalities and the increasing marketization and educationalization (Labaree 2008) of more and more aspects of young people's everyday lives appears to have intensified these competitive and divisive tendencies. Reformers are not unaware of these dynamics, but many of the forces that animate division tend to be marginalized, if not excluded, during reformers' processes of problematization and rendering technical. Because parental contributions to the production and connection of enclosed learning environments largely escape reformers' control and knowledge, parental contributions also tend to fall by the wayside when reformers attempt to design networks of interconnected learning environments.[18] As we have begun to see, these spatial fixations—along with pedagogic fixations, fixations about the project's intended beneficiaries, and fixations about

participation by the local community—contribute to all sorts of unanticipated trouble for reformers as soon as their philanthropic intervention is
launched into the world. The following chapters examine how these excluded forces destabilized reformers' carefully crafted plans and yet how
reformers largely responded to these destabilizing forces in ways that allowed them to keep their optimism for their intervention more or less
intact.

4

PEDAGOGIC FIXATIONS

About a week after the Downtown School opened, I was sitting with students in a class that focused on science. The class began much like a traditional middle school science class. The teacher, Cameron, controlled a PowerPoint presentation from the front of the room, and the students and I sat quietly on stools around elevated tables with slate tops and sinks in the middle. Cameron explained, "We are going to go over some classroom procedures that are boring and not fun." The procedures included step-by-step scripts for how we were supposed to enter and exit the classroom. He also explained that each table was a group and that each member of the group would have a job. In response, a few students asked questions such as, "Will we get a paycheck?" and "Can we get fired?" Cameron did not answer these questions but instead clapped his hands in a pattern that the students had learned to repeat back. The room quieted and Cameron continued listing the jobs. The first two jobs were Paper Collectors, to which one of the students at my table whispered to the rest of us, "One, two, three, not it." The next job was called Material Master, and the final job was called Clock Watcher. The students at my table debated who would be the Material Master—nobody wanted to be the Clock Watcher or the Paper Collectors—and eventually a coin toss by Cameron settled the issue.

After jobs were assigned, Cameron showed a slide with a picture of Isaac Newton and asked students if they knew the person in the image. At this point I noticed one of the school's designers, the principal, and another adult—who I later learned was a reporter—quietly enter the back of the room. Cameron told us that while we all knew about YouTube, we probably did not know that there was also a Web site called TeacherTube. Cameron then started a video clip titled "Newton's First Law," which opened with a shot of dominoes knocking each other over in a chain reaction. At first, the video looked like a typical instructional video, except that glitches occasionally disrupted the image and the sound seemed muddled and distorted. Suddenly, odd-looking sock-puppet characters—which I later learned had been appropriated from the popular video game Little Big Planet 2—bounced across the screen while making unintelligible squeals. The students looked as perplexed as I was. Cameron stopped the video, said, "That's weird," and then fussed with his computer. As he did so he casually shared that perhaps an e-mail he had received that morning could help us figure out what was going on. Cameron projected the email onto the Smart Board at the front of the classroom, and we read that there was a hidden package in the back of the classroom.

Everyone was looking at Cameron, their backs erect, and a few even stood on their feet. One student called out, "Why are you doing this?" Cameron did not answer the student but instead told the class that he was going to form a search party to look for the hidden package. He asked for volunteers, and nearly all the students' hands went up. The four students that Cameron chose for the search party quickly scrambled to the back of the room and scoured the tables, chairs, and cubbies. Soon, one of these students found a large manila envelope that had been taped under a table. Cameron asked the student to bring him the envelope, from which he retrieved a letter that was adorned with pictures of the sock-puppet characters that we had seen in the video. According to the letter, these characters needed our help because their houses kept falling down. According to Cameron, the students would spend the rest of the trimester trying to help the sock-puppet characters learn how to build better houses. To do so, we would have to learn about physics.

At the back of the room, the designer, principal, and reporter smiled and whispered among themselves before leaving. Cameron quieted the class and then asked several students to pass out a worksheet that had also been included in the package from the sockpuppet characters. The worksheet asked us to make identification badges, and Cameron told us that if we did not finish our badges during class time, then we could finish them at home. The next time the class met Cameron passed out a second worksheet, also purportedly from the sock puppets. This one asked the students to look at a technical diagram and answer questions such as, "What information can be gathered from the picture?" Cameron told us we had eight minutes to do the worksheet and that if we did not finish, it would be homework. He projected a countdown timer onto the Smart Board and we got to work.

———————————

Tracing the processes by which yearnings for philanthropic disruption are translated into interventions that paradoxically tend to help remake and extend existing institutional arrangements and power relations, chapter 3 examined how reformers' spatial fixations largely exclude the ways in which the production of space is always part of more extensive political processes that reformers' cannot control. These oversights were made visible once the production and connection of learning environments was viewed not only from the perspective of reformers and designers but also from the perspective of parents and caregivers. This chapter examines how similar tunnel vision is entailed in reformers' pedagogic fixations. Like spatial fixations, pedagogic fixations occur through processes of problematization and rendering technical, but pedagogic fixations focus on changing persons rather than on spaces per se. Pedagogic fixations help reformers act, think, and feel *as if* the activities they are imagining and designing for others are both novel and in the best interest of their recipients. Philanthropic interventions that aim to transform and improve a target population often entail these pedagogic fixations, and yet, as we will see, these fixations are also remarkably fragile and hence have to be repeatedly repaired in practice in order to survive.

While pedagogic fixations help reformers and their backers act as if they are participating in a project that is innovative and beneficial for the target population, factors and forces excluded by these fixations create countless unanticipated problems for reformers as soon as their intervention is launched. Once an intervention is set down in the world, these unanticipated forces overflow the project and destabilize reformers' carefully designed activities, so much so that reformers can even worry that their project will collapse. In theory, these moments of instability are opportunities when reformers can reexamine their pedagogic fixations, and to some extent they do. But the dominant tendency is not so much to question the fixations that arose during processes of problematization and rendering technical as to engage in a different sort of fixation: reformers quickly reach for stabilizing resources wherever they can. Ironically, many of the resources that are ready-to-hand come from canonical practices in the figured worlds that reformers aim to disrupt (DiMaggio and Powell 1983). As such, attempts to disrupt the status quo in open and improvisational ways can have the paradoxical consequence of refixing activity into rather enduring and tightly scripted forms.

Curiously, many of the people who committed themselves to the Downtown School mostly maintained their pedagogic fixations throughout these processes, particularly their sense that the school's pedagogic activities were both unconventional and philanthropic. From a social practice theory perspective (Holland and Lave 2001), the endurance of these pedagogic fixations cannot be reduced to dogmatism or simplistic notions of ideology. Rather, we must look for how these fixations are maintained and repaired in practice, in part through what the ethnographer Amanda Lashaw (2008) has characterized as "the ample production of hope." Ironically, it is partly through this ongoing revitalization of optimism that reformers often end up helping to remake and extend that which they hope to disrupt.

DESIGNING BENEFICIAL EXPERIENCES

As discussed previously, the Downtown School's most distinctive innovation was to try to redesign the pedagogic activities of schooling as if they were an engaging and beneficent game. Like the reformers' spatial fixations, this pedagogic fixation partially arose through processes that problematized not only conventional schooling but also modernist state institutions more generally. Like many other social reformers who have been inspired by the seemingly dynamic organizations and work cultures of Silicon Valley, the designers and backers of the Downtown School problematized reformers of the past for creating organizations that were hierarchical, rigidly scripted, and, hence, controlling. These previous attempts at social and organizational engineering were seen as inhibiting, rather than enhancing, the capacities of the people who worked in bureaucratic organizations as well as the people those organizations claimed to serve. By contrast, games appeared to offer an inspiring alternative model for how experts and managers could design and organize experiences for others. Game design, and experience design more generally, appeared to offer a way for experts and managers to craft activities that were organized and goal driven but also flexible, improvisational, creative, and even fun. Most importantly, doing so would allow experts to redesign activities that benefited people in ways that more Tayloristic approaches to organizing activity did not. Games and experience design, proponents argued, would help unleash people's inherent creative capacities and would thus amplify innovation, learning, and personal satisfaction.

Of particular interest to the reformers who designed the Downtown School was the work of the sociolinguist James Paul Gee, who had written an influential book on the educational potential of video games (2003). Gee had also received large grants from one of the philanthropic foundations that was sponsoring the Downtown School, and he served as an advisor on the project. By turning pedagogic activities into a game, the school's designers hoped to overcome conventional schooling's emphasis on tightly scripted and obedient behavior as well as its related reliance on surveillance and coercive disciplinary techniques, which, as we know from Foucault (1977), are not features unique to schools. According to Gee and the school's founders, well-designed games would allow students to actively and creatively explore a "problem space" that became incrementally more difficult as the players progressed and as their skills developed. Moreover, these games would provide students with a context for their activity and, thus, with resources for constructing personal meanings and emotional investments in their school-based activities. By taking on the identity of the game's characters, students would not only be motivated to participate in schooling, but they would also produce beneficial personal transformations, conceptualized as learning, as they did so.

The vignette at the opening of this chapter begins to illustrate how the Downtown School's designers tried to implement this hopeful vision of pedagogic activity. Near the beginning of a trimester, the teacher in each course would introduce a "mission" for that course. These episodes, which typically lasted for twenty to thirty minutes, were meant to introduce students to the designed game world that would frame the students' schoolwork in that course for the trimester. The designed game worlds would consist of characters that did not belong to the school and who needed the students' help. For example, the sock puppets described in the vignette at the opening of this chapter needed the students' help so that their houses would stop falling down. In another class, a set of fictional characters needed the students' help decoding messages in order to solve a mystery about a missing character. In still another class, professional editors at the transnational media conglomerate Pearson supposedly needed students' help designing educational comics, and so on. Guided by teachers, students would interact with these nonschool characters through Skype phone calls, video chats, recorded videos, blogs, e-mails, physical letters, and other telecommunications. In practice, these episodes were a noticeable break from conventional classroom activities, and, as evinced in the opening vignette, many students did appear to be alert and engaged when they occurred, much as the reformers had hoped.

But when considered in terms of the school's everyday routines, a very different picture of the school's pedagogic practices begins to emerge. Most noticeably, these unconventional and less-scripted moments were rather fleeting and negligible compared to the abundance of conventional, highly scripted, schooling activities. After brief episodes in which students communicated with characters from the designed game worlds, daily life would quickly return to familiar school routines in which managers, here teachers, issued subordinates a near constant succession of fine-grained commands. In the vignette just described, the sock puppets assigned the students paper worksheets that could be completed as homework if they did not finish them in class. In the school's math class, which had been framed as a code-breaking academy, one of the students' first challenges was to take a paper and pencil test on fractions. In class after class, a common pattern emerged: after an unconventional and improvisational exchange with characters from the designed game worlds, educators returned to conventional schooling practices with familiar power relations and adult-scripted activities, but these schooling practices had been relabeled as if they were part of the game.

Consider, for example, how the school's designers attempted to transform the familiar disciplinary practices of hierarchical observation, normalizing judgments, and examinations (Foucault 1977). According to the school's designers, their goal was to help all students become masters in the school's various knowledge domains. Much like a video game, students would get feedback rather than grades, and progress would be measured in terms of moving through various stages and levels in the game. Moreover, this feedback would supposedly come from within the designed game worlds. Instead of teachers assessing students, characters in the designed game worlds would supposedly evaluate students' work. The beforementioned paper-and-pencil test for the code-breaking academy is an example of this sort of symbolic transformation of a familiar disciplinary technique. The teacher presented the test as if it were an entrance exam to the code-breaking academy, but it was also a formative assessment for the school's educators. Moreover, the feedback students received on their various assignments did not use letter grades or points out of one hundred, as is done in conventional schools, but it was still organized on a linear scale with five ranked categories—master, senior, apprentice, novice, and prenovice—each of which also had the equivalent of pluses and minuses—Level 1, Level 2, and Level 3. The labels had changed, but the underlying practices had not.

The school's designers envisioned a similar transformation in how they organized the curriculum. All students were required to take the same five courses, and they had little say over what they were expected to learn in each course. While the reformers referred to these courses as *domains* and assigned imaginative new labels to each one, the content of these courses was defined mostly by state standards and to a lesser degree the school's designers and educators. One course covered New York State's standards for sixth grade science education, another class focused on the state standards for math education, another combined social studies and English and language arts, and another course blended physical fitness with what educators referred to as "socioemotional learning." The school's most unconventional course focused entirely on media production, which in the school's first year consisted of game design. The reformers also tried to incorporate what they referred to as "twenty-first century literacies" within these domains, which in the school's first year consisted of teamwork, systems thinking, and time management. Each domain was supposed to focus on these literacies as well as the state-mandated content. In any case, students had no voice in shaping the curriculum, despite reformers claims to be student centered.

Spatial and temporal routines also mostly resembled conventional schooling practices; if anything, they were even more tightly scripted by adults than I recalled from my own experiences in public middle school. Students were expected to be within the physical boundaries of the school from 8:30 in the morning until 3:30 in the afternoon. During this time, adults required students to participate in a nearly continuous succession of tasks that educators defined and oversaw. A standardized schedule co-ordinated the movement of classes between rooms and the transfer of authority between adults at nine points during the day. Thirty minutes at the beginning of each day was scheduled for a schoolwide assembly, called Morning Meeting, and a follow-on 10- to 15-minute advisory period. There were then four 50-minute academic periods, followed by 45 minutes that was split between lunch and recess, followed by two more 50-minute academic periods, before ending the day with a 15-minute advisory session. Throughout the week, individual classes would oscillate between 50 and 100 minutes, taking up one or two scheduled periods. Within each of these time blocks, teachers directed students to work on scripted tasks that typically lasted 20 minutes or less, and many of these scripted activities were broken down into successive step-by-step procedures that resembled algorithms.

Typical pedagogic activities consisted of small projects, minilessons, and short assignments. Projects were the least adult-scripted activities and yet adults had a heavy hand in managing these activities as well. Students usually worked on a project in increments of thirty minutes or less over several class periods. Educators defined project goals and often the roles of teammates. In many cases, teachers also assigned students to different roles, provided directives on how to reach those goals, and assessed the quality of students' work. Minilessons, which were a daily routine in most classes, followed the familiar lecture format. Teachers provided information and modeled phenomena as students took notes and sometimes asked questions. Minilessons were typically shorter than projects. Many were approximately ten minutes in length, and in longer periods teachers would sometimes do more than one minilesson per class. Assignments tended to be highly scripted information-seeking tasks or problem set exercises. For information-seeking assignments, teachers typically provided students with a book, a photocopied packet (usually copied from a textbook), or a specific Web site. Students would then answer questions by extracting information from the designated source and transferring it, often with minimal interpretation or translation, to a preformatted answer document. Sometimes students would answer these questions on paper handouts and sometimes they would use the school's laptops to answer questions in a Google Doc that was accessible to the teacher. When using the Internet, the teacher would define which Web site and even which Web page the students should access, and students would be reprimanded for leaving the specified Web page. Problem sets mostly resembled standardized tests and were primarily used in the math-themed class. These, too, tended to be relatively brief, with most lasting twenty minutes or less.

This sketch of the quotidian pedagogic activities at the Downtown School shows a puzzling discrepancy between the reformers' vision of unprecedented creativity and fun and the striking conventionality of daily life in the school, a conventionality that educational historians David Tyack and Larry Cuban (1995) referred to as the "grammar of schooling." While the reformers championed student agency and creativity, students had very little say about what they could do, and most of what they were supposed to do was quite similar to the very schooling practices that reformers criticized and aimed to replace. Most of what reformers had changed was the language used to describe these conventional practices.[1]

Later we will see how reformers managed to work with and through these seeming contradictions but, for now, it is important to emphasize two key points that are central to this later analysis. First, forces that reformers could not control often structured the practices that they most overlooked. Just as the reformers tended to downplay their school's entanglement in competitive processes of social selection, so too they tended to overlook and underemphasize the ways in which their entanglement in educational systems structured much of the project's pedagogic activities. Newly available means, as I have been emphasizing, tended to fix reformers' energy and attention on what they could foreseeably control and transform with these new tools. Second, it is worth noting how reformers' optimistic vision of disruption obscured the ways in which those who enacted the project would exercise power over those that they figured as beneficiaries of their philanthropic intervention. If games had especially strong motivational powers and if contemporary youth voluntarily played games for hours on end, then a gamelike intervention would seemingly escape the ethically thorny issue of coercing participation. Similarly, if feedback came from fictional game characters, then educators did not appear to be exercising power over students through grading practices, and so on. This downplaying of the power relations inherent in pedagogic interventions was an optimistic oversight that left reformers unprepared to deal with people who resisted the reformers' philanthropic offerings, as we will now see.

OVERFLOWING AND RETROFITTING

Not long after the school opened, it became evident that the school's gamelike pedagogy did not have the motivational powers that the school's designers had hoped. Almost immediately after the school opened, many school leaders, teachers, and parents worried that students were out of control. Some students talked back, made fun of the designed game characters, ignored or played with directives from teachers, and generally asserted themselves in ways that made it difficult for teachers to stick to the scripted activities that they, game designers, and curriculum designers had jointly crafted. Students were exercising their creativity and agency, but not in the ways that the school's designers had anticipated or desired. Instead, students were transforming the reformers' carefully designed activities toward their own interests and sensibilities. Here, for example, is a snippet from my field notes not long after the school opened:

> We're lined up in the hallway waiting for Sarah [the teacher] to take us to the gym. Before heading up the stairs Sarah reminds us of the procedures we're supposed to follow after we arrive: place our bags and jackets against the wall, run three laps around the perimeter of the gym, then get in a big circle and quietly wait for her instructions.
>
> Sarah goes on to tell us about the main activity for the day. She tells us we're going to split into two lines and play a game with basketballs. Troy shouts out, "Knockout!" Several other students follow his lead and also shout out "Knockout." Sarah ignores them and starts explaining what we're going to do: a student at the front of one line will shoot the basketball, then the person from the front of the other line will rebound the ball and give it to the next person in the shooting line. Each student will then go to the end of the opposite line and the process will repeat.
>
> "That's not Knockout," Troy says.
>
> Sarah says that this is what we'll be "playing" today. Troy counters that Knockout is more fun.
>
> Sarah responds by telling Troy, "When you grow up and become a teacher then you can have everyone play Knockout." Sarah also reminds the students that gym was part of their grade.
>
> Raka blurts out, "Who knew so much fun stuff would be part of our grade?"
>
> Sarah tells him to, "Knock off the attitude."

A similar dynamic played out in every class: when students tried to question or bend reformers' and educators' scripted activities, educators corrected them and tried to compel their participation in the school's version of fun. Many educators equated student resistance with personal disrespect or with spoiling the fun of the group. For example, when one of the students called out, "This is so fake!" as the teacher showed students a blog message that had supposedly been written by a master game designer, the teacher snapped back, "Stop ruining it for everyone!" Similar tensions played out in all classes, especially at the beginning of the year.

Reformers' and educators' concerns about control also extended beyond the pedagogic activities of classrooms. As just mentioned, the school's designers had allocated forty-five minutes for lunch and recess, which they roughly split into two equal time blocks. At the beginning of the year students could more or less do what they liked during recess so long as they hung out in a designated classroom or the gym, both of which were monitored by adults. The students who hung out in the gym produced a heterogeneous assortment of activities that often bled into one another. Students moved around noisily and fluidly, many improvisational games emerged, and participants moved in and out of various activities, changing their own course and the course of the activities in the process. Some students shot basketballs, some played with jump ropes, others did cartwheels, some roamed the perimeter of the gym, and others hung out with friends in small groups. Many students moved between activities and social groups and there was no clear overarching plan or structure, perhaps suggesting opportunities for breaking down preconceptions about class, gender, and race.

However, some of the school's designers and educators worried that this arrangement was too chaotic, noisy, and out of control. As one of the school's designers mentioned to me as we watched the students play during recess, "I don't know if they [the students] can handle this. I could hear them from the street when I went to get lunch." These moments of concern evince the dilemmas that contemporary institutional reformers face as they try to reconcile, on the one hand, their aspiration to design activities that promote creativity, agency, and transformations toward self-realization among an intervention's intended beneficiaries and, on the other hand, the more instrumental mandate to control, measure, and develop those persons into particular idealized subjects.

While these dilemmas could theoretically be moments in which reformers questioned their assumptions, and particularly the enduring yearning to create apolitical and philanthropic mechanisms for learning, the dominant tendency was to engage in a different sort of fixation: the school's designers and educators quickly searched for resources that would stabilize the project against the unanticipated turbulence of students' unsanctioned behavior. In response to students' resistance to the adult-scripted activities—all of which evinced the student-centered agency that reformers championed—the school's designers, leadership, and educators quickly attempted to establish the authority of school adults in order to regain control of students and hence their project. Ironically, they mostly did so by retrofitting the project with the very techniques of discipline and control that were common at the conventional schools against which they had defined their project and themselves.

In several classrooms, desks were rearranged from inward-facing clusters of five desks—an arrangement which put some students' backs toward the teacher but also allowed for easier peer communications during student-driven project work—into sequential rows that all faced the teacher at the front of the room. Further, educators intensified their efforts to orchestrate a seamless flow of adult-scripted activities, even during moments when students had previously enjoyed some autonomy, such as recess and the brief passing period between classes. Within a week after one of the school's designers expressed concern that students might not be able to handle recess in the gym, educators introduced adult-scripted activities for recess in the gym. Half the gym was organized into a football game that one of the educators administered. In the other half of the gym, students were allowed to organize their own smaller games, so long as they remained relatively quiet and spatially contained. Most students who did not play football stopped going to the gym after these changes, and some social divisions among students, notably gender divisions, became more spatially calcified during recess. During passing periods, which educators saw as moments when they could lose control, teachers introduced a script in which they organized students into quiet, forward-facing, single-file lines before they left a classroom. After such a line was formed—which could take some time—teachers marched students down the hallway to their next class, where they then waited quietly against a wall until the next teacher allowed them to enter. All teachers introduced this script at the same time, about a month into the school year. Further, in the middle of the fall, all the educators established a pedagogic script where they directed students to begin a silent, individual, teacher-defined task for five minutes immediately upon entering a new classroom.

In addition to extending practices of surveillance and control to spaces and periods where students had previously experienced some autonomy, educators also intensified their grip in domains where they had already been exerting their authority, albeit in the obscured ways discussed in the past section. In classrooms, educators not only continued to define and enforce scripted activities for students, but in a Tayloristic fashion instructors started breaking down these scripts into ever-smaller step-by-step procedures. In many classes, educators accompanied these fine-grained scripts with techniques intended to facilitate a heightened awareness of "clock time" (Thompson 1967) among students. While modernist institutions have long emphasized clock time, this orchestration became more fine-grained and explicit than I expected. The reformers referred to their focus on clock time as a twenty-first century literacy called time management, but time management typically had a lot to do with classroom management, in which students ironically had little say over how they managed their time. Many educators saw clocks and timers as a useful way to keep students on task during scripted activities as well as when they transitioned between these activities. What educators facilitated was a near-constant awareness among students of how much clock time they had left or had spent on a given task. When directing students to do a scripted activity, educators would almost always tell the students how much time they had for the activity. Many would use their laptops to project a digital countdown timer for the activity onto the whiteboard at the front of the class, which functioned as a continuous animation of clock time slipping away. Many educators also wore stopwatches around their necks and routinely referred to their stopwatches as they called out how much time was left before the scripted activity ended. Educators expected students to be in their assigned seats and listening for the next directive when a timer ended.

Not only were these references to clock time much more pervasive and evident than I had anticipated, but they somewhat surprisingly had the "gamifying" effect of adding a sense of urgency and competition to what were otherwise rather trivial and boring tasks. The approaching termination of the timer could turn an otherwise boring and scripted activity into a race against the clock, and as timers approached zero you could sense a palpable rise in the energy of the students, an emotional rush that I also felt when I participated in these rote routines.[2] Several teachers even punctuated the end of a countdown timer with the visualization and sound of a large explosion, further adding to a sense of excitement, even though the tasks that we were completing were often quite rote and meaningless. This rush against the clock was sometimes reinforced by a manufactured sense of competition among students and classes. For example, at one point during the year, an educator made a game out of how quickly students could line up quietly before entering his classroom. He taped a large piece of butcher paper on the wall outside his classroom and wrote how many seconds it took for each class to line up quietly before being admitted into the room. This went on for several weeks as classes competed against each other to see which class could be the most disciplined, until the winning class had achieved a time of less than four seconds.

Of course, these processes for creating order and discipline were in glaring contradiction to the reformers' pedagogic fixations—which purported to cultivate student agency, creativity, improvisational problem-solving capacities, and so forth—and yet, seemingly paradoxically, the designers of the school were often complicit in the introduction of these highly scripted practices. What is more, many of these techniques were either replicates, if not enhancements, of the techniques used in the more traditional schools against which the reformers had contradistinguished themselves. In keeping with DiMaggio and Powell's (1983) notion of "mimetic isomorphism," many of these canonical management techniques were introduced either by reformers and educators who had worked at other schools or by representatives from the Downtown School's School Support Organization (SSO), the latter of which was meant to replace school boards within New York City's autonomy for accountability exchange (chapter 2). And the techniques were introduced in a coordinated and standardized fashion across the entire school, often right after the school's weekly professional development session.[3] Here, for example, is a portion of an e-mail that one of the school's leaders sent to the school's faculty and staff; in it, the leader explicitly calls on educators to tighten their scripting of students' behavior:

> During [our professional development period] we discussed the importance of the directions we give students. Are directions given both orally and in writing or are they only being delivered orally? Are they broken down into small steps or are there many steps embedded in narrative? Every lesson at The Downtown School thoughtfully considers what students are being asked to do. Please remember to review how you are asking them to do it.

This purposeful import and deployment of canonical disciplinary practices raises the curious question of how reformers managed to reconcile their practices with their ideals. In the words of Bennett Berger (2004), who studied similarly wide gaps between ideals and acts in his study of a group of countercultural communards in northern California, such reconciliation requires a lot of ideological work.

REPAIRING IDEALISM

Part of the answer to the question I just posed has to do with the occluding effects of fixations. As I have been arguing, reformers tend to fix their imagination and attention on aspects of the world they can foreseeably transform in morally sanctified ways with their seemingly innovative remedies; correspondingly, they tend to overlook and take for granted whatever they cannot so easily control and transform with these newly available means. As we have seen, the school's designers did not have the power to change many of the factors that structured canonical pedagogic practices. The state and the DOE, rather than the school's designers, determined much of the curriculum, as well funding for student-teacher ratios, the allocation of space, and many other resource provisions. The built environments that they inhabited—consisting of multiple similar classrooms, each of which had been designed for a single educator teaching several dozen students— were inherited and built with canonical models of schooling in mind.[4] Additionally, the school had to be able to interoperate with other schools in the broader New York City schooling system as well as with colleges and universities. Part of its mandate involved receiving and delivering students in age-graded cohorts and producing standardized outcome metrics that made students and educators legible, hence differentiable, in processes of social selection and managerial oversight that extended beyond the space of the school. Reformers and educators had to comport themselves to these more entrenched strictures, and they deliberated how to do so, but reformers, in particular, did not tend to see such practices as central to what their project was all about.

How so?

For one, despite their professed student-centered ethos, more widespread and deeply sedimented ideological edifices about age relations and developmental temporalities helped reformers and educators downplay aspects of their pedagogic practices that were particularly at odds with their ideals. As sociologists of childhood and youth have documented, modernist practices of disciplining and controlling children and young people are legitimized, and hence often taken for granted, in part because of a more general tendency among adults to infantilize children and young people, a tendency that emerged alongside broader historical changes in the social and cultural organization of age relations (Zelizer 1985; Qvortrup 1994; James et al. 1998; Corsaro 2005). Figuring children as particularly underdeveloped and vulnerable is especially common in figured worlds that take the care and development of children and young people as their raison d'être. There were too many of these infantilizing practices to enumerate, but the reformer's previous comment that the students couldn't handle recess in the gym is one such example. Additionally, some educators routinely addressed the students with labels that positioned them as immature and inexperienced because of their age—terms such as boys and girls—and one educator even reminded the students that they were being addressed with these terms because they had not yet proven themselves worthy of a more mature and autonomous status. More commonly, educators routinely subjected students to didactic lessons on topics that students were presumed not to know but were, in fact, quite knowledgeable. One such episode was a schoolwide assembly in which educators made students perform small skits in which they acted out norms for polite social etiquette, such as how to hold the door open for someone and how to acknowledge the act with the phrase "thank you." Students already knew about these normative conventions, even if they sometimes did not enact them, in part, I believe, to demonstrate their autonomy from adult-imposed strictures. As we will see in the next chapter, these sorts of infantilizing practices produce conditions for oppositional behavior, especially for subordinates who can gain status among their peers by demonstrating resistance to supervisory power.[5]

Additionally, experienced reformers and educators routinely made a distinction between practices of control and practices of care, the former of which they classified as classroom management and the latter of which they classified as pedagogical or learning activities. In practice, classroom management and pedagogic practices were one and the same, with purportedly caring pedagogic practices taking forms that helped sustain authorities' control in crowded conditions. Yet experienced reformers and educators tended to classify management practices as a separate but necessary precondition for administering pedagogic practices, and the latter was widely seen as beneficial for all students and hence as morally caring. For experienced reformers and educators, classroom-management practices seemed to be understood as a necessary, sometimes ugly, but also fairly mundane aspect of being a professional educator. And, if anything, experienced reformers and educators seemed to see those of us who were newer to their figured worlds—such as reformers who came from the worlds of technology design, as well as myself—as a bit naïve. As I spent more and more time in the school, I often got the sense that learning how to discipline and control students was treated by experienced educators as a sort of sub rosa aspect of being an experienced member of their figured world.[6] Indeed, new reformers and educators became more experienced old-timers in part by learning to make the distinction between classroom management and pedagogic practices as well as by learning how to be comfortable exercising power over young people. Perhaps recalling their own experiences as novice teachers and knowing that I was new to middle school as an adult, several of the experienced educators would make comments to me such as, "Teaching is crazy, right?" after I witnessed an educator deploy a variety of rather domineering disciplinary techniques in an attempt to corral and pacify students. When I agreed, I felt as if I was beginning to be let into their club in part by treating the exercise of power over young people as a normal, and even skillful, aspect of being an experienced educator.

While less-experienced reformers seemed to share my sense that many of these disciplinary practices were odd, if not unsettling, the division of labor in the philanthropic intervention also made it easier for these reformers to downplay and overlook the extent to which their project involved exercising coercive and disciplinary techniques on those it was designed to help. At the Downtown School, there was a fairly sharp and spatialized division of labor between the people who designed and supported the intervention and those who implemented it. By and large, the school's design team spent little time managing everyday life at the school, even though they held considerable power over those who did. The founders of the school spent increasingly little time in the school as the project aged, and the practitioners who did spend their days in the school were split between, on the one hand, a group of game designers and curriculum designers who were largely responsible for crafting the school's innovative pedagogy and, on the other hand, teachers and administrators who enacted the designers' pedagogic scripts, managed students, and were charged with keeping the school running. It was the school's philanthropic backers, its game and curriculum designers, and its founders who remained the most enthusiastic about the school and its innovative philanthropic potential, and yet they also had comparatively little responsibility for, as well as less exposure to, its quotidian functioning. Additionally, those of us who were newer to educational reform were able to treat canonical practices of discipline and control as respectfully belonging to the world of professional educators. For example, one of the school's founders, a media technology designer, noted to me that they also found educators' classroom-management practices curious but then quickly distanced themselves from the remarkability of such practices by suggesting that they were an oddity of what professional educators do.

Finally, and as noted earlier, the school's isomorphic drift was partially obscured and discounted because many of these familiar features had been recoded with terminology borrowed from technology design, especially game design. This terminology downplayed the ways in which educators not only remade canonical practices but also controlled others through those practices. All these dynamics help explain how reformers and educators were able to reconcile tensions and contradictions between the project's ideals and its acts. All have the effect of occluding, normalizing, translating, and generally downplaying the ways in which the school's pedagogic activities were shot through with the very techniques that reformers aimed to disrupt. Yet practices that occlude, distort, and overlook do not adequately account for how reformers and educators also manage to maintain and repair their sense that a philanthropic intervention is both cutting edge and morally sanctified. Oversights can help such fixations persist, but they do not provide experiences that renew a collective sense of moral optimism. The maintenance and revitalization of such feelings depend on the collective accomplishment, and ritualized valorization, of what I call sanctioned counterpractices.

SANCTIONED COUNTERPRACTICES

At the end of every trimester the Downtown School's educators thoroughly reconfigured the school's social, spatial, and temporal routines. All normal classes were suspended and students were assigned a single challenge to work on with a small team of their peers for the rest of the trimester. For the first trimester, educators challenged teams to build a Rube Goldberg machine out of everyday materials that parents and educators had donated; for the second trimester, students wrote and produced short plays based on fairy tales that they had remixed; at the end of the third quarter, students produced a field day consisting of physical games that they had designed. This was Level Up, a special weeklong period that was staged at the end of each trimester.

Level Up periods were the times during the year when the school's pedagogic practices most closely resembled reformers' pedagogic fixations. They were also the moments that drew most heavily on idealizations of creative and high-tech work practices that have been valorized as a new model of work and citizenship in many parts of the globe (Irani 2015; Lindtner 2014). Socially, educators organized students into groups of eight to ten, each of which had an adult advisor. Adults still defined the overall challenge for each Level Up, but much of the design and building of the projects was left up to the students. In keeping with the school's ideals of a student-centered pedagogy, educators mostly played a supportive, rather than a controlling, role. They waited for students to request their assistance and stepped in only when conflicts between students seemed to be especially tense. The students negotiated with each other about what they should do next, struggled to implement their decisions, failed to produce expected results, passed judgments (both positive and negative) on each other's ideas and efforts, revised their plans, argued with each other about who should do what, and so on.

Students also spent a lot more time talking than they did during a normal school day, and the overall volume in classes was noticeably higher. At one point, a teacher who was running a class on the floor beneath the Downtown School even came upstairs to complain about the noise because his students were taking an exam. The organization of students into teams also broke with the individuating tendency of many of the school's other pedagogic practices. While there were many internal disagreements over the direction of each team's project, each group oriented toward a common production. A common stake and say in the outcome of the project supported these more cordial relations.

Assessment was also more open ended and distributed during Level Up. At the end of the first Level Up, the school showcased the students' Rube Goldberg machines for parents and an outside panel of judges (mostly professional designers). The judges offered verbal feedback about what they did and did not like about each machine, and they awarded one team a prize for the best machine, but as far as I know, no individual grades were given. Further, students and teachers talked informally about the various projects, but they did so more as partners than in normal routines in which educators were the presumed experts.

In terms of space and equipment, educators reorganized classrooms so that rows of forward-facing desks were broken apart and clustered into workspaces. Educators gave each team one-half of a classroom that they could use as a dedicated workspace for the entire Level Up period. Educators also provided teams with a hodgepodge of scrap materials, from cardboard tubes to toy cars, PVC pipes, rulers, tape, weights, marbles, and so on. Educators allowed students to make a mess and leave their materials and in-process productions in their workspaces throughout Level Up. Unlike normal classes, educators did not confine students to their seats, and many students moved fluidly around the classroom. Temporally, the school day had only a few divisions. Students worked on their projects for hours at a time and educators made few references to the urgency of clock time. At any given moment, some students were off task, but educators generally did not intervene. Some students told their peers to stop wasting time, and sometimes a student asked an educator to direct their peers to participate. In general, though, Level Up felt much less scripted and less rushed than a typical school day.

Some other schooling practices also approximated reformers' pedagogic fixations, albeit not as closely as Level Up. For example, the episodic moments in which classes communicated with characters from designed game worlds were substantively unconventional for a school. Similarly, the requirement that all students take a media arts course focused on game design was somewhat unique. Other unconventional practices included the occasional small projects, the few times during the trimester when classes used the school's "semi-immersive embodied learning environment," and the school's after-school programs that focused on making, hacking, and remixing media and technology.

As shorthand, I refer to these moments when the daily life of a disruptive intervention most closely approximates reformers' philanthropic idealizations as sanctioned counterpractices. The phrase is meant to draw attention to how these activities are indeed different from the more conventional, and bureaucratic, processes that reformers aim to disrupt; they are counterpractices. Yet they are also deviations that are permitted and valued by people in positions of institutional authority: sanctioned counterpractices.

The project's designers and backers tended to treat these unconventional practices as indicative of what the project was all about, but I found them more of a carnivalesque inversion of disciplined routines and orders[7]. While moments of sanctioned counterpractice were often inspiring, they were also relegated to a few carefully bounded times during the day or school year, reformers and educators were not able to expand them, and, if anything, they became less a part of the school's routines as it aged.

Sanctioned counterpractices became less prevalent as the school aged for several reasons. For one, and as already discussed, the school's designers had assumed that their gamelike pedagogy would motivate subordinates' voluntary participation in managerially scripted activities. When this did not happen, educators ratcheted up discipline in an attempt to restore managerial authority and enforce compliance. Additionally, and as we will see in chapter 6, privileged parents mapped their anxieties about some of the school's less-privileged students onto assumptions about educator permissiveness, thus pressuring educators toward more adult-controlled models of schooling. Third, the mandate to produce competitive scores on state exams constantly hung over reformers' and educators' heads, and both privileged and less-privileged parents pressured educators to devote more time and attention to preparing students for these exams. These parents did so not necessarily because they saw the state exams as indicative of what their children had learned but because they saw them as key to their children's mobility in broader educational systems. As one professional parent wrote in an email to other parents and school's leaders, "I don't like these tests more than anybody else. I actually pretty much despise them. But these are the rules made by the State. I don't make them. I just follow them." Many less-privileged parents and caregivers were especially concerned about test scores because their children's access to other middle and high schools were so dependent on these scores. More-privileged families, by contrast, had greater access to various educational alternatives, as well as private tutoring for test preparation, and yet many privileged families also pressured educators to focus more on testing. Further, the marketlike choice system was designed to increase competition between schools and, subsequently, between students, largely on the basis of test scores. As such, as the school aged, educators dedicated less time to sanctioned counterpractices and more time to test preparation, especially after the school's first-year scores fell below those of peer institutions. In the school's second year, educators even dedicated the entire Level Up period at the end of the second trimester to test prep.

Against the magnitude of these unwieldy forces, sanctioned counterpractices begin to look less like seeds of transformative change and more like rituals that not only release the pressures generated by an increasingly disciplined and oppressive social order, but which also help affirm and repair many people's moral feelings about the project and hopes for change. One of the most striking characteristics about the Downtown School's sanctioned counterpractices was that despite being relatively marginal and insubstantial compared to the school's daily routines, they were overwhelmingly featured in the school's publicity materials, showcases for parents, festivals, open houses, tours for the press, planning documents, e-mail blasts, academic reports, journalists' stories, and other venues and rituals where the reformers and educators staged self-representations of the school.[8] By contrast, the school's more canonical practices were almost entirely absent from these self-representations.

The vignette at the opening of this chapter illustrates this dynamic playing out. The school's designers, leaders, and a visiting journalist entered the back of the classroom right before the teacher introduced the gamelike interaction with the sock puppets, a moment that was playfully unconventional for a school. Yet they left as soon as the class returned to familiar schooling practices. The vignette at the opening of chapter 2 also illustrated a similar process as journalists and tour guides focused on and staged the school's most cutting-edge technologies and practices while overlooking and even actively excluding its many conventional features—for example, by moving the student working on video-game design out of the classroom and into an empty hallway. What is more, these stagings were always celebratory and they often, but not always, featured the project's distinguishing technologies, such as the semi-immersive embodied learning environment, which, as noted earlier, was rarely used. Additionally, design and media professionals who worked for the nonprofit that designed and helped run the school crafted many of these self-representations, and their sophisticated media-production skills lent the representations a heightened sense of professionalism and, hence, legitimacy.

Some readers may be tempted to interpret this elevation of sanctioned counterpractices over more-conventional everyday routines as mere propaganda or public relations. I do not find such interpretations convincing, at least not in projects where many practitioners make significant personal and professional sacrifices in order to practice a form of work that they see as caring and philanthropic. In practice, the periodic elevation of sanctioned counterpractices over everyday routines did not seem to so much conceal reformers' real intentions as help the school's designers, educators, and powerful backers realize the collective experience of having good intentions and being cutting edge. These seeming verifications of the project's idealized potential mattered to reformers, educators, and their supporters because the celebration of sanctioned counterpractices helped produce and sustain the sense that they were committing themselves to something that was both morally good and original. The unusual amount of outside attention, and especially media attention, that the school's sanctioned counterpractices received also helped reaffirm these sentiments.

It would not be a stretch to suggest that sanctioned counterpractices— and the celebratory rituals that surrounded them—often had a quasi-religious inflection to them, in the sense that, when they worked, they helped produce a collective sense that we were participating in something larger and good; I found that they engendered feelings of belonging not just to one another, but also to a forward-looking moral project. Not coincidentally, similar moral sentiments animated the entrepreneurial reformers' (Becker 1963) calls for disruption, and they were repeatedly reinforced by the media's upbeat stories about the school.[9] Given that the school's designers' relied on these powerful outsiders in order to follow up on their insights and yearnings, the collective celebration of sanctioned counterpractices likely helped sooth some of the discomforts of inhabiting this compromised position as it engendered feelings of harmony across various divisions of power.

A brief account of one of my own experiences participating in a sanctioned counterpractice will help illustrate these last points. As mentioned earlier, educators rarely used the school's most spectacular technology, the semi-immersive embodied learning environment, even though it was prominently featured in many public-facing representations of the school. But when the technology was used, nearly everyone treated the occasion as special. One of the school's well-known founders usually ran these sessions, along with two technologists who worked at one of the local universities. The technology required a large white mat that took up about half the room to be laid across the floor, onto which the visuals of an educational game were projected from overhead. Players would interact with the projection on the floor by moving highly reflective Styrofoam balls that a series of cameras around the perimeter of the room could detect, hence allowing the projected imagery to respond, seemingly magically, to the players' gestures. Normally, I did not participate in these games since only a few people could play at a time and I did not want to detract from the students' time with the system. But on one occasion I joined a group game that involved trying to navigate a virtual boat to collect virtual coins while avoiding virtual alligators.

While playing the game with several students, I lost my sense of self-awareness and social differentiation. I felt as if I were part of a collaborative endeavor that was greater than myself, even though the other players were eleven and twelve years old and who, under normal circumstances, were socially differentiated from me. I am fairly certain the other players felt the same, as did many of the other students and staff who cheered us on.[10] When I wrote my field notes that evening, I had an unusually hard time recalling the specifics of the game or how it worked, but the intense feelings of excitement, wonder, and belonging that it engendered were still vivid. I am sharing this anecdote not to add yet another account of what play or flow feels like as a psychological experience—the school's founders called it the rise—but instead to help illustrate how collective experiences with unfamiliar and awe-inspiring technologies can help produce a sense of belonging and enthusiasm not just for the sanctioned counterpractice, but also for the larger collective undertaking that the unconventional practice seems to represent.[11] Later in the day, the designer who had helped design and run the game said to me with seeming excitement, "It was great to see you get lost in play today!" Her comment stayed with me not just because it had indeed been great to be lost in play, but also because our shared enthusiasm seemed to join us in a way that I had not felt previously. To me, it felt like the enthusiasm that people share after having attending a good

concert or sporting event, an excitement rooted in part in the shared recognition that they had together experienced the rise. When experienced as
part of a disruptive philanthropic undertaking, these enchanting and exhilarating feelings seemed to epitomize the project's novel and moral promise.

Such feelings surfaced on numerous occasions throughout my time
in the field, especially when media outlets visited the school or when the
school staged festivals of the students' sanctioned counterpractices for parents and other outsiders. During such moments I often could not help but
share good feelings about the project, and my memories of these moments
have repeatedly tempted me to write a more celebratory account of the
school. Doing so not only felt like a kind thing to do for the well-intentioned people who had so generously welcomed me into their project, but
it also would have helped me feel more hopeful about, and pleased with,
the sort of work I have tried to do for much of my professional life.

CONCLUSION

I am convinced that most people who design and implement disruptive
philanthropic interventions sincerely want to promote what they consider
to be beneficial social change. But their ability to do so is compromised
from the start by the outsized expectations that are placed on them, as well
as by the fairly limited means that they have available. Experts' reliance
on powerful outsiders for resources and recognition allow the former to
imagine and launch new experiments, but they do so at a cost. In responding to these outsiders' calls for disruption, experts translate broader concerns with the present and hopes for the future into technical diagnoses
and prescriptions: they problematize what is wrong with existing remedies
while imagining seemingly new and better ones that will take advantage of
the unprecedented opportunities of recent technological breakthroughs.
In doing so they promise social transformations that their philanthropic
interventions do not have the power to bring about.

The reformers who founded the Downtown School translated broader concerns with the present as well as hopes for a promised democratic polity into
a seemingly disruptive pedagogy. They problematized dominant pedagogic
approaches for failing to live up to democratic ideals and designed what they
imagined would be more engaging, relevant, and equitable pedagogic practices. They saw in video games and new digital media unprecedented opportunities for doing so. And yet most of daily life at the Downtown School
ended up looking much like daily life at a more-conventional school, and
it became even more conventional as the Downtown School aged. Despite reformers' aspirations for a student-centered pedagogy, students had

little say over either the goal or the mode of their activities. At nearly all points during the day, educators directed students to enact tightly scripted behaviors, often these scripts were broken into fine-grained step-by-step instructions, and noncompliance was increasingly reprimanded. Even during recess students were subjected to near constant surveillance and strict limitations on their behavior. Much of what ended up being playful and unconventional about the Downtown School was the terminology that reformers used to describe canonical schooling practices. And yet, despite all this conventionality, many of the people who had committed themselves to the project maintained the sense that the school's pedagogic practices were both philanthropic and cutting edge. How should we make sense of this rather wide gap between ideals and acts?

I have been arguing that reformers become fixated on what they can foreseeably control and transform with the new means that they have available. In the context of a concrete reform project, reformers translate broader yearnings for social change into narrow problems and solutions that their new tools can foreseeably fix, even though many of the factors and forces that will constitute the project, not to mention the social problems that a project is designed to address, extend far beyond reformers' reach. Reformers tend to conceptualize their projects as if they can dismantle and reassemble inherited worlds and systems when their projects are also, and more so, assembled by these worlds and systems. The reformers and educators who founded the Downtown School could not control much of the curriculum, many aspects of the school's physical space, the mandate to administer state tests, the age-graded organization of schooling, the allocation of funding per pupil, or, critically, whether students would desire and enjoy the version of fun that the school was offering. What reformers and educators could more easily transform was some of the terminology and equipment that they used within the school. They could also more easily transform how they represented themselves to themselves and outsiders. And they were able, more or less, to realize their pedagogic ideals during small and bounded periods that temporarily held at bay aspects of the project that they could not otherwise control.

An important feature of these pedagogic fixations is that they entailed substantial blind spots that revealed themselves only once unanticipated forces overflew reformers' plans and started destabilizing the project in ways that appeared to threaten its survival. In facing this instability, the dominant tendency of reformers and educators was to engage in a different sort of fixation: reformers and educators quickly reached for resources that could stabilize the project; ironically, many of these resources came from canonical versions of the institution that reformers aimed to disrupt. Set against such tensions and contradictions, moments that more closely approximated reformers' pedagogic ideals, what I have been calling sanctioned counterpractices, took on an experiential and symbolic significance that far exceeded their role in the project and that was in no way commensurate with their potential to bring about substantive social change.

As the next several chapters explore, this interrelation among idealized fixations, overflowing, attempts to stabilize a project, and the selective elevation of sanctioned counterpractices over everyday routines helped produce numerous unintended, and often problematic, consequences, not the least of which was the further entrenchment of inherited systems of power and privilege. Such effects were not the real but hidden intentions of reformers, nor did they reveal that reformers were especially naïve. Rather, they testify to what can happen when sincere yearnings to improve the world are wished onto technological breakthroughs that many people hope are capable of fulfilling those yearnings, when, in fact, they are not even remotely equipped to do so. The next chapter examines how processes of problematization and rendering technical produce fixations about the people that a disruptive intervention aims to help, in this case students. It explores how these intended beneficiaries exert unanticipated pressures on a philanthropic intervention and how reformers tend to respond to those unanticipated pressures in rather retrograde ways. Chapter 6 investigates how powerful factions of the local community, in this case privileged parents, can grab onto a philanthropic intervention and wrestle it toward their own ends and how reformers are often positioned in such a way that they are compelled to acquiesce to these demands.

5

AMENABLE AND FIXABLE SUBJECTS

It is now anybody with access to a fifteen hundred dollar computer who can take sounds and images from the culture around us and use it to say things differently. These tools of creativity have become tools of speech. It is a literacy for this generation. This is how our kids speak. It is how our kids think. It is what your kids are as they increasingly understand digital technologies and their relationship to themselves.

—FROM LAWRENCE LESSIG'S TED TALK ON "REMIX CULTURE"

I first heard the preceding quote during one of the Downtown School's after-school workshops. The school had invited a local media artist—a young white man who wore blue jeans, sneakers, and a T-shirt emblazoned with the logo for Creative Commons—to lead a workshop on remixing videos. Before letting the students loose on the computers, the instructor gave a short lecture on what he referred to as remix culture. During his presentation the artist showed several example videos as well as a segment of the legal scholar and activist Lawrence Lessig's TED Talk. After Lessig said, "This is how our kids speak," the instructor paused the video and told the students, "That's you," before resuming the clip. After the video ended, the visiting artist told the students that it was their civic duty to remix media.

That evening I wrote about the incident extensively in my field notes. I found it ironic that the instructor was trying to persuade the students to participate in a practice that, according to the video he had just shown them, defined not only how their generation spoke and thought but also who they were. I also found it curious that he associated a particular media-production activity with a more general responsibility for contemporary citizenship. It seemed that the instructor, and also the school, wanted to have it both ways: on one hand, to better serve the young by being sensitive to their presumed interests with new media technologies but on the other hand, to mold students into the kinds of workers and citizens that reformers thought the world needed. It was a tension that I saw over and over again while conducting fieldwork, especially when reformers and educators tried to figure out how to deal with students who seemed less than fully amenable to the reformers' philanthropic prescriptions.

As we saw in the last two chapters, in designing a disruptive philanthropic intervention, experts translate more widespread yearnings for social change into concrete programs in part by imagining and rendering spaces and activities in terms that are seemingly transformable and controllable with the new tools that they have at their disposal. We also saw how these fixations inevitably leave out much of the complexity of life on the ground and thus lead to unanticipated challenges for reformers once a project has launched. It was also shown how reformers tend to respond to these unexpected forces by quickly reaching for resources that will help stabilize the project, even though many of these resources come from inherited versions of the institutions that reformers aim to supersede.

This chapter examines the workings and consequences of another thread of disruptive fixation: rendering the intervention's intended beneficiaries as if they are especially in need of, amenable to, and fixable with the new technical remedies that reformers have on hand. While spatial fixations allow reformers to imagine environments that can be designed, linked, and governed and while pedagogic fixations allow reformers to envision and script the experiences that will supposedly take place in those spaces, subject fixations allow reformers to imagine a population of beneficiaries that will (often voluntarily and agreeably) take part in those designed experiences. This chapter explores how reformers often knew very little about the people they aimed to help, nor could they with the resources they had available, despite their claim to put students' interests at the center of their concerns. Instead, processes of problematization and rendering technical allowed them to imagine those persons as especially in need of, amenable to, and fixable with their gamelike pedagogy and digitally themed offerings more generally. Such fixations not only led to further unanticipated pressures and dilemmas for reformers and educators once the school had launched, but they also encouraged reformers to respond to these dilemmas in ways that helped remake many of the institutional processes that they aimed to disrupt as well as the social divisions that they hoped to bridge.

One of the curiosities of these subject fixations is that the designers of the Downtown School were aware that many past educational reforms had failed in large part because they had privileged the viewpoints of experts and managers over the viewpoints of those they aimed to help. In their processes of problematization, the founders of the Downtown School stressed that their approach to reform was unlike the paternalistic and top-down approaches of many other social reformers, both past and present. They were clear that their project had been designed with the presumed needs and interests of contemporary children and young people in mind. This vision of reform drew on popular discourses in the worlds of technology design, and expert-planned interventions more generally, that advocate for putting students, users, humans, citizens, or the community at the center of designed interventions (Norman and Draper, eds. 1986; Norman 1988; Sandholtz et al. 1997). As we saw in chapter 2, these democratizing discourses dovetail nicely, if not necessarily explicitly or intentionally, with modes of governing that have gained influence in recent decades, particularly those that emphasize consumer sovereignty and community involvement (Rose 1999, 137–96). This resonance has allowed reform projects like the Downtown School to take root in, and thus to give material shape to, policies that promote marketlike solutions for the perceived shortcomings of statecraft—and top-down planning more generally—even though such goals are not necessarily reformers' professed aims (Rose 1999; Sennett 2006).

While such approaches to social reform attempt to invert, or at least balance, the power relations of top-down interventions and hence to escape the latter's much-discussed shortcomings (Scott 1998), reformers and designers who advocate for various human-centered philanthropic interventions still face the problem of how to understand the lives of the people they aim to help while also maintaining that their model of change can be generalized. On one hand, and in a more postmodern gesture, these reformers often claim to want to design interventions that are suited for the contingencies of local conditions and the dynamic multiplicity and hybridity of cultural differences. On the other hand, and in keeping with the high modernist social reformers that they often problematize, these reformers want to produce models of intervention that can be replicated and spread. The former could perhaps address problems associated with top-down planning, but doing so would be costly, time consuming, and not easy to replicate. The latter could be "scalable," to borrow a popular term, but they privilege the perspectives of experts over those of a project's imagined beneficiaries.

Like many other techno-philanthropists, the founders of the Downtown School rendered this problem fixable by invoking popular ideas about the unprecedented possibilities of new innovations in information technology. If contemporary youth were first and foremost members of a digital generation, as numerous social and cultural commentators like Lawrence Lessig had suggested, and if new media technologies permitted a seemingly infinite proliferation of opportunities for cultural participation, and hence learning, then a model of philanthropic intervention centered on new media technologies seemed to be both generalizable and adaptable to cultural specificities and personal idiosyncrasies. From such a perspective, the designers of the Downtown School did not need to know much about their students' lives while they were designing their intervention, nor did they have the means to acquire such an understanding. Instead, they could design a "school for digital kids" that would teach students from any background how to build on their presumed affinities with new media in order to pursue their diverse interests. In imagining and crafting such a plan, the designers of the Downtown School built on the work of technologists and scholars that had heralded the "long tail" (Anderson 2004) character of new media ecosystems. According to this popular and influential view, networked digital media now made it possible for just about anyone to participate in rewarding and diverse forms of cultural production (Benkler 2006) and, hence, learning (Ito et al. 2010). At the same time, scholars problematized unevenness among those who pursued such opportunities as the "participation gap" (Jenkins et al. 2006), a problem that designed educational interventions could perhaps remedy. With these technical problems and solutions in mind, the designers of the Downtown School imagined that subjects from various backgrounds would be in need of, amenable to, and fixable with programs such as the after-school workshop on remix culture, as well as many of the school's other digitally themed pedagogic offerings.

This chapter examines how these reductive renderings of the project's intended beneficiaries excluded much of what mattered to many students as they negotiated identity and difference with each other at school and online. As such, reformers were especially unprepared and ill equipped when students attempted to configure identities that did not match reformers' idealizations. This chapter explores the limitations and consequences of these subject fixations by examining processes of subject formation, not just from the perspective of reformers and designers but also from the perspective of those targeted by philanthropic intervention. The chapter first looks at the practices through which students negotiated differentiated social identities—and, hence, divisions—in the context of schooling before considering the role of school-sanctioned counterpractices in the production of these identities. Throughout, I draw attention to how reformers' processes of problematization and rendering technical simplified and mischaracterized both students' and educators' contributions to processes of identity construction and, hence, to the production of social division.

IDENTITIES-IN-PRACTICE

Ethnographers who have conducted research in schools have repeatedly shown how students often develop an intimate perspective on the salient social divisions of the adult worlds for which they are being prepared, in part through their participation in the school-based cultural worlds of peers, which, especially in middle school, tend to organize into informal peer groups, or cliques (Willis 1977; Eckert 1989; Corsaro and Eder 1990; Thorne 1993; A. Ferguson 2001; Lewis 2003; Pascoe 2007).[1] According to Paul Willis, in capitalist societies with compulsory education, larger political-economic processes, such as social reproduction, are accomplished in part *through* these informal peer groups or, more precisely, through the partially autonomous cultural productions of these groups. From such a perspective, subjects are not simply stamped out, or interpellated, by schools and then delivered to different locations in a capitalist social order, as social reproduction theorists from Althusser (1971) to Bowles and Gintis (1976) to Bourdieu and Passeron (1977) have, in different ways, implied. Nor are gendered (Thorne 1993; Pascoe 2007) and racialized (Lewis 2003) identities made and remade simply because of unexamined institutional biases. Rather, young people play an active, which is not to say independent, role in making, remaking, and reconfiguring these identifications and divisions, in part by participating in the differentiated and differentiating cultural worlds that young people form as they navigate schools and other adult-controlled institutional settings (Sims 2014a, 2014b).

These cultural worlds are connected to, but also partially autonomous from, the adult-designed scripts and modes of control that characterize official activity in institutional settings that have been designed for young people. In the United States, semiautonomous cultural worlds of young people became much more extensive in the nineteenth and early twentieth century when compulsory schooling, and its age-graded social organization, was institutionalized. Correspondingly, many children and young people were moved out of places of paid and unpaid labor, which were more age heterogeneous, and assembled together in shared settings (Qvortrup 1994). One consequence of this transformation was that children and young people now spent much of their lives with people of similar ages and in institutional settings where they far outnumbered those in positions of authority. Under such conditions, semiautonomous, and often age-graded, cultural worlds, or youth cultures (Coleman 1961), emerged, a development that was aided and accelerated by entrepreneurs aiming to create and expand markets for everything from clothing to food to media (Cook 2004). While children and young people have largely remained materially dependent on adult family members for longer periods of their lives, and while they are routinely subjected to adult-defined scripts in settings such as schools, they also construct cultural practices and understandings that are somewhat independent from these scripts as they navigate age-segregated schools and adult-controlled settings more generally (Qvortrup 1994; Buckingham 2000; Corsaro 2005; Thorne 2009).

From a social practice theory perspective, the partially autonomous cultural worlds that young people make and configure in these settings are integral to how the subject positions and divisions that they come to inhabit—what Holland and Lave (2001) refer to as "history in person"—are learned, embodied, made, and changed (Eckert and McConnell-Ginet 1995; Holland et al. 1998). By negotiating participation in the practices of informal peer groups, students learn how to fashion themselves, speak, and act in particular ways that articulate belonging and difference. From this social practice theory perspective, social identities are always *identities-in-practice*, that is, coconstructed and contested by way of ongoing negotiations and struggles over who does what with whom in situ. As such, identities are always multiple, relational, and in processes of ongoing construction as students negotiate participation in some forms of group life and not others.[2] Students cannot fashion any identities they like since participation in the social practices of a clique partially depends on embodied knowledge and material resources that have been learned and provisioned outside of school. Participation also depends on acceptance by others who coparticipate in the shared social practices of these informal groups. Further, while participation is partly a matter of belonging, it is also a matter of differentiation. Students are identified and make their identities in part to say whom they are and in part to say whom they are not. Changing participation in peer groups changes both identities and peer groups, and yet some social divisions, notably gender and racialized class divisions, remain fairly consistent over time despite having to be rebuilt in situ (Eckert 1989; Thorne 1993). Given the power relations inherent to all philanthropic interventions, one especially salient factor in the ongoing negotiations over identity-in-practice among those targeted for intervention is how to orient toward the expert-designed scripts, as well as the authority structures more generally, of the intervention (Willis 1977). As we will see, it is in part by taking different stances toward these power relations that peer groups distinguish themselves from one another as they relationally construct different—and differentiating—criteria for status, recognition, and value.

While reformers' processes of problematization and rendering technical had considered the salience of young people's cultural worlds in processes of learning and identity making, they also idealistically imagined that they, the experts, could design and manage the cultural worlds that facilitated such processes. In particular—and in a manner that is akin to business managers' misguided attempts to design "communities of practice" within workplaces (Duguid 2008; Lave 2008)—the founders of the Downtown School imagined that the game worlds that they designed and into which they attempted to conscript students would furnish students with the cultural resources that they needed for identity construction and learning, a vision that was highly influenced by the renown learning theorist and video-game advocate James Paul Gee (2003). Doing so, the school's designers argued, would remedy a problem with conventional schooling: the expectation to learn skills and acquire knowledge that is divorced from a culturally meaningful context of application. According to this combination of problematization and rendering technical, designed game worlds could fix this problem by providing the missing cultural context.

Once again we can see how reformers' processes of problematization and rendering technical entailed partial critical insights into the limitations of the expert-designed interventions that they aimed to disrupt. But we can also see how these insights were narrowly fixated on what reformers could foreseeably control and transform with their new sociotechnical remedy, in this case a gamelike version of schooling. Such a vision of learning and identity formation did problematize the vision of learning and identity formation that underwrote conventional schooling—the idea that identity transformation is reducible to knowledge acquisition—but it also overlooked and ignored the lessons that Willis and other ethnographers had taken pains to establish: that subordinates in formal organizations form their own informal groups and cultural worlds in part to cope with the power relations and shortcomings of managerial attempts to formally organize their activity (Orr 1996; Suchman 2006). The limitations of these more contemporary attempts to design, construct, and control cultural worlds as a means of managing activity and learning are made apparent once we consider processes of identity formation from the perspective of those targeted for management and improvement.

Just about every day that I conducted fieldwork at the Downtown School, I made a point to eat lunch and attend recess with the students. These were the main times during the day when students had greater autonomy over their activities and thus more opportunities to negotiate friendship and difference with their peers. At lunch, students could more or less do what they liked so long as they stayed in their seats, kept the volume of their voices down, did not make a mess, and did not have more than six students at a table. Within these adult-defined rules, individual tables became like small islands. Persons and practices from proximal tables would sometimes spill into each other, but typically the practices of more distant tables remained fairly opaque to other students, even though much of what happened at different tables was fairly similar: students ate; they traded and gifted food; they conversed about a variety of topics from homework to gossip about their peers, commentary on teachers and other school adults, sharing details about family life, and expressing and arguing about their tastes for, knowledge of, and previous experiences with everything from food, TV shows, music, YouTube videos, fashion, travel, afterschool and weekend adventures, violence, and sexuality.

Yet despite these similarities, many students cared deeply about where they sat. As the period immediately prior to lunch approached its end, I would line up with the students and wait for the teacher to lead us down several flights of stairs to the cafeteria. Upon entering the cafeteria, many students would quickly rush to claim seats for themselves and their friends; yet it often took several minutes to settle who was going to sit with whom. While the entire school attended lunch at the same time, some classes arrived slightly before the others and some students, notably ones from less-privileged families, got in line for the hot lunch, which led students to try various tactics for holding seats for their friends. Sometimes, when a high-status student arrived after a table had filled, the bulk of a table's occupants relocated, awkwardly leaving behind one or two. More marginal students in a clique made bids for inclusion at a coveted table by offering to share food, candy, and other small treats with more established table dwellers. Having a friend who was already a regular member of a table was perhaps the most common way for a new person to gain a seat. Similarly, one of the most frequent sources of drama was when a friend joined a new table but did not bring along the friends with whom he or she had sat previously.

After twenty minutes for lunch, the cliques that formed at tables in the lunchroom migrated to recess with some reworking. Students could choose to go to either the gym or a classroom, both of which adults monitored. Activity in the gym centered on a regular game of touch football that was run by an educator. Activity in the classroom was not as scripted by adults, but the school counselor and often a teacher or the principal roamed the room and intervened if students talked too loudly, touched each other in ways deemed excessive, or noticeably insulted one another. Typically, students in the classroom hung out in inward-facing huddles that mostly matched the groupings they formed at tables during lunch. Pairs and trios of "besties" would sometimes break off from a huddle and roam the room before reuniting with their larger friend group. In a bid to cross these group boundaries, individual students sometimes ran up to someone in a cluster to ask a question, offer a gift, deliver news, or play a prank.[3] For the most part, though, groups of students carved out distinct territories within the crowded classroom. Some groups fortified themselves between a table and a wall, which kept both unwelcome peers and adults at a distance. These huddles were usually tightly knit and hard for outsiders, and especially monitoring adults, to observe, let alone enter.

I paid a lot of attention to these informal peer groups, or cliques, that congregated at lunch, recess, and other moments in which students had relative autonomy, including after school and online. While reformers' processes of problematization and rendering technical had largely overlooked such practices, these groupings seemed to matter deeply to many of the students. As such, I thought they could not be separated or diminished from an attempt to understand an intervention that billed itself as student centered. Peer groups mattered to students in part because these groups provided opportunities for friendship, belonging, and collective ways of undergoing and interpreting the always-changing experience of being a student, a child, a sibling, and a friend. But they also mattered because they involved open-ended—and hence uncertain, dramatic, and risky— processes by which students came to develop sentient perspectives on their relationship to social identification, division, and status hierarchies, not only in the school, but in their worlds more generally. Negotiations over participation in cliques at school were closely tied to students' out-of-school lives, and they shaped students' futures not just in the school but also beyond it (Sims 2014a). Peer groups were not just shared expressions of individual affinities; rather, they were produced in relation to all the potential opportunities for participating in group life that existed within the shared space of the school. Some of these opportunities were taken, others were not; sometimes bids for inclusion were accepted, other times they were rejected. In any case, the outcome of each of these indeterminate moments said something about who the student was and was not. Finding a table to join at lunch was just one of many recurring moments during the school day when these processes unfolded.

ASSEMBLING AFFINITIES AND DIVISIONS

Within a few months of the Downtown School's opening, four dominant cliques emerged and continued to orient the social worlds of students for much of the first year. The divisions students made within the school mostly mirrored the divisions that structured their out-of-school lives, but the process of assembling these groups was always ongoing and never fully settled. There were two cliques of predominantly boys and two cliques of predominantly girls, and each clique was largely segregated in terms of racialized social class. Like social worlds more generally, these cliques formed as students negotiated different standards of performance, status, and authenticity as they faced the shared challenge of how to be good at navigating middle school (Strauss 1982). These processes also produced factions and hierarchies within cliques, and sometimes these processes produced splintering and subworlds. Through these processes, which were never fully settled, a few students tended to be elevated as exemplars of performance within the clique, and often, but not always, students who were not members of a clique would identify these stars as representative of the clique as a whole. However, and as we will see, outsiders tended to stereotype these exemplars, and hence the clique, pejoratively and reductively, in part because they appeared to offer models of how to be a good middle school student that were at odds with their own standards.

While these four cliques constituted the main opportunities for students to participate in group life with peers at school, many students avoided regular participation in these cliques, failed in their attempts to win acceptance, or moved in and out of participation in a clique's activities. Several students formed small clusters of two or three friends, and a few students primarily kept to themselves. While these more interstitial groups and individuals exemplified the diversity of ways that students could navigate life with their peers at school, students who did not participate in the main cliques often paid the price of social isolation, lack of recognition, and low status among their peers. In interviews, many students referred to students who kept to themselves as loners, nobodies, and lonely people if they recognized them at all; small clusters of friends were often similarly overlooked or stigmatized.

The formation of these group divisions was not intended nor anticipated when the reformers imagined the beneficiaries of their intervention, and reformers and educators spent much of the first year trying to figure out how to deal with these unanticipated processes. Through their processes of problematization and rendering technical, the school's designers had assumed they were taking students' out-of-school lives and interests into account in a way that would bring students from diverse backgrounds together. These aspirations were, in my opinion, sincere, but they were premised on the assumption that reformers knew what students were up to in their out-of-school lives, which they mostly did not and could not with the resources that they had available. Of the four main cliques, only one group resembled the generational stereotype that underpinned the reformers' imaginings of a "school for digital kids." This group, which other students sometimes referred to as "the Geeky Boys," was the largest clique at the school and was also the most diverse economically and ethnically.[4] Only one girl, Nita, occasionally hung out with this group, and the majority of the clique's regular participants, about seventy percent, had professional parents, most of whom worked in the culture industries. All the regular participants in the school's after-school programs—which, as a reminder, focused exclusive on media and technology production—were participants in this clique, and, indeed, many of the clique participants had become friends in part by attending the after-school programs. Other students primarily stereotyped participants in this clique for their distinctive affinities for certain digital technologies and media, especially video games but also manga, anime, and transmedia franchises such as Pokémon. As Christopher, a boy from a less-privileged family who regularly hung out with the other main clique of boys, noted to me about this group during an interview, "I think a large part of the school body is the kids who are into game design and stuff like that, kids who are really into that." Similarly Sacha, a girl whose parents were creative professionals but who nevertheless struggled to gain acceptance by any of the main cliques, said, "[They're the] kids who like Pokémon, or are Bakugan loving," and as Troy, one of the higher-status members of the other main clique of boys said, "They talk about TV shows. Like let's say Naruto probably."[5]

Participants in this clique described themselves in similar terms, but they valued their differentiating practices and interests in certain forms of media and technology proudly and positively at school even as they did not reduce themselves to these interests. Many self-identified as gamers or even hardcore gamers, and they routinely used material culture—such as clothing, stickers, and games—as well as talk in order to express their distinctive enthusiasm for, knowledge about, and expertise with video games as well as new digital technologies more generally. As Raka, a member of this clique whose parents were both professionals, told me when I asked him about his favorite digital technologies, "I use everything." When I asked him to identify his favorite media technology, he continued, "Oh, that's hard," before pausing, seemingly to think it over. After a moment of reflection he suggested that it was probably his laptop, a fairly new Apple MacBook, before elaborating, "But I'm at the cutting edge of technology. My dad has three plasma-screen TVs for his computer and this computer that has not even come out yet. And since me and my brother are really good gamers we have Alien computers. Whenever a game comes out we get it. We beat it in two days. We're done."[6] Raka was among the students that most regularly showed enthusiasm for new media technologies to his peers at school, but his enthusiasm was indicative of a more general, if sometimes more muted, affinity among members of this clique, and his performances of affinity for and skill with new media technologies appeared to help him win recognition and status within the group.

The main nonschool media practices for which many of these clique participants shared affinities and expertise focused on gaming, especially playing hypermasculine first-person-shooter games like Modern Warfare II, action and adventure games, and, for some, massively multiplayer online role-playing games like World of Warcraft. They frequently discussed these games while hanging out at school, some played with other clique members in person and online out of school, and many prominently expressed their interest in games and new tech gadgets on Facebook and other social media. For example, many of these boys used pictures of characters from their favorite video games as their profile photo on Facebook, and some also uploaded images from a game to their profile and then tagged the various characters with the names of their friends. Modern Warfare II was so popular among a subset of this clique that one of the tables in the cafeteria even came to be known among members of this clique as the Modern Warfare II table.

The participants in this clique were by no means the only students to use new technologies extensively outside of school, nor were they always the most skilled and knowledgeable users of many of these technologies. But participants in this clique were the only students that routinely expressed an affinity and sophistication for certain new media as a basis for social distinction within the school, and they were the only ones to avidly pursue and develop these affinities and skills through expert-designed pedagogic interventions that were not required, such as the school's after-school programs that focused on media production. Nearly all students at the school had played video games, and many still played them frequently. Most students had cell phones, and several had considerable experience on social media. Many of the students who produced the most sophisticated media projects in the school's required game-design course were girls who hung out together in one of the other main cliques, and many of the most sophisticated users of social media were girls who qualified for free or reduced-price lunch and who hung out in another of the major cliques. And yet, despite these areas of relative experience and expertise, these other students were not typically recognized by their peers for their technical acumen, nor did these students routinely and prominently express their technical sophistication at school or online, and none regularly participated in the school's nonrequired but adult-scripted media-production activities. Instead, they participated in a diversity of other out-of-school activities, and their peers at school generally described these students in nontechnical terms.

The clique of girl students who predominantly came from homes where one or both parents worked in professional fields—which included two less-privileged girls, who were twin sisters, but no boys—was primarily known by their peers as being studious and obedient toward school adults. Both students who did and did not participate in this clique often referred to them as the "good kids," although many students who did not participate in the clique viewed their more obedient orientation toward school adults as too eager to please. For example, in an interview, Star, a girl from a lower-income household who rarely hung out with this group but who also avoided the other main clique of girls, described this group pejoratively, calling them the "Goody Two-shoes," before explaining, "You know like the coupons, they're always in a rush to get them. And they're always the same people who win them." Star was referring to a classroom-management technique that one of the teachers had implemented midway through the year. The teacher gave students paper tickets, called coupons, as a reward for obedient behavior, and the teacher named whoever accumulated the most coupons by the end of the week the Student of the Week. The winner got a poster with their name, avatar, and accumulated coupons posted on a bulletin board in the hallway. After several months of this contest, nearly all the winners were regular participants in the clique that Star called the Goody Two-shoes, and several of these girls had won the contest so many times that their posters in the hallway were covered in coupons.

The Goody Two-shoes more-obedient orientation toward school authorities, as well as the more general gendering of techno-scientific expertise, may help explain why their peers did not recognize this group as being distinctively technical despite their impressive accomplishments on adult-assigned media-production projects. The students who successfully claimed a distinctively technical identity in the eyes of their peers all avidly pursed media and technology projects in realms of their life over which they had more autonomy and control, notably after-school programs and leisure activities. In these more voluntaristic realms of activity, this clique of mostly privileged girls oriented toward activities that were neither focused on new technologies nor supported by the school. The privileged members of the clique participated in private classes for dance, music, foreign language, swimming, ice skating, tennis, snowboarding, and horseback riding. Many also had extensive experience with international travel, sometimes for tourist purposes and sometimes for their parents' work. When asked to name their hobbies and interests in interviews, many noted a similar list of out-of-school activities and experiences and, much like their peers, also tended to feature their out-of-school activities on their social network profiles (once they got them) and discussed these activities while hanging out with their friends at school; several participated in the same out-of-school activities, in part because of their parents' facilitations (chapter 3). Reformers' rendering of students as digital kids did not anticipate these out-of-school interests and practices, and, as such, they were not initially institutionally supported or recognized within the school. Consequently, many students who did not participate in this clique were largely unaware of their out-of-school lives, and they primarily associated these students with an obedient orientation towards school authorities—hence pejorative labels such as Goody Two-shoes.

Participants in the other two main cliques were primarily from lower-income homes and most qualified for free or reduced-price lunch. Like the Geeky Boys and the Goody Two-shoes, these two cliques helped remake gendered divisions, but unlike the more-privileged cliques, these cliques interacted with each other rather frequently. The participants in the clique of girls were all from less-privileged families, with the exception of two girls, Hannah and Chloe, both of whom had professional parents and had recently moved to the United States from Europe. All the participants in the clique of boys were from less-privileged households, but some were more materially disadvantaged than others. Many of the students in these cliques were high-achieving students, and some produced complex media productions as part of required coursework, but students who did not participate in these cliques did not tend to see these students as overly obedient to educators, as they did the Goody Two-shoes, nor did they associate them with a distinctive expertise with or affinity for new technologies, as they did with the Geeky Boys. Most of the participants in these cliques made extensive use of digital media in their out-of-school lives, just not in the ways that the subject fixations of the school's designers and educators had assumed. Some of the less-privileged students, and especially less-privileged girl students, were the most experienced and sophisticated users of social and communications media such as Facebook, MySpace, Twitter, a video-chat program called ooVoo, mobile phones, various instant messenger programs, and so forth. They used these tools to develop and maintain a diversity of relationships with friends and family, adjusting technologies and practices according to their interlocutors. Their early adoption and sophisticated use of these tools was partly supported by their relative freedom from organized activities in the afternoon hours and partly by a less-rigid mapping of social media practices onto age divisions within their families. While privileged families, and especially professional parents of girls, tended to view sites like Facebook as a youth-centered social space to which their children should be prohibited access until they were older (which ended up happening in seventh or eighth grade for many of these students), many of the less-privileged students had already been on Facebook for several years by the time they arrived at the Downtown School. Many of these early adopters had been introduced to social media by family members so that they could stay in touch with extended family members that were geographically distributed, and many had received hand-me-down cell phones so that various adult members of their families could coordinate child rearing alongside work schedules and other commitments. Like the students who participated in the Geeky Boys clique, many of the students who participated in the clique of less-privileged boys also continued to play video games extensively outside of school, and many had done so even more when they were younger.

But many of the students who participated in these cliques also had out-of-school interests, experiences, and skills that did not center on digital media. Like their more-privileged peers, several of the less-privileged girls had years of experience with dance, music, cheering, and performing arts, but unlike their more-privileged peers, these students primarily accessed these activities through their elementary schools, not the private market, and some also attended enrichment programs sponsored by churches and organizations like the Make-A-Wish Foundation. In general, though, girls from less-privileged families were the least involved in organized after school programs once they arrived in middle school, in part because the

Downtown School did not support programs that aligned with their interests and in part because many increasingly took on work responsibilities at home. Several aided their parents, aunts, and uncles with chores and with looking after younger relatives, and several went home, to the park, or the library after school. None of the members of this clique participated in the Downtown School's suite of after-school programs focused on media and technology production.

Similarly, none of the participants in the clique of boys from less-privileged homes participated in the Downtown School's after-school programs. Instead, many of these students participated in sports, particularly basketball and football, outside of school. Many had done so for years and had numerous family members with extensive athletic histories. When I asked a student named Jamal if he ever worked on media-production projects outside of school he replied, "I don't really do stuff like that outside of school, because, really, my family, like on my mom's side and on my dad's side, our talent is in sports. So usually I'm playing sports, or I'm playing sports games."

Some of these sports programs were sponsored by a local Boys Club, which charged $10 a year and also offered programs that helped underprivileged boys prepare academically for college, a program that several of the highest status members of this clique had been involved in for years. Other sports programs, such as football as well as a competitive basketball league, were more expensive and run by private organizations. Finally, several of the less-privileged boys were also involved in youth groups for their church. Again, and like their peers, participants in this clique prominently displayed many of these out-of-school interests and experiences both online and at school, for example, by wearing a football jersey to school, by posting pictures of themselves in their basketball uniforms on Facebook, by posting pictures online of their favorite professional athletes and gear, and so forth. And yet none of these areas of distinctive affinity and expertise were supported by the school's student-centered intervention, and none were celebrated in the school's more public festivals and ceremonies, which, as noted in the last chapter, focused almost exclusively on the school's sanctioned counterpractices. All these interests and practices were not especially centered on new media, and, as such, they largely escaped reformers' renderings of subjects that were amenable to their innovative intervention.

Given the lack of institutional support and valorization for many of these students' out-of-school experiences and interests and given that the bases of recognition and status in the other main cliques were rooted in material privileges, these students put forth alternative bases for recognition and status among their peers at school. The main ways these students promoted alternative bases for recognition and status were by emphasizing to their peers that they were more precocious in certain realms and, in a related vein, that they enjoyed more autonomy from the controlling scripts that adults routinely attempted to place on the students' lives. In keeping with Eckert's (1989) analysis, many less-privileged students had access to kinship and friendship networks that were more age-heterogeneous than privileged students, and this age-heterogeneity likely allowed some less-privileged students to observe and emulate the knowledge and practices of older youth in ways that their more-privileged peers could not. Acceptance by older youth and cousins also offered support for alternative temporalities and trajectories of learning to the ones promoted in the school and normatively encouraged by more-privileged parents. Here, for example, was how Troy, one of the high-status members of the clique of less-privileged boys, explained how he got the nickname of Kobe, a reference to the professional basketball star Kobe Bryant, while playing basketball at a local park, "When I was nine, I used to play [basketball] with [this boy who] was about 14 years old. After I played with people that are really good, I started to get better myself. That is when they started calling me Kobe." By drawing on these out-of-school networks and practices, some of these students from less-privileged households attempted to construct alternative bases of recognition and status from the ones that the school's designers and educators were attempting to construct inside the school. But, as we will see, because reformers' and educators' subject fixations mostly excluded these bases of recognition and status, less-privileged students' attempts to construct alternative criteria were increasingly seen by reformers and educators as problematic and deviant.

Participants in these cliques of predominantly less-privileged students demonstrated their relatively superior precociousness and independence in numerous ways, many of which drew attention to the fact that their out-of-school lives provided them with experiences, knowledge, and expertise that their more-privileged classmates lacked. For example, one of the main ways they did so was by being the first students in the school to dabble in flirting and dating. While students in the Geeky Boys and Goody Two-shoes cliques rarely interacted with students outside of their gendered group boundaries until seventh and eighth grade, participants in the two cliques of predominantly less-privileged students routinely interacted with each other in sixth grade, especially at the beginning of the year. These interactions often centered on the possibility of whether a high-status member of each clique was going to "go out" with the other. These courtship rituals primarily consisted of members of each group speculating about and trying to facilitate the coupling of high-status members of their respectively gendered groups. The students that clique participants identified as potential couples often played a fairly passive and silent role in these processes, and on the rare occasions when two students did finally agree to go out, I got the impression that they did so in large part because they risked losing their high standing in their respective peer groups if they did not acquiesce. For example, the first couple to go out did so after several weeks of pressuring by friends, but the relationship only lasted for a few hours before the boy ended things. The boy's status in his gendered clique was elevated and, perhaps more importantly, the prospect of emasculation by his peers, which could have occurred if the girl had ended the relationship first, was avoided.

In addition to interacting across gendered clique divisions, albeit in ways that often helped construct and affirm heteronormative gender and sexuality binaries, members of these cliques performed their precociousness by drawing attention to the areas in which they had, or sought, more autonomy and independence from adult prescriptions. For example, while students from privileged homes had traveled internationally much more extensively than their less-privileged peers and while they often referenced and displayed these worldly experiences for their peers at school, privileged students were comparatively inexperienced when it came to knowing how to navigate New York City, let alone the broader world, without the help of adults. Some students from less-privileged homes latched onto this difference as a basis of social distinction. In one such moment, three high-status members of the clique of predominantly less-privileged girls recalled their attempt to get together over the weekend without having an adult coordinator. Hannah and Chloe—who, as mentioned before, were from privileged backgrounds but hung out with a clique of predominantly less-privileged girls—did not know how to instruct their friend Niki—who qualified for free lunch—on how to get to Hannah's house, nor did they yet have enough experience with mobile phones or navigating transportation options to overcome the challenge. As the girls playfully recalled the episode, Niki teasingly drew attention to the areas where she was comparatively more precocious and worldly.

"You don't use your phone!" Niki exclaimed, in teasing disbelief.

"Yes I do, I text people," Hannah countered, "It took like an hour texting you to come to my house. You were like, 'Okay, what bus do I take?' And I was like, 'Okay, um, take this bus.' Hello? I don't know a lot of this stuff. And it's hard texting on my phone."

"And then you were like, 'I'm going to take a taxi,'" Chloe said, inserting herself into the conversation, "and we were both freaking out, like, 'No! No! Don't do that!'"

"Why?" Niki asked, perhaps genuinely confused or perhaps goading her friends.

"Hello?" Hannah said, seemingly exacerbated by Niki's refusal to understand what appeared to be commonsensical to Hannah. "You can't take a taxi alone at that young age."

"Why? I always do," Niki retorted, challenging Hannah and Chloe's assumptions about what sorts of practices were accomplishable and acceptable for people of their age.

Less-privileged members of these cliques not only routinely referenced similar experience and knowledge in areas where they were more precocious and worldly than their more privileged peers, but they also performed their greater precociousness and independence from adults by demonstrating a willingness to resist the scripting of activities that adult authorities attempted to impose on them, especially at school. These autonomy displays ranged from challenging educator prescriptions (e.g., not following directions, questioning directives, etc.) to breaking prescriptions behind the teacher's back (e.g., talking to each other, throwing notes back and forth, listening to music while on the computers, cursing, etc.), playing with the prescriptions (finding exceptions not covered by the literal meaning of directives, referencing alternative interpretations of the directives, fidgeting with binders, rulers, and other school supplies, etc.), or going along with the rules but in a manner that signaled resistance. These tactics often had the feel of dancing with the limits of what adult authorities would permit, and they often involved playing with the tacit assumptions of adult prescriptions, especially with unstated assumptions about temporality. For example, sometimes a student would walk more slowly than was tacitly expected, they would take longer than they were supposed to while providing an answer to a teacher's question, and so forth.[7] Many of these transgressions of adults' prescriptions were, in my opinion, fairly minor, but they carried significant weight in the processes by which students distinguished themselves from one another at school, and, as such, they provided means for gaining status and recognition from their peers that were not only absent from, but also resistant to, many of the assumptions and values entailed in reformers' imaginings of amenable and fixable subjects. While many other students also played with small transgressions of adults' explicit and tacit prescriptions, they tended to do so more tepidly, and they did not tend to develop a reputation among their peers as being especially independent from, and resistant to, authorities' attempts to control them.

CROSSING BOUNDARIES

While these negotiations over participation in school-based cliques often remade the social divisions that organized students' lives outside of school, some students managed to cross the divisions that organized their out-of-school lives as they participated in the peer cultures that organized in and around the school. In some cases these crossings appeared to affirm reformers' fixations of subjects that, regardless of background, would be amenable to and fixable with their remedy, and, as such, reformers and educators often celebrated these students as examples of their intervention's idealized promises. As already mentioned, two sisters who were on free lunch, Amina and Malika, regularly hung out with the Good Two-shoes, a handful of less-privileged boys and one less-privileged girl, Nita, typically hung out with the Geeky Boys, and two girls with professional parents, Hannah and Chloe, mostly hung out with the main clique of girls from less-privileged homes, at least initially.

While I found these cases encouraging—as did many educators and reformers—taken as a whole they revealed more about the mechanisms that divided the students than they did about the intervention's potential to mend entrenched social divisions. The students from less-privileged households who participated in groups of primarily privileged students had the burden of adapting to numerous practices that the privileged majority more or less took for granted, whereas privileged students who participated in groups of predominantly less-privileged students tended to retain the respect of their privileged peers and could fairly easily participate in the practices of their privileged peers when they wanted, an option not readily available to their less-privileged friends. For example, Amina and Malika could not afford the regular ice-skating trips that the mother of one of their more-privileged friends organized for some members of the friend group, so they went across the street to a public library and waited for their mom after school instead. And ice skating was just one among many expensive out-of-school practices—from summer vacations in Italy to weekend snowboarding trips, dance classes, and eating at downtown restaurants—that their privileged friends talked about at school, posted to Facebook, and sometimes participated in together.

Material disadvantages also hindered less-privileged students from participating more fully in the Geeky Boys clique. For example, Robert, who came from one of the most economically disadvantaged families at the school, was accepted and respected by coparticipants in this clique in large part because he was widely recognized as the best Modern Warfare II player in the school. And yet his family did not have a working personal computer in their home, let alone a high-end computer like those that privileged members of his clique, such as Raka, proudly owned and sometimes used for media-production projects with friends. These material disadvantages were both a source of longing and potential embarrassment for students who crossed racialized class divisions inside the school. For example, when I visited Robert's apartment, I noticed that he had adorned his Playstation 3 with Apple stickers, even though he did not own any Apple products, which were expensive, and he made a point of rightly emphasizing to me that his phone was also a computer. Similarly, several boys from less-privileged homes who hung out in the Geeky Boys clique told me that they wished they had iMovie, Apple's proprietary software for video production, at their homes. And many students from less-privileged homes yearned for cell phones that matched those of their more-privileged friends. Similarly, and as an example of what Thorne (2008) has referred to as "shame work," Nita routinely exaggerated the toys and gadgets, particularly Legos, that she had at her home when she was bidding for inclusion and respect from some of the members of the Geeky Boys clique, something I learned only once I visited her house and got to know her family. In a related vein, Amina, who primarily hung out with the Goody Two-shoes, opted to not bring a cell phone with her to school even though her mom had purchased a less-expensive and less-coveted pay-as-you-go phone for her as a fifth grade graduation present.

As students and the school grew older, several of these initially encouraging cases of students crossing more entrenched out-of-school social divisions began to deteriorate. For reasons that are discussed in the next chapter, by the end of the first year, both Chloe and Hannah had distanced themselves from Niki and many of the other less-privileged girls as they increasingly hung out with members of the Goody Two-shoes, Robert had to repeat sixth grade for academic reasons and thus no longer shared classes with the friends he had made during the school's first year. Most of the other less-privileged members of the Geeky Boys increasingly hung out with each other and less with their more-privileged friends in subsequent years. Similarly, in seventh and eighth grade, Nita shifted away from the clique of mostly privileged boys and toward the clique of mostly privileged girls. While this move allowed her to continue to participate in a clique that was primarily composed of more-privileged peers, it also led her to perform a more-normative gender orientation. Whereas she had once posted geeky content to her Facebook account, including examples of media that she had made, after she switched peer groups she started posting pictures of pop stars like Justin Bieber.

A few less-privileged students, such as Amina and Malika, as well as a boy named Issac and a boy named Ato, continued to hang out with cliques of predominantly more-privileged students. While these cases were encouraging, they were also exceptional, and yet reformers and educators routinely featured these students as model students when they presented their project to broader publics. These selection processes were especially noticeable whenever journalists and other influential outsiders visited the school, but they were also present in internal assemblies and showcases, all of which focused on the school's sanctioned counterpractices. While being featured and celebrated was likely flattering for these students, I also suspect that some may have begun to feel tokenized, especially after being repeatedly put forth as promising success stories. The important point here is that while students' out-of-school lives structured the processes by which divisions were produced within the school's peer culture, reformers' and educators' fixations about amenable and fixable subjects excluded much of students' out-of-school experiences. In the majority of cases, the reformers' student-centered reform had little connection to students' out-of-school lives, and the majority of the students for whom their intervention did resonate were boys with creative professional parents. Even in the realm of new media practices, the school's sanctioned and valorized uses of new media technologies entailed unexamined class, race, and gender biases. In keeping with more middle-class parenting practices, precocious uses of social and communications media, especially by less-privileged girls, were either overlooked or stigmatized by educators, and in the school's second year reformers and educators even devoted part of one of the special Level Up periods to the theme of "online safety and civility" in social media. By contrast, educators did not offer lessons about the safety and civility of playing masculinized video games, and if anything reformers and educators helped legitimize such practices as educational. In keeping with more-general cultural biases, technological practices associated with middle-class masculinity were applauded while those associated with femininity as well as more working class masculinity tended to be overlooked or discouraged (Wajcman 2007; Sims 2014b).

CONDITIONS OF SANCTIONED NONCONFORMITY

The examples discussed before draw attention to the salience of students' out-of-school lives in the processes by which students constructed affinities and divisions with their peers in and around the school. While I have begun to draw attention to how reformers' fixations of amenable and fixable subjects helped reinforce broader structures of privilege, the relations between reformers and their intended beneficiaries deserve further comment in this chapter and the next. The identities and divisions just discussed were produced in conditions that were not unlike the conditions that many people, regardless of their age, face everyday as they navigate institutional life: the students spent the majority of their days responding to the prescriptions of authorities in a bureaucratic organization, and they would remain subordinates, albeit with changing privileges, for as long as they remained a part of those organizations. One of the things that peer groups do in these circumstances is provide subordinates with different modes for coping with the experience of being monitored, assessed, and directed, often for hours at a time, day after day, for years on end. Peer groups provide collective ways for subordinates to not only make these conditions meaningful and livable but also with ways in which they can work through dilemmas about when and how to conform, or not, to processes of subjugation.

Interestingly, a similar dilemma animated the reformers' attempts to design a new model of pedagogic intervention. On the one hand, the designers of the Downtown School championed nonconformity among those that they targeted for pedagogic intervention. In problematizing the rigid strictures of bureaucratic organizations, they claimed that contemporary organizations could not function, let alone innovate, unless knowledge, creativity, and learning were distributed, that is, unless subordinates in an organization could act creatively and in ways that their managers had not anticipated and scripted. In keeping with broader management discourses about the new economy, the designers of the Downtown School wanted to craft subordinates that were quirky, creative, and independent. Yet, and on the other hand, organizations require subordinates to comply with organizational demands, and managers are responsible for orchestrating and motivating that compliance. This tension puts both authorities and subordinates in the odd bind of being expected to conform to an organization's demands and yet to break with its strictures of conformity. While conformity and creativity are not mutually exclusive, they are also difficult to reconcile in many cases.

The designers' attempts to make schooling gamelike can be seen as one attempt to work through the preceding structural tensions. Yet, and as we just saw, of the main peer groups that formed at the Downtown School, only the group of mostly privileged boys, and really only portions of this group, attempted to resolve the conformity/nonconformity tension in ways that resonated with how reformers and educators also hoped to resolve the same tension. The school's sanctioned counterpractices, particularly those practices that embraced gaming and certain forms of new media production, did provide this group of students with institutionally sanctioned ways to experience degrees of creativity and nonconformity. As the school's designers had hoped, these sanctioned counterpractices afforded students opportunities to act in ways that were not tightly scripted by adults, and thus the students who embraced these practices as a means of differentiation could do so without feeling as if they were merely conforming to the bidding of those who held power over them in an institutional setting.

Yet other students, and even some of the students who hung out with this clique of predominantly privileged boys, did not resolve tensions between conformity and nonconformity in ways that both satisfied their attempts to participate in peer groups and matched reformers' expectations about sanctioned nonconformity. Some responses were seen by other students, as well as many educators, as too conformist, whereas others were seen as not conformist enough, and there was no evident principle as to how to do nonconformity in the "right" way. As noted earlier, many students, and particularly students from less-privileged homes, often saw the Goody Two-shoes as too conformist, a view that some educators ironically also shared. This group's lack of participation in the school's nonrequired clubs and after-school programs focused on media production meant that they and their work were not often featured in many of the educator-sponsored festivals and showcases that celebrated the school's sanctioned counterpractices. As such, this group came to be known and to know themselves as good students, but not as the rule-breaking innovators that are so often lionized.

In contrast with these students, other students came to be seen by many educators, involved parents, and students as not conformist enough. Instead of doing nonconformity by embracing the school's sanctioned counterpractices—which again favored students, and especially boys, from privileged households—the cliques of predominantly less-privileged students navigated the conformity/nonconformity tensions by resisting, challenging, playing with, and sometimes transgressing the implicit and explicit prescriptions of the adults who held power over them, even though doing so risked punishment. Such an approach had the feel of a dance, especially at the beginning of the year. Counter to some popular accounts (Ogbu 1987), many of these students did not appear to have a counterschooling orientation, at least not yet. Most cared about getting good grades and aspired to attend college, and a few wanted to someday become doctors. Several routinely scored among the highest of their peers on exams, they congratulated each other for getting good grades, and they encouraged their friends who did less well on assignments and tests that they could do better. But they also oriented to school authorities in ways that demonstrated to themselves and their peers that they were not docile subjects.[8] Their willingness to participate in counterpractices that school authorities had not designed and scripted complemented their presentations of themselves as more mature and autonomous than their peers, and initially these practices won them a cool status among many of their peers. Yet, and as I detail in the next chapter, after months of pressure from privileged parents, educators started ratcheting up punishment for these unsanctioned responses, and as they did so these students' cool status among their peers changed from one of ambivalent respect to one of institutionally sanctioned dismissal, a repudiation that often consolidated stereotyped ascriptions of minority coolness, deviance, and race, even though there was a general taboo against using racial identifiers. By the end of the school's first year, such ascriptions were commonplace among students who did not participate in this clique.

For example, when I spoke with Elinore and Joanna about the school's cliques toward the end of the school's first year, both girls expressed what appeared to me as a noticeable change in the ways they viewed the cliques that many students had come to refer to as the "Cool Kids." Both girls identified as white, but they were less privileged than most of the other students at the school who also identified as white, and throughout the year they had periodically made attempts to hang out with the Cool Kids cliques, sometimes with success. For Elinore, there were two main types of cliques at the Downtown School. "There's the smart and nerdy," she told me, "and there's the cool." As she said this last word she raised her hands and made quotation marks with her fingers in the air, seemingly mocking the idea that the group of students were *actually* cool.

Given that she had previously appeared to admire these students, at least to a degree, I asked her why she had used the air quotes.

Her friend Joanna quickly chimed in, "Because they *think* they are so cool."

Fairly rapid changes in judgments towards one's peers are common among middle school students, but Joanna's and Elinore's apparent change of heart also paralleled privileged parents' increasingly vocal critiques of these students as well as educators' subsequent attempts to discipline members of the Cool Kids cliques.

"I'm not trying to be racist," Elinore added, "but most of them are black."

"Yeah," Joanna quickly added, "I'm not trying to be racist but . . . "

Elinore cut her off, "I'm just saying like the color."

Sensing their uneasiness with racial labels, I asked them what made the group cool, but Joanna quickly reiterated her earlier point that they weren't *actually* cool, they just thought that they were.

"They think they are tough," Elinore elaborated. "They think because they curse that they are awesome."

I had long observed that a willingness to curse, albeit typically when adults were not around, had been one of the small transgressions of adult strictures through which these groups of students differentiated themselves from, and were differentiated by, other groups of students. It was one of the symbolic practices by which members of these groups presented themselves as comparatively mature, and it was through these small acts of transgressions that some of these students had initially won a somewhat respected cool status among many of their peers. Earlier in the year Elinore and Joanna seemed to be somewhat impressed with these small acts of transgression, and I had even seen Joanna try to emulate their unsanctioned responses.

"They think that since they are black," Elinore continued, "like in the movies you see, oh the big tough people are black. Like the bullies and stuff." As we will see in the next chapter, this consolidation of stereotypes about race, toughness, and bullying were supported and accelerated by many of the privileged parents and, subsequently, educators, both of whom were especially anxious about bullying. Over the course of the school's first year, this label, which legitimated the ratcheting up of educator-enforced discipline, became shorthand for many of the unsanctioned counterpractices of students from less-privileged backgrounds. As it did, the term also increasingly became part of students' lexicon, although when students made similar ascriptions they were less careful than adults about combining them with explicit racial identifiers.

"There is even a song that is called White and Nerdy," Joanna explained, "and it's about black and white people." I had not heard of the song, which I soon learned was by Weird Al Yankovic, a musician and video producer who frequently parodies popular culture. Joanna offered to play me the song on her iPod. "It is just a stupid video," she said, perhaps recognizing that the song parodied racial stereotypes as it affirmed their existence, "but I like it."

As reductive and pejorative ascriptions of race, coolness, and deviance became more consolidated and pervasive, the students who were the targets of such ascriptions responded with attempts to maintain the positive valuation of their various counterpractices while also exhibiting a reluctance to be fixed by their peers and educators as irredeemable delinquents. Ultimately, however, their efforts did not succeed. By the end of the first year, many of their peers dismissed them with labels such as "bad," "low," "bullies," and "troublemakers." The two participants in these cliques who seemed immune to these processes of racialization and status degradation were Hannah and Chloe, both of whom were from privileged homes. Even after the status of their original clique had been diminished, most students continued to treat both girls with respect, and most considered Chloe, who was white, the most-popular student in school.

CONCLUSION

This chapter has explored how reformers tend to imagine the people they aim to help as if they are in need of, amenable to, and fixable with the reformers' novel means of intervention. In the case of the Downtown School, reformers imagined the project's intended beneficiaries as digital kids, a population that presumably would be especially amenable to the intervention's focus on gaming and new media production. Through these subject fixations reformers overlooked and distorted much of what many of their intended beneficiaries' were interested in, as well as much of what their lives were actually like. At the Downtown School, families with boys were much more attracted to the school than families with girls, and most of the students that attended the school divided themselves into cliques that largely mirrored the structural divisions that divided their out-of-school lives. Only one clique of students took advantage of the school's after-school programs focused on media and technology production, and the participants in this clique were primarily boys with creative professional parents. Many students who either could not or did not wish to partici-pate in this clique formed groups of their own, with alternative criteria for recognition and status and different orientations toward the reformers' version of learning and fun. Like the students who gelled so well with the reformers' sanctioned counterpractices, those who formed other groups drew extensively on their out-of-school lives as they worked to create dif-ferentiated identities in a community of peers. In doing so, all helped make realms of social life in which they could improvise practices, and hence selves, that had not been fully scripted for them by adults. But unlike the students who participated in the clique of predominantly privileged boys, students who participated in the other cliques, as well as many students who did not find a dominant clique to which to belong, improvised prac-tices without much recognition or support from the adults who held power in the school. In some cases, and especially for the cliques of primarily less-privileged students, school authorities increasingly attempted to eradicate their unsanctioned responses.

Reformers' fixations about digital kids not only occluded much of what mattered to many students, including, ironically, many uses of digital media, but they also limited the ways that reformers and educators un-derstood students' negotiations with each other over identity and differ-ence at school. As we have seen, peer cultural practices were inextricably tied to students' lives outside of school, and these lives were highly shaped by broader structures of power and privilege and particularly entrenched racialized social class and gender divisions. In making bids for belonging, recognition, and status within the school's peer culture, different groups of students attempted to elevate different ways of doing middle school as worthy of admiration and respect, and they did so not only in relation to each other but also in relation to what reformers and educators held up as esteemed practices. While these negotiations over participation in school-based peer cultures could be seen as part of broader historical and political struggles, reformers' processes of problematization and rendering technical largely excluded such an analysis.

As we will see in the next chapter, reformers' fixations about their inter-vention's intended beneficiaries were particularly limiting when reformers and educators had to figure out how to respond to students who did not embrace the school's sanctioned counterpractices as a means for construct-ing their identities at school. Despite the reformers' critique of authorita-tive pedagogical interventions and even though they had a sincere desire to right social injustices, the reformers did not tend to see students who resisted aspects of their remedy as creative and risk-taking innovators, nor did they recognize these practices as in-school attempts to reconfigure out-of-school inequities. Instead, they tended to either dismiss such responses as deviant or use them as evidence to problematize the shortcomings of some of the officials and educators who ran the school. At the same time, reformers' fixations about the project's intended beneficiaries helped reinforce the identity construction processes of students who were more enthusiastic about the school's sanctioned counterpractices. This institutional sanctioning of particular ways of doing creativity and nonconformity helped many privileged students—and especially boy students who had creative professional parents—see themselves as counternormative even as they mostly conformed to the prescriptions of organizational authorities and accepted organizational hierarchies.

As I have argued elsewhere (Sims 2014b), the students' constructions of classed and racialized peer groups also intersected with the processes by which students experimented with different ways of doing gender. Here, too, reformers' fixations about the intervention's target population unintentionally helped remake some of the very divisions they aimed to bridge. By sponsoring and celebrating a few digital media practices, and especially particular forms of gaming, as creative and original, the school provided the clique of mostly privileged boys not just with opportunities for forging friendships with peers at school, but also with an institutionally sanctioned way to construct themselves as masculine subjects. Not only were the media and technology practices that the school sanctioned a prime example of what Judy Wajcman (2009) has described as "both a source and a consequence of gender relations," but they were also taken up by privileged boys as a way of working through tensions between, on one hand, masculinized pressures to assert autonomy from authorities and institutional strictures, while also, on the other hand, appeasing those authorities in order to use the resources of the institution to elevate their status.

On this last point a comparison with Eckert's (1989) important study of adolescent identity formation is interesting as it highlights the ways in which school-sanctioned identities can shift over time and yet produce similar effects. For Eckert, who conducted her study at a high school in the US Midwest during the 1980s, jocks were the students who more often than not successfully navigated the gendered tension between autonomy and institutional demands, whereas the students who attempted to present themselves as jocks at the Downtown School were primarily both less-privileged and unsupported by the school (Eckert 1989, 494). Instead, at the Downtown School it was the students presenting themselves as enthusiasts of gendered forms of media and technology practice who were best positioned to simultaneously assert independence and reap institutional rewards, perhaps suggesting a shift in class-structured assumptions about normal ways of expressing adolescent masculinity. At the same time, similar attempts to exert autonomy while also accommodating pressures to be feminine were either overlooked or stigmatized by educators—even though these practices sometimes involved sophisticated uses of digital media—while approaches to femininity that mostly acquiesced to educator scripts did not reap the benefits associated with an enthusiastic embrace of the school's sanctioned counterpractices. Finally, attempts to accommodate masculine pressures from nondominant positions were increasingly stigmatized as threatening and punished.

These varying responses to the students' peer cultural practices bring to light a familiar paradox in philanthropically sanctioned educational interventions. Many people tend to see these interventions as enculturating mechanisms that can bring people of different backgrounds into some kind of local, national, or even global harmony. Yet in many ways educational interventions presuppose that very enculturation, assuming that everyone ought to understand the intervention's demands and values in the same ways. As such, unsanctioned responses can be overlooked or dismissed as deviant, rather than as quite understandable responses given the perspectives and locations of those responding. If such a paradox is familiar, then what makes a disruptive educational intervention new is not that reformers have finally found a way out of this paradox, but rather that new technologies provide reformers, and many others, with new ways to reductively imagine philanthropic beneficiaries.

6

COMMUNITY FIXATIONS

At the end of every school day, the carefully designed and scripted world of the Downtown School momentarily came into direct contact with the world beyond the school. The process was highly routinized. Educators escorted their advisory groups in single-file lines down three flights of stairs and through a door that exited onto the sidewalk on the north side of the building. As advisory groups approached the door, educators' control waned, the pace of descent quickened, and the single-file lines stretched and frayed. As students streamed onto the sidewalk, the educators came to a stop just beyond the doorway. Across the sidewalk, a handful of parents chatted with each other as they faced the exit. Some crossed the sidewalk to strike up a casual conversation with one of the educators. On some days the principal came outside and crossed the sidewalk to talk with the waiting parents. These parents were regulars, and I got to know most of them quite well. All were active in the PTA and showed up regularly for the school's various assemblies and showcases. Most were creative professionals with flexible work schedules.

When students spilled out of the building, they typically forked and pooled into inward-facing clusters to the east and west of the exit. As these students waited for friends and commute partners, some took cell phones, music players, and portable gaming devices—all of which were banned during the school day—out of their pockets and bags. Friends shared gossip about their day at school, resumed conversations that classes had interrupted, joked around, and participated in small games such as chase. These forked clusters mostly matched the cliques that I discussed in the last chapter. Participants in the cliques of predominantly privileged students clustered to the west of the exit. Some greeted waiting parents and chaperones and eventually departed down the sidewalk to the west, and several parents left with a few of their children's friends in tow. In contrast with these students and families, almost all the participants in the cliques of predominantly less-privileged students clustered to the east of the exit.

When they departed they headed east, without adults, in one or two large groups. On most days they headed to a nearby pizza parlor or bodega for a snack and then took various bus lines home or to organized after-school activities.

I suggest that these clusters mostly matched the clique divisions that formed during the school day because students who crossed racialized class divisions inside the school typically would not do so on the sidewalk. For example, while Hannah and Chloe regularly hung out with the Cool Kids cliques inside the school, they usually clustered to the west of the exit after dismissal. Some of the waiting parents knew these girls and their parents, and I got the sense that Hannah and Chloe wanted to keep aspects of their school friendships private from their parents. Occasionally their friends called out to Hannah and Chloe from down the sidewalk, eliciting a blush from the more privileged girls and laughter from their less-privileged friends. Similarly, students from less-privileged homes who avoided hanging out with the Cool Boys and the Cool Girls cliques during the school day nevertheless tended to depart to the east after dismissal. As their more-privileged friends headed off to ice-skating lessons, dance classes, and other private after-school activities, these students tended to head to a nearby library, where they waited for their parents to get off work. Others headed home.

Thus far we have examined several dimensions of a cyclical process that I am referring to as disruptive fixation. We have seen how powerful people from outside the figured worlds of reformers call upon and offer to support disruptive interventions that leverage the seemingly unprecedented philanthropic possibilities of recent innovations in media technology. We have seen how reformers respond to these calls by assembling teams of experts that include participants who are relative newcomers to the worlds they are asked to redesign but who specialize in the new techno-cultures that the powerful outsiders extoll. We have seen how these specialists engage in the interrelated processes of problematization and rendering technical as they go about imagining and designing a philanthropic intervention that can seemingly disrupt the status quo. We have seen how fixations about space, pedagogy, and the people reformers aim to help occur through these processes, and we have seen how these fixations exclude numerous factors and forces that will grip and destabilize an intervention in practice, often in ways that thwart reformers' aims. We have begun to see how the people who plan and execute a disruptive intervention respond to these unanticipated forces not so much by examining the limits of their fixations as by engaging in a different sort of fixation: they quickly reach for resources that will help stabilize the project against the turbulent forces that their fixations have excluded. We have seen how many of these resources and techniques ironically come from canonical versions of the organizations that reformers aim to reinvent. And we have begun to see how many of the people who design and support a philanthropic intervention manage to mostly repair and maintain their sense that a project is both innovative and beneficent despite these apparent tensions and contradictions. We have seen, for example, how they tend to overlook and downplay the canonical and controlling features of the intervention while ritualistically celebrating what I have been calling sanctioned counterpractices—those aspects of the project that most closely approximate reformers' idealizations. If history is a guide, the swell of idealism for a particular disruptive philanthropic intervention will eventually retreat, but history also suggests that it will not take long for new swells to rush forth once again.

While this sketch outlines a cycle of disruptive fixation, it does not yet sufficiently account for the roles that local elites play in perpetuating these cycles. In polities that see themselves as liberal and democratic, a new round of disruptive fixation can take root only if reformers can win political support from some members of the local worlds into which they intervene. Some contemporary reformers value this local participation, and, indeed, they often problematize other reform efforts for not taking local concerns and perspectives sufficiently into account. Yet reformers also do not fully anticipate the compromises they will be asked to make in order to win this support (Li 1999, 2007), and, indeed, they probably would not have been able to imagine their projects as disruptive and democratic if they had fully anticipated the extent to which these locals would steer the project toward their own ends.

This chapter explores how processes of fixation simplify and distort the political partnerships that reformers will form with members of the worlds into which they intervene. While simplifications of the population of intended beneficiaries appear to be an enduring feature of processes of problematization and rendering technical, the prevailing rationalities and discourses that guide and legitimate these processes also appear to have changed somewhat in recent decades. As Nikolas Rose (1999) has argued, in the last several decades many Anglo American (and likely other) social reformers have advocated for a third way between, on one hand, top-down statist interventions that expect local populations to accept the interventions that technocrats have planned and, on the other hand, purely market-based approaches that leave the governing of a population entirely up to individuals and the private sector. According to Rose, third-way scholars and reformers have argued that some of the responsibilities for governing should be delegated to communities, which could stand for anything from voluntary and charitable organizations to the presumed groups of multiculturalism. We see a similar ethos in the importance that many contemporary technology designers grant to notions like participation, commons-based peer production, and participatory cultures (Jenkins et al. 2006; Turner 2006, 2009; Kelty 2013). From a governmentality perspective, ordinary people are now expected to participate in the governing of their communities, however conceived, in order to contribute to the common resources, meanings, and values shared by members of the group.

As Rose observed, such discourses have the paradoxical quality of treating the notion of community—and, by extension, we could say participation—as, on one hand, a quasi-natural and extra-political phenomena, and, on the other, a key component in a particular mode of governing (1999, 167–68). According to Rose, the notion of community—which has a long history in liberal political discourse—becomes part of a particular governmental mode when reformers render it technically, that is, when they treat it as something that can be studied, formalized, designed, and managed (175). In the case of cutting-edge educational interventions that target young people, notions like community and participation are rendered technical in part by the ways that designers and reformers study, imagine, and plan ways for parents and caregivers to be involved in the governance of an intervention. When these interventions focus on redesigning schooling, parents and caregivers are often rendered as harmonious members of the "school community" and should thus work in partnership with reformers and educators to accomplish the task of governing the intervention and rearing the young. As part of this process of rendering community technically, those designing educational interventions create mechanisms for parents and caregivers to participate in the governance of the intervention. Some of these mechanisms, such as Parent Teacher Associations (PTAs), have a long and institutionalized history, whereas others, such as fundraising and various forms of volunteering, are more emergent and are thus subject to more interpretative flexibility as various parties attempt to establish and legitimate appropriate modes of parental involvement (Lareau and Muñoz 2012). As part of these broader historical changes in modes of governmentality, sharing in the responsibility of governing schools has increasingly come to be seen as an aspect of good parenting in the United States, especially among more middle-class parents (Lareau 1987, 2003; Hassrick and Schneider 2009; Posey 2012; Posey-Maddox 2014).

This chapter explores the theme of community fixations by examining reformers' ambivalent relationships with local elites, who, in the case of the Downtown School, were primarily privileged parents. Reformers rendered both families and educators as part of a harmonious and, hence, apolitical school community, and both were also idealized as participants in a broader learning network. As part of reformers' community fixations, parents and educators were imagined as connectable to each other in unprecedented ways thanks to recent advances in information and communication technologies (chapters 2 and 3), although the reformers also planned to offer more conventional mechanisms for parental involvement, such as the PTA. Reformers' imagined this relationship with the project's intended beneficiaries as mostly symbiotic and apolitical, and, as such, they did not anticipate that factions of parents would exert considerable destabilizing pressures on the project as soon as it was launched. In an attempt to stabilize the project against these unanticipated and often divisive forces, reformers and educators once again engaged in a much more pragmatic form of fixation: they allied themselves with factions of powerful parents that offered to help stabilize the project in exchange for considerable power sharing. As we will see, such alliances undermined reformers' democratic aspirations and tended to reinforce existing structures of power, privilege, and division. That these parents' participation steered the project so far away from reformers' original aspirations but also helped reformers mostly keep their idealism for the project intact complicates not only assumptions about the transformative potential of disruptive philanthropy but also assumptions about the inherently democratic character of community involvement and local participation.

BEING INVOLVED

As the vignette at the opening of this chapter helps illustrate, some privileged parents had routine access to school officials, including the principal, through quotidian practices such as picking up their children after school. Some of these parents also came by the school during the day for seemingly innocuous purposes, such as dropping off their children's lunch. While parents and many educators often saw these practices as harmless and even dutiful cases of good parenting, they also provided some parents with regular access to school officials as well as unique perspectives on what was happening inside the new school.

"It's pretty easy at the school to be in touch," one of the professional mothers told me when I accompanied her to her family's house after one of the school's PTA meetings. "I often can't get their lunch together in the morning, so I have to go drop it off, then I stop in the classes," she added. The mother was a frequent visitor to the school, and after several months I had gotten to know her quite well, as had the teachers, principal, and reformers. The mother and I would frequently chat on the sidewalk after school had ended, and when we did she often gently pressed me for information on what was going on inside the school, both in classrooms and among the school leaders. In addition to picking up her children after school and dropping off lunches during the day, she acted as a volunteer for field trips and open houses for prospective families, and she was a regular attendee at, and sometimes volunteer for, the school's various showcases, festivals, and parties. She was also a regular, and often vocal, participant at official forums for parental involvement, such as meetings for the PTA and the School Leadership Team (SLT), the latter of which was charged to provide guidance on the curriculum. Within a month or so of the school's opening, privileged parents like this one held all the top leadership positions in both the PTA and the SLT.

These highly involved parents also played an outsized role in shaping other parents' understanding of what was going on inside the school. As I briefly discussed in chapter 3, many of the school's privileged families met and established an informal coalition several months prior to the school's opening. Privileged parents with quotidian access to the school played an influential role within this coalition since their status as quasi-insiders positioned them as valuable sources of information about what was going on at school. Obviously students also routinely moved between the school and homes, and they often shared accounts of what happened at school with their families. While adults often considered students' stories less reliable, student accounts gained validity as parents shared their children's stories with each other, primarily through e-mails and phone calls, and especially when parents with quotidian access offered similar accounts. "I get a lot of e-mails," the same mother just quoted continued. "I'm generally referred to as 'the bridge.' So I feel like a lot of people contact me from different factions."

This mother's reference to the e-mails she received evinces how new media technologies did indeed shape the dynamics of parental involvement in the project's governance, but they did so in ways that had been largely excluded in reformers' renderings of a fluid and harmonious informational network connecting parents and educators. While reformers had imagined, and attempted to implement, information and communication technologies that frequently updated parents about what their children were doing at school, they had not anticipated that a coalition of privileged parents would use similar tools in order to coordinate and amplify their political power. Like any coalition, this collection of parents had its internal disputes and divisions, and yet its members typically presented a common front—one that they professed spoke for all the parents—when they voiced their ideas and demands to school officials. Deliberations and coordination among coalition members typically took place through e-mails, phone calls, and various face-to-face discussions among the parents who were members of the informal coalition. As such, reformers, school officials, and parents who were not part of the coalition had limited means for knowing about, let alone shaping, these political processes until after the coalition announced their proposals and concerns in a collective, and often fairly consolidated, manner.

One feature of this communication dynamic is that it tended to propagate rumors and amplify anxieties among the parents who were networked to each other, especially when the stories that they told each other appeared to fulfill some parents' stereotypes about students from less-privileged homes. I spoke with a few privileged parents who were reflexive about this tendency, even though they also participated in it. As one creative professional father put it, "There was kind of this flywheel vortex developing. Things would be put out, and innuendo turned into these fantasies: a school in chaos, bullying and all this." Despite this reflexivity, when adults with quotidian access offered accounts that confirmed anxious suspicions, the coalition mobilized to confront reformers and educators with a flood of e-mails and phone calls; members of this coalition also used more official venues for parental involvement—namely, the PTA and the SLT—to make forceful demands on reformers and educators.

While the parents who participated in this informal coalition did not always succeed in getting their demands met, reformers' processes of problematization and rendering technical had not come close to anticipating the extent to which these parents would exert political pressures on the school, nor did their cutting-edge innovations offer a way to counter these forces once they became aware of them. As such, reformers and educators often found that they had little choice but to cede to many of the demands of these parents, even though doing so undermined reformers' idealizations of disruptive and just social change. This capitulation to the demands of local elites and the associated compromising of the project's ideals happened for several reasons.

For one, while these parents' attempts to shape and control the project were clearly political acts, they were often depoliticized by both institutionalized mechanisms for parent involvement as well as more generally accepted ideas about the importance of community involvement in the governance of schooling. Because the coalition controlled the PTA and SLT, they could advance their perspectives and aspirations through institutionally sanctioned channels for community involvement. When they did so, they often presented their demands as if they represented all the parents, when in fact they were the consensus views of a faction of predominantly privileged parents. As such, resisting parental demands could give the impression that reformers were undemocratically installing the sort of top-down technocracy that they had problematized.

Second, the demands of privileged parents had teeth. Privileged parents had better "voice" and "exit" (Hirschman 1970) options than most other parents, and the two advantages reinforced each other. In terms of voice, parents who stopped by the school frequently and engaged in lots of volunteer work cultivated relationships with reformers, school leaders, and teachers, and these relationships allowed them to voice their ideas and concerns more frequently, privately, and informally. Additionally, many of the privileged parents held advanced graduate degrees, and several pointed to their professional expertise as legitimating their contributions to the school's governance. Again, parents did not tend to present these attempts to be involved as a form of politics but rather as a generous service that they were offering on behalf of the school community. "I felt with an architectural design background, I could be helpful," one of the creative professional parents shared when we were discussing the school's planned relocation. The conversation quickly turned to other areas to which the professional parents attempted to lend their credentialed expertise: "And then there were a couple people like Curtis, Donny's stepdad, who's a lawyer, and a good kind of advocate type. He and I basically, along with Anne, handled a lot of that. And now with the bullying and all this, I've brought in Jorge, Ivan's dad, who's a mental health professional, with a lot of experience with schools and juvenile psychiatry, to kind of advise and consult with and help get them interested to advocate and deal with the issue." Educators and reformers sometimes rebuffed these offers by parents to volunteer their expert assistance, but doing so was also difficult given the valorization of community participation.

In addition to offering these professional services, seemingly as generous gifts, highly educated parents routinely presented themselves with written, verbal, and body language that displayed their high cultural capital, and these displays helped them win influence in their relations with reformers and especially school officials and teachers. Because much of the correspondences among parents and between parents and school officials took place through e-mail, parents who were skillful writers gained influence in part because they wrote so effectively. Similarly, parents who could voice their positions in the manner of a formally educated person tended to wield extra influence in PTA and SLT meetings. And, as already noted, the coalition further buttressed these advantages by allowing privileged parents to consolidate their voices in private and then amplify a unified voice when interacting with the school.

By contrast, less-privileged parents and caregivers tended to have greater difficulty making their voices heard by educators and privileged families. Most were not part of the informal coalition of parents, and most did not, and often could not, regularly attend PTA and SLT meetings. Not only did gaining quotidian access to the school require a lot of unpaid work, which was difficult for less-privileged parents to offer, but so too did all the back channeling among parents. As the mother who referred to herself as "the bridge" suggested, "I get 100 e-mails a day from school parents. It's unbelievably labor intensive." Because these practices were so labor intensive, participation was highly structured by parents' working lives and their material circumstances more generally. For the most part, the parents

who had regular access to the school and school officials were professionals who had a fair degree of control over their work schedules. Mothers
also did most of this volunteer and support work, although some fathers
with flexible work schedules were also actively involved. There was one
less-privileged father who worked in construction and who often stopped
by the school when he was not employed, and there was one unemployed
single mother who dropped in on the school quite frequently, but neither
of these parents occupied a bridge position in the coalition, and I am fairly
sure they were left out of most of the back channeling that took place
among more privileged parents. Neither parent held leadership positions
in the PTA or the SLT.

When parents and caregivers from less-privileged homes were able to
attend more official forums for parental-educator relations, such as schoolwide meetings for parents, most of the less-privileged parents sat toward
the back of the auditorium and rarely spoke; by contrast, most privileged
parents who had quotidian access to the school sat toward the front of
the auditorium, and some sat next to educators and school leaders. These
parents often spoke before and more often than less-privileged families,
and a few carried on casual conversations with educators and school leaders before, during, and after the meetings. Moreover, when parents who
were underprivileged did speak, more privileged parents would sometimes
trivialize their concerns, sometimes in public and sometimes in private
conversations with me or with each other. For example, after one schoolwide meeting, a professional mother told me that one of the less-privileged
mothers who had spoken during the meeting was "truly insane" before
joking that I should interview her for my project. The privileged mother
elaborated on her comment by telling me about a conversation where the
less-privileged mother had interpreted some of the taunts that students
made to each other at school as "normal kid stuff." This interpretation
exasperated the professional mother, who saw such taunts as completely
unacceptable. The professional mother told me that she thought the less-
privileged mother had a "severe mental illness," a claim that she then attributed to another professional parent, a psychologist, who, according to
the mother with whom I was speaking, had formed this diagnosis based on
the manner in which the less-privileged mother had been smiling while she
was talking. All these factors contributed to amplifying the voice of more-
privileged families while damping, if not silencing, the voices of those who
inhabited significantly less-privileged circumstances.

Privileged families also had better exit options than the less-privileged
families, and threats to leave the school reinforced their voice. As I will
shortly discuss, in the school's first year a large faction of professional
parents threatened to pull their children from the school if educators did
not make the changes they demanded. Here, too, the informal coalition

benefitted privileged families because it allowed them to threaten to exit
en masse. Privileged parents could make this threat because they lived in
District Two and hence could access other quality public schools. Further,
several privileged families could (begrudgingly) pay for private schools,
and indeed one disaffected family departed for a private school during the
school's second year. As such, privileged parents were empowered with the
sort of consumer sovereignty that proponents of school choice have celebrated, and choice increased the power of their voice to influence the
school. By contrast, families from less-privileged backgrounds, and especially families living outside of District Two, had much more limited exit
options than the school's privileged families, and hence they did not enjoy
nearly the same power within the choice system. Since less-privileged parents
did not enjoy nearly the same choices, their voice was also comparatively
weakened.

While reformers and school officials generally welcomed parental involvement, the appropriateness of parental influence in the school's governance was also highly ambiguous, especially when this participation took
place outside of the official forums of the PTA and the SLT. I often got
the sense that involved parents did not want to come across as if they were
overbearing, disrespectful of reformers' and educators' expertise, or attempting to shape the school unfairly in their children's favor. Involved
parents often emphasized to me that they were not the stereotypical PTA
or "helicopter parent" that had been widely disparaged in the media, and
they often stressed that they preferred a hands-off approach. "I'm so not
the PTA mom," the mother quoted earlier told me after explaining all the
ways she was involved in shaping the school's governance. "I've never been
involved. I turn my children over to the educators. I trust that the educators know something about education, which I don't. Take care of them,
and I'll pick them up at the end of the day." But because the Downtown
School was new, she said, she felt she needed to be more involved. Because
the school was new, it also did not yet have standard protocols for parental
involvement, and, as such, it was fairly easy for parents like this one to
insinuate themselves into positions of influence. Plus, since the school's
planners and educators were so busy trying to get their project up and running, the extra help was often needed and appreciated. "I feel like I have a
sense of what's going on in the school more than I did when they were in
fifth grade," the mother continued, "just because it's new and very open,
and I'm pretty involved."

In short, the school's privileged parents were much better equipped
than the school's less-privileged parents and caregivers to access school
officials and to participate in the school's official and informal modes of
governance. Some used their flexible work schedules to routinely drop by
the school and to volunteer at school events. By being networked to each

other as well as to powerful people beyond the school, these families were better able to share information, form consensual viewpoints, and mobilize collective action. They used these connections to help win leadership positions on the PTA and SLT, and they wrote, spoke, and carried themselves in ways that signaled their high cultural capital. Finally, the classed geography of their District Two residences provided them with exit options that could be used as leverage in negotiations with reformers and educators.

In many ways, these advantages are not that surprising. Privilege, after all, is precisely the advantages available to some groups and not others. It is also not surprising that privileged parents did all that they could to provide advantages for their children. But what is more curious is how these practices were tolerated by reformers and educators who designed and morally legitimated their philanthropic intervention in large part by appealing to concerns about social justice. I do not believe the reformers and educators who designed and worked at the Downtown School were insincere in these aims, nor did they appear especially eager to capitulate to privileged families' demands. In one case, one of the school's leaders was even reported to have "had a breakdown" after trying to resist the pressures of privileged parents for several weeks. Yet time and again, reformers and educators not only mostly gave in to these demands but also managed to mostly repair their idealizations of the project. Examining a particularly contentious episode between the reformers and the school's privileged parents helps illuminate how these seemingly contradictory outcomes were accomplished. While other contentious episodes—such as the relocation battle discussed briefly in chapter 3, as well as struggles over how much emphasis should be given to preparing for the state's standardized tests—revealed internal fissures among the coalition of privileged parents and, hence, led concerned parents to back down on their demands, when privileged parents consolidated their voice, as they did in the following episode, reformers and educators had little choice but to capitulate.

FUELING FEARS OF IMMINENT COLLAPSE

I was introduced to the prospect that the intervention could imminently collapse on the morning of the second day of school. An hour or so earlier, one of the school's leaders had held an emergency early-morning meeting for all educators. A mother had called the night before suggesting that her son, who was white and comparatively privileged, had been bullied on the first day of school (later, the boy's father suggested to school officials that perhaps the boy's mother had overreacted). The school leaders wanted to coordinate an immediate response, and, as part of that response, one of the school's leaders visited all the advisory classes to address the purported bullying issue with students. The school leader's address to the students began by comparing bullying to a pollutant: "Did you notice the bags of garbage on the street in front of school today? Garbage is stinky and unsightly, right? Well we've been dealing with our own garbage this morning." After noting that they had received complaints about bullying, the school leader went on to compare the school to a house. The leader emphasized that bullying threatened the very foundation of the house, "You can always replace the roof, the walls, and the bathroom. But if the foundation goes, the whole structure comes down." Bullying, from this perspective, was a moral pollutant and an existential threat to the school as an idealized community.

While I knew that bullying was a hot topic in the media before I started fieldwork, I had not anticipated the degree to which fears about bullying would build into panics that substantially altered the political direction of the school, often in ways that undermined reformers' philanthropic idealizations. For concerned parents and some educators, bullying was not just an unfortunate, but common, aspect of children's and young people's peer relations, something that could be called out and hopefully corrected when observed by adults. Rather, bullying was often presented as a moral and existential threat to their children as well as the school community. Starting from the first day of school, stories about bullying quickly spread among parents in the informal coalition. For some privileged parents, these reports appeared to confirm their preconceived anxieties about the presence of lower-income students of color. Privileged parents habitually ascribed the specter of the bully to members of the cliques of predominantly less-privileged students, and especially the clique of boys, even though I observed students from all backgrounds being mean to each other and even though most of the antagonistic actions by members of the Cool Kids cliques were directed in quasi-jest towards other students who hung out in these cliques.[1] Hyperbolic stories of these students' dangerous nonconformity—their "cursing," "fresh," "obscene," or "shocking" language; their "disruptions in classrooms"; their "intimidation" and "sexual harassment"—circulated among privileged parents throughout the fall.[2] Some privileged students had shared stories about these students' transgressions with their parents, and a few of the parents with quotidian access to the school lent credibility to these students' accounts, even though these parents had spent only brief moments inside the school and did not have a good sense of what daily life was like inside the school.

By winter, the seeds of panic had grown into a crisis. The involved parents' demands were clear: they demanded that school leaders implement zero-tolerance policies in order to to quickly purge unsanctioned behavior and, if need be, to remove the purported perpetrators. Here, for example, is a snippet of an e-mail that one of the creative professional parents sent to educators and parents; the subject line of the e-mail was written in all caps: OF UTMOST IMPORTANCE: BULLYING:

> We as concerned parents and educators take these complaints with the greatest gravity, and will not abide by such behavior in any way, shape, or form. We all agreed that there should be zero tolerance for such behavior. Not one child at the Downtown School needs to suffer at the hands of another student. Not one child needs to worry about intimidation, sexual harassment, racism, or bullying in our school. Our school should be a safe haven, a sanctuary of learning and security for our children, and we all agreed to work toward this end. . . . The culture of television, rap music, the street, is not the culture of the classroom and does not belong inside the school walls.

Several aspects of this parents' e-mail deserve comment. For one, despite the fact that many of the school's sanctioned counterpractices were particularly well attuned to the out-of-school interests and practices of boys from privileged families and despite the fact that privileged parents routinely crossed into the school as they attempted to shape the direction of the project, the parent appealed to an idealized learning environment that reformers also yearned for: that the school could be an apolitical and culturally neutral sanctuary of learning and security. In doing so, the parent helped reaffirm the promise of reformer's spatial fixations (chapter 3) even as he called for changes that seemingly undermined their pedagogic fixations (chapter 4), as well as their broader commitments to social justice. At the same time, he problematized reformer's inability to accomplish their spatial fixations by suggesting that an abject alterity—the culture of television, rap music, the street—had punctured and contaminated that sanctuary. He linked unsanctioned behaviors to an illegitimate, and thinly coded, racialized culture that presumably came from and belonged to another space, the streets, properly located beyond the school walls. Not only did professional parents routinely suggest that a polluting culture had infiltrated their idealized learning environment, they also hyperbolically suggested that this unwelcome alterity threatened to infect their children. As one mother, a professor, said at a PTA meeting, "How do you deal with the infectious tendency of this behavior, that spreads horizontally, and infects others? It's transmitted from generation to generation and from person to person." In another e-mail, a professional parent described the issue as follows: "potent cliques seem to have arisen and feed off the preying on others." Such hyperbolic language did not tarnish the prospect of creating the idealized and harmonious community that reformers had envisioned; rather, and in an all-too-familiar tendency with utopian undertakings, it repaired this fixation by calling for measures that would purge purportedly corrosive elements while also policing the community's borders.

This work of repairing idealized fixations about the project also entailed efforts to prevent a more-direct consideration of how the project was a site of politics and, hence, how their acts and demands were themselves political. While students' acts of resistance toward authorities and their taunts and put-downs toward each other were an opportunity when reformers, educators, parents, and students could address the problematic and contentious social divisions that organized students' lives outside of school, privileged families actively closed off a consideration of such factors by calling for zero-tolerance policies and other universalizing dictates. When I asked one creative professional couple what zero tolerance meant, the father replied, "It just means you don't say, 'Oh, kids are kids! That's okay.' There's some disciplinary action, and some threat to the kid to say this doesn't happen in our school."

The mother jumped in, "There's a hard line of response to behavior that's not tolerated, and there's no excuse. You don't make an excuse for the child."

"'Oh they're street kids,'" the father continued. "'Oh, they are tired.' 'Oh, they're just boys.' 'Oh, they're just from this part of the world.' 'Oh, they're just a certain age.' It's basically—it's not cool. It doesn't happen here. It happens again, you're out of here."

Similarly, as one creative professional parent wrote in an e-mail to the principal, with members of the design team carbon copied:

> Please realize, allowing such out of control, blatant misconduct to persist endangers our whole school and everything you and everyone else involved has worked so hard for. . . . We as caring parents and dedicated educators cannot let this go on. This kind of behavior has nothing to do with a certain disadvantaged segment of our population. It is not age-related. Nor hormone related. It is not economic bound. It has nothing to do with race. All members of our society, rich, poor, middle class, pink, blue, rainbow-colored, yellow, brown, black, red, white, must be respectful and tolerant of others. . . . Zero tolerance should be our policy and real punishment must be our credo.

In this quote we can again see how idealized appeals to a harmonious and morally just community are entwined with appeals to close off a consideration of power and politics: the attempt to exclude a consideration of how social class, race relations, age, and other structural factors that extend beyond the site of the school might have shaped the issues transpiring within the intervention; the linking together of parents and educators with the pronoun *we* and the moral framing of their collective efforts as acts of parental care and professional dedication; the claim that transgressive elements threatened to bring down the whole project, as well as its moral promise; the demand that authorities use the full extent of their institutionally sanctioned power to discipline and, if need be, purge, those who took part in unsanctioned responses; and the legitimation of using power in such ways through appeals to the presumed universal standards of tolerance and respect. In other words, despite being drawn to the philosophies and approaches of a student-centered intervention that was connected to the world, privileged parents considered authoritarian zero-tolerance policies and disciplinary techniques, as well as attempts to police the school's borders, as a legitimate means for creating an idealized sanctuary of learning founded on purportedly universal norms of respect and tolerance—which can easily be read as contemporary versions of "civilized"—even if those accused of showing disrespect were routinely subjected to disrespect, intolerance, and symbolic violence by the dominant culture more generally and by the privileged parents in these very instances. Perhaps sensing that such calls were at odds with the pedagogic ideals that attracted privileged parents to the school, one of the creative professional parents told educators at an emergency meeting about bullying, "We're all behind you cracking down, cracking the whip, showing that it's not tolerated," at which point he paused for a moment before adding, "It's not fun, and it's not about learning, but it affects learning." Like educators' reconciliation of classroom-management practices with their pedagogic idealizations (chapter 4), this parent justified calls for disciplinary power by classifying such practices as a separate, but necessary, precondition for what the intervention was really about: the facilitation of supposedly apolitical and beneficent learning activities.

Initially, reformers and educators mostly tried to resist these professional parents' attempts to influence the governance of the school, and several privately shared with me that they thought some of the parents' comments were racist. The reformers and educators that I knew well were frustrated by these parents' aggressive attempts to shape the school, and they were also much more willing to consider the ways in which social divisions in the world structured tensions within and around the school. One of the school leaders, who had a background in social work and who was responsible for instituting the called for disciplinary measures, was especially reluctant to accept privileged parents' diagnoses and acquiesce to their prescriptions. But reformers' idealized fixations had also led reformers to be blindsided by these parents, and the cutting-edge aspects of their intervention offered few resources for fending off such pressures once they became evident.

"They're trying to dictate, absolutely," one of the school's designers shared with me toward the end of the school's first year. The reformer seemed annoyed with these parents, understandably so, and also surprised. "Parents have made a lot of inappropriate comments about kids who are lower income and of color," the reformer continued, "comments that you think we're done with those kinds of things. But we're so obviously not done, even in progressive Manhattan, the bluest of the bluest places in America." Offering a glimpse into how the designers' fixations excluded consideration of such forces, the reformer continued, "It's just that we didn't suspect that—we were all so wild doing all sorts of innovative things with the curriculum and the structures of a school—we were also going to be dealing with a social experiment, which is integrating kids truly, truly having an integrated school. That has been challenging for parents," the reformer said. It seemed to me that the reformer was caught in an especially compromised position. While the reformer was clearly annoyed and even offended by some of these parents' behavior, this person and other reformers seemed reluctant to forcefully rebuke these parents, probably because they feared that if they did so, then a large faction of these parents would make good on their threats to leave the school.

Despite reformers' and educators' insights into the problematic character of these privileged parents' participation in the project's governance, in January of the school's first year, and after several months of trying to resist privileged parents' demands, reformers and educators finally capitulated and rapidly introduced a slew of canonical disciplinary techniques. The tipping point occurred shortly after two of the widely recognized leaders of the Cool Boys clique, both of whom were high-achieving students of color, were given weeklong "superintendent suspensions" for allegedly sexually harassing two of the girls who hung out in the Cool Girls clique. One of these girls identified as white and had creative professional parents, while the other identified as black and qualified for free lunch. For months, the four students had been central players in their cliques' courtship dramas (chapter 5). While I do not know the full extent of the incident that led to the suspensions, I heard from students that one of the boys had "touched one of the girl's butts during a game of Truth or Dare at school." I also heard from parents that the boys had been sending lewd, aggressive, and inappropriate text messages to the white girl with creative professional parents. While school officials, professional parents, and many students labeled the incidents as sexual harassment, the students involved did not see them as clearly defined. When the incident came up in conversations among peers at school, one of the suspended boys pleaded, "I didn't harass her!" Additionally, while the girls involved initially put distance between themselves and the boys, especially at school, they remained friends with the boys and continued to interact with them, especially online. Whatever actually happened, a consolidated mass of privileged parents threatened to leave the school, and reformers and educators finally acquiesced to their demands.

This particular crisis was eventually eased by the departure of core members of the Cool Boys and Cool Girls cliques, especially those who held high-status positions within their respective cliques. The three students who had emerged as leaders of the Cool Boys during the first several months of school, two of whom routinely received some of the highest scores in the school on exams, transferred to larger, less-resourced schools that had sports teams, more of a dating scene, and much smaller proportions of children from professional families. They did so after months of repeated suspensions, pervasive surveillance by educators, toting around behavior cards, and the other disciplinary measures discussed in chapter 4. In contrast with the ambiguous playfulness that characterized their unsanctioned practices earlier in the year, by the spring their status as disruptive and dangerous deviants who needed to be pacified or purged had become fixed in the eyes of many anxious professional parents, educators, and peers. Although I was not at the school as often during the school's second year, I heard from several parents that members of the Cool Girls clique who were from less-privileged homes were the ones figured as bullies in the school's second year, and by the end of the second year several of the most influential members of this clique, some of whom were also high academic achievers, had also left the school.

While several reformers and educators shared with me that they were disappointed over these students leaving, the school's design team, as well as many of its educators, continued to champion the school as a cutting-edge model of philanthropic intervention, and they did so with all appearances of sincerity. Even after the school's contentious first year, reformers and educators continued to celebrate the school's sanctioned counterpractices in various venues where the school staged self-representation of itself, and they even developed digital resources, which they called kits, to help spread their model of reform to other reformers and educators. Some of the school's designers and their wealthy backers launched a second version of the school in another major city, and the foundations that supported the school's planning continued to direct large grants toward the nonprofit organization that was run by one of the school's founders. In one case, one of these foundations even hired a member of the school's design team to locate and fund similar innovations in digital media and learning.

That the contentious political struggles just discussed did not appear to substantially tarnish the idealism of the school's designers and backers deserves comment. As discussed in chapter 4, the recurring and ritualized celebrations of the school's sanctioned counterpractices did much to help repair hopeful feelings about the project. Additionally, broader rhetorics about choice appeared to have helped deflect more sobering self-reflection.

Many reformers, educators, and parents from privileged backgrounds suggested that the students who had left the school had done so because they
had been a bad match for the school's innovative model. Similarly, the parents of the students who left the school also suggested that the school had
been a bad fit. "The Downtown School could work for some other kid,"
the mother of one of the departing students shared with me, "but it just
wasn't working for my son." Instead, and with help from leaders at the
Downtown School, her son enrolled at an older and more-conventional
school that, ironically, was called School of the Future. That school had
been founded in the early 1990s, likely with a similar, if less intense, fan-
fare to that which now surrounded the Downtown School. But unlike the
Downtown School, the School of the Future was not currently a coveted
option among privileged parents living in District Two. "School of the
Future is a more traditional school," the mother of the departing student
added, "which works for this kind of kid." Another mother of one of the departing students expressed that she was also looking for a more traditional
school, with high standards, good test scores, sports teams, a debate team,
"and all that good stuff." When framed in terms of market logics, this sort
of educational segregation is easily depoliticized as a product of individual
preferences, a move that deflects responsibility for those divisions away
from the actions of privileged parents, reformers, and educators.

In addition to depoliticizing the students' departures as matters of personal choice, the criterion of a good cultural fit justified new efforts to
seal the school's borders and to control who and what passed through. In
addition to demanding stricter discipline within the school, several of the
involved professional parents took an active role in trying to shape admissions and recruitment. They brokered relationships with elementary
schools in District Two that had high percentages of students from creative
professional families, they recruited friends to apply, they volunteered to
meet with prospective families at open houses, and they helped shape how
school officials defined selection criteria. As these parents gained influence
in the school's admissions' processes, school leaders and some of the highly
involved parents gradually changed how they talked about inclusion.
Instead of saying that the school was for "kids these days," as the school's
designers had stated in the school's planning documents, they started
saying things like, "We'll take anybody, but we want to make sure they get
what we're about."

This comment, which was made to me by one of several parents who
held a PhD and worked in academia, was echoed by several of the other
highly involved professional parents. "They can't do the unscreened thing
anymore," another involved parent, who also held a PhD, told me in an
interview in the spring of the school's first year. "Our selection criterion,
our only selection criterion is 'informed choice,'" she added, referencing

the Department of Education's policies for how new schools in the choice system could influence their admissions processes. "What we think would make sense, the parents who've been involved in the discussions about this," she continued, "is that you define 'informed' in a particular way, so that you're getting kids who are a good fit with the school." The school had only been open for a few months, but these parents were already trying to influence how school leader's interpreted and applied the informed-choice criterion. They also tried to shape admissions to their liking by volunteering at open houses, where they could subtly encourage and discourage different families from applying. Even though these parents had pressured reformers and educators to make the school more isomorphic to conventional schools, at open houses they emphasized the school's alterity and sanctioned counterpractices, which, as we saw in chapter 3, primarily appealed to other creative professional parents. "I did all these open houses," she continued, "and at every open house I said to people, 'Just think about whether this is a good fit for your child. It's game-based learning, these are not your mother's jeans, this is a totally different way of being in school. You need to feel comfortable with it.'"

Once again we can see how a magnified and idealized emphasis on the school's unconventional features—and especially its sanctioned counterpractices—played an important, if unexamined, role in the remaking of social divisions. Even though the pedagogic practices of the Downtown School were more similar to than different from conventional models and even though the school's routines became more conventional in part because of pressures from privileged parents, involved parents and school officials increasingly conveyed that the school was a good fit for some families and not for others by emphasizing the school's supposedly unique features. And, as we have seen, the uniqueness of the school's sanctioned counterpractices, particularly their geeky resonance, primarily appealed to parents who worked in the culture industries, especially if they had boys.

Partnering with these local elites did help stabilize the philanthropic project against the prospect of a sudden and embarrassing collapse, and these alliances did help repair idealizations of community among those who continued to commit themselves to the project. After educators finally gave into the demands of privileged parents, nearly all the students from privileged families remained enrolled in the Downtown School through eighth grade, several had younger siblings enroll, and some of their parents, especially parents of boys, became among the school's biggest supporters and champions. In large part because of these families' involvements and endorsements, in subsequent years more and more creative professional families in District Two sought a spot at the Downtown School, to the point that the school became a hot option and was quite difficult to get into. As one creative professional said to me after they heard me give a short talk on the school during the school's third year, "Everybody I know who has kids that age want their kids to go to that school, and it's really hard to get in." As we chatted, she suggested that some professional families were even moving to District Two just so their kids would have a chance to attend. "It's like a private school in the public system," she explained. I agreed and mentioned that the schools shared a pedagogic philosophy that was similar to the private Waldorf and Montessori schools. "Yes," she replied, "but they're incorporating technology."

IDEALIZATIONS AND CONDITIONS OF COMMUNITY INVOLVEMENT

I have been arguing that reformers' political partnerships with local elites were partly accepted and legitimated because of more widespread assumptions about the inherently democratic character of community involvement and local participation in the design and governance of a philanthropic intervention. The founders of the Downtown School were part of a growing collection of social reformers who advocate for philanthropic interventions that are participatory, user-centered, community-based, citizen focused, and so forth. A similar ethic, but from the other direction, pervades what has become a mark of good-parenting practices in the United States, especially among middle- and upper-middle-class families (Lareau 1987, 2003; Lareau and Muñoz 2012; Hassrick and Schneider 2009; Nelson 2010; Ochs and Kremer-Sadlik, eds. 2013; Posey-Maddox 2014). Such idealizations of community participation in the design and governance of philanthropic interventions are understandable, especially given the well-known shortcomings of top-down attempts at technocratic social reform (Scott 1998). But an unreflexive endorsement of terms like community and participation can also obscure the ways in which sanctioned forms of community participation often reinforce and legitimate privilege as well as exacerbate social division. At the Downtown School, many parents did not have the time or resources to be extensively involved in shaping and running the school, and those who did have these advantages did not use them to simply enrich "the school community." Instead, involved parents promoted their political interests as if they were the interests of all the parents, even though their demands often had detrimental consequences for other students and families who did not enjoy their advantages. As with the other fixations that this book has been examining, idealizations of community and participation converted diverse experiences, divided interests, and unequal power relations into seemingly more tractable and apolitical entities—the community, the parents—as they overlooked the conditions that made sanctioned forms of participation something that could and should be desired, learned, and practiced.

What the highly involved parents at the Downtown School shared was not so much a gendered, raced, ethnic, or national identity—although these identifications did sometimes matter—as similar class conditions and corresponding cultural predispositions. Complicating stereotypes, several of the highly involved parents were fathers, numerous families had lived significant periods of time outside the United States, not all were white, and others were citizens from other countries. Most were doing quite well compared to the vast majority of the people in the world as well as to other practitioners in their respective professions. Yet their positions of relative privilege were also tenuous (Neff 2012), and their ability to reproduce a similar social standing for their children was by no means guaranteed. Most did not have large sums of money to bequeath to their children, nor could most buy their children into elite private schools. Several lost their jobs during the course of my study, and others were frequently scrambling for career opportunities, sometimes even moving across the world to do so. In trying to provision educational advantages for their children, they had little choice but to navigate a schooling system that was intensively competitive. Privileged parents often bemoaned how competitive schooling now seemed: the insanity of having to apply to middle school as if it were college, another round of competitive applications for high school, the eventual rat race of getting into a good college, and the further uncertainty of what sorts of meaningful occupations would exist on the other side of college, the other side of graduate school, or the other side of who knew what.

For many of these parents, the Downtown School seemed like as an appealing educational alternative to what one creative professional parent called "the race toward medical school." After a contentious meeting in which some parents pushed school officials to spend more time preparing students for the state's standardized tests, a frustrated creative professional parent shared with me why their family had been drawn to the Downtown School in the first place. The parent told me about one of their older sons who had gone to "one of these fancy schools" where they stressed competition and lots of homework. He said that the son became a nervous wreck and that he was still suffering from these earlier schooling pressures even though he was now in college. The father said he did not want that for his child who attended the Downtown School; he did not want their younger child to become "that type of kid."

When such concerns and yearnings are considered in the context of an increasingly competitive, disciplined, and unpredictable political and economic order, some privileged parents' intense involvements in the Downtown School no longer appears as simply crazed effort to give their kids a leg up. Rather, they can also be seen as entailing critical insights into the broader political and social conditions in which they lived, insights that were much like those of the school's designers and reformers. Many could see that conventional schooling systems were organized as a hypercompetitive race that produced a few winners and many losers. All could see that this race had negative consequences for nearly everyone involved. And all were motivated to direct substantial energies towards efforts to disrupt these unwanted processes. But their attempts to do so ironically helped sustain and spread the very conditions that generated those afflictions. Their responses were not unlike that of a person who, discomforted by the effects of climate change, installs a more powerful but ecofriendly climate control system in their home. They did not challenge the political and economic orders that have made schooling and their lives ever more competitive and precarious, and, if anything, they helped circulate claims that legitimated such arrangements: self-realization through creative entrepreneurship, unprecedented opportunities thanks to new technologies, lifelong learning (e.g. reskilling), and so forth. Problems generated in part by a more-widespread acceptance of these claims were understood narrowly as problems with conventional schooling or particular individuals and, as such, these parents fought for remedies that may have helped them temporarily secure some relief for their children but that left the sources of their concerns intact. In doing so, they not only helped sustain the conditions that generated their concerns, but they also divided themselves from other families that were also trying to cope with precarious conditions, but from significantly more disadvantaged positions.

The increasing entrenchment of spatialized social divisions into fortified enclaves and networks makes attempts to bridge these widening divisions ever more challenging (Davis 1990; Graham and Marvin 2001). Not only did these spatialized social divisions discussed in chapter 3 facilitate the stereotyping of people who primarily lived their lives in other spaces, but also, and in a related vein, many of those in positions of relative privilege were quite palpably afraid of having their children share spaces with children from less-privileged backgrounds, especially, as we have seen, when issues of race, gender, and sexuality were involved, as they often are in schools and other enclaves for youth. One of the school's designers referenced these dynamics while recalling a conversation they had had with one of the involved parents. "He was afraid for his kid to be around kids of color," the designer said, "just literally afraid of other kids because of their backgrounds." The designer went on to reflect on how such fears can take root when families spend the majority of their lives separated along lines of racialized social class. "Like he actually was very innocent in his concern," the designer explained, "I had to remind him that eighty-plus percentage of the inner city are those kids."

In the Downtown School's second year, one of the creative professional parents who had been gripped by the panic over bullying during the previous year found himself at the center of a new moral panic, this one centered on girl bullies. In part thanks to his eloquent e-mails condemning bullying in the school's first year, the father was elected to one of the leadership positions in the PTA. When the new panic broke out, the father decided to check out the situation in person and spent several days sitting in on classes and moving with students throughout their days, much as I had. When we later discussed these forays into the school, the father told me that he had changed his perspective on the bullying frenzies. "Sure some students act out," he said, "but they're just kids," reversing his early arguments in favor of zero tolerance. The father added that the professional parents had a tendency to gossip with each other, get worked up, and then overreact.

While this parental engagement with students from diverse backgrounds produced a hopeful personal transformation, I do not want to suggest that such an approach could easily solve the problems I have been addressing. Most parents and guardians did not and could not spend extensive time inside the school. Further, marketlike choices for educational services offer families, and especially privileged families, options that allow them to avoid dealing with discomfiting issues of privilege and cultural difference. Finally, once removed from direct participation—a consequence of spatialized social divisions—the negative feedback amplification of self-selected communication networks can produce hysteria that is difficult to dislodge. Toward the end of the father's year as the PTA officer, I asked him how things had gone being involved. "I hate it," the father said, noting privileged parents' recurring hysteria, "There are a lot of neurotic parents."

CONCLUSION

While privileged parents routinely figured bullying as an invasive force that threatened to destroy the school, it was more their own hysteria about bullying and threats of exit that fueled reformers' anxieties about an early and embarrassing collapse of their philanthropic project. Not only had these parents' threats to leave pressured reformers into deploying canonical resources and practices that ironically made the school much like more traditional urban public schools, but it also bolstered some privileged parents' attempts to seal off the school in ways that they could control. The noteworthy point here is that reformers capitulated in ways that undermined their philanthropic ideals not because they were duplicitous or totally unaware of tensions between their ideals and their actions, but because they found themselves in a crisis that was only partly of their own

making. Like other well-intentioned reformers, their fixations did not anticipate the numerous forces that would overflow, grip, and twist their philanthropic intervention in all sorts of unexpected directions. Over and over
again during the school's first year, it felt as if the project was weathering
a blustering storm, springing leak after leak and teetering on the verge of
collapse. In an attempt to control these volatile forces and avoid an embarrassing collapse, reformers quickly assembled stabilizing resources from
wherever they could.

As we saw in chapter 4, some of these resources came from canonical versions of the institution that reformers aimed to disrupt, particularly
the disciplinary techniques whose genealogy Foucault (1977) traced. As we
saw in this chapter, other stabilizing resources came from local elites who
offered their support on the condition that they could take a prominent
role in shaping the project's governance. At the Downtown School, the
local partners who were best positioned to offer this support—and also
the best positioned to withdraw it—were privileged parents. Reformers
did not partner with these local elites without reservations, nor were they
unaware of their project's entanglement with forces whose control and
generation extended far beyond their reach. When recounting the school's
challenges, reformers often acknowledged the magnitude of the divisions
that structured students' out-of-school lives, and some commented on how
these divisions likely contributed to the contentious struggles that they
were trying to handle in the school. But the dominant tendency, especially
when reformers worried that the future of the project was at stake, was to
try to stabilize the project by just about any means available. Most turned
to technical diagnoses and fixes that left optimistic feelings about the philanthropic nature of their intervention intact. The school needed better
leadership, some said, or they needed more teacher training because the
model was so new, they needed more rules and strictures or a more developed school culture or better admissions policies, or less bureaucratic
oversight, or, as is all too familiar in the case of schooling, they figured
some of their intended beneficiaries as especially deficient or irredeemable
with their remedy, and so on. The deployment of stabilizing resources, and
especially partnerships with local elites, helped dampen these volatile
forces and avoid an embarrassing collapse, but what endured was not a
shining new model of schooling or an innovative mechanism for fixing
social divisions, but rather a version of canonical schooling retrofitted with
seemingly cutting-edge material and symbolic forms.

7

CONCLUSION: THE RESILIENCE
OF TECHNO-IDEALISM

In late June 2012 I attended the Downtown School's first eighth-grade graduation ceremony. I was about to move across the country for a new job and the ceremony offered a last chance to say goodbye in person to the school's designers, educators, parents, and students. Graduation ceremonies tend to be festive occasions, and this one was especially cheerful. The ceremony was the first graduation for the first school of its kind. The graduating students were, and always would be, that school's very first class. Various people who had committed themselves to the project since its early days were now seeing the fruits of their efforts. After a tumultuous start, the school had mostly stabilized. Instead of a mass exodus of privileged families, the school now enjoyed the ambiguous blessing of being a hot option among families in District Two, especially among creative professional parents with middle-school-aged boys. An impressive portion of the graduating class had been accepted by New York City's selective public high schools, and some students who could have been accepted into these schools nevertheless preferred to remain at the Downtown School for high school.

Nearly everyone at the graduation ceremony seemed pleased and proud. We clapped and cheered loudly when students crossed the stage to receive their degrees or to pick up an award, and we cheered equally loudly when school leaders recounted the school's accomplishments. During one such moment, a school official announced the results from that year's standardized state exams. Loud applause once again filled the auditorium when the official announced that this year's scores were up from last year's and that the Downtown School was now competitive with well-regarded peer institutions. Like others, I applauded these accomplishments, and I felt genuinely happy for everyone who had worked so hard on the philanthropic project. It felt good to celebrate each other, and hence the project, as a successful, beneficent, and cutting-edge experiment, and it felt equally off-putting—petty, churlish, and even misanthropic—to focus on the project's shortcomings. Sure the school had some problems, but it was not as if the people who had made the project what it was were especially greedy, self-ish, or unscrupulous. Parents were just trying to offer their children the best educational opportunities that they could, and designers and educators were spending much of their lives in professions that paid comparatively modestly, did not confer especially high social status, and were frequently subjected to public attacks even though they were trying to help others. Surrounded as I was by all these positive feelings and good intentions, how could I focus on the negative?

And yet I also remembered how the school's philanthropic backers and designers had imagined and justified their new school in large part by problematizing what they called the testing regime. Similarly, I recalled how many of the privileged parents who now cheered for the school's improved test scores had been drawn to the Downtown School because it seemed to deflect that regime's normative prescriptions and competitively divisive pressures. I recalled how these designers and parents had championed the school's focus on games, technology, and design because it supposedly facilitated students' creativity and improvisation, modes of activity that the testing regime seemed to foreclose. Once again I felt I was participating in a seeming paradox: as designers, educators, and parents worked to make daily life at the school more and more conventionally scripted, many of these same people continued to celebrate the school as if it were radically new and disruptive. I also began to think about who was not at this graduation cer-emony: students such as Corey and Niki, both of whom had once been near the top of their class academically and socially but who had left the school after privileged parents, and then educators, fixed them as threatening delin-quents. And I thought of Corey and Niki's group of friends, many of whom had also been driven from the school during its first several years. Similarly, I wondered who had been kept out, whether through concerted efforts by in-volved parents, structural impediments such as school district borders, or the more quotidian workings of unexamined biases. When I considered these more prescriptive and divisive aspects of the school, I could not shake the sense that we were celebrating our own contributions to remaking the status quo *as if* those contributions were disruptive and philanthropic. I have been unable to shake that feeling since, and, if anything, I have come to feel that those of us who contribute to these processes extend far beyond the people who design and implement cutting-edge philanthropic interventions.

We have tried this before, repeatedly. The demand to fix education in order to fix society is as old as public schooling. The claim that the new media technologies of an era represent unprecedented opportunities to do so is equally as old. Despite well over a century of educational crises, countless reforms, endless experiments with the new media of the moment—radio, film, television, computers, the Internet, games, mobile phones, tablets, MOOCs, and virtual reality—public education has never come close to its idealization as society's great equalizer and unifier, and new technologies have never managed to fill the gaps.

But maybe next time will be different?

The case examined in this book suggests that the next time will not be so different. It is hard to imagine a philanthropic endeavor better equipped to fulfill recent calls to disrupt education than the Downtown School. The school had smart, skilled, and dedicated designers, reformers, and teachers. They had an abundance of resources, including some of the most cutting-edge educational technologies in the world. They had a pedagogic approach designed by some of the world's most respected learning theorists and technology designers. And yet, despite these resources and an abundance of good intentions, the designers and backers of the Downtown School mostly overlooked, rather than overcame, their intervention's contributions to remaking the status quo. The reformers had promised unprecedented creativity, improvisation, and fun, and yet daily life at the school turned into a lot of rote and scripted behavior (chapter 4). They believed they were opening the school to the world, but in several highly problematic areas educators and, in particular, privileged parents worked to seal it off (chapters 3 and 6). They hoped to appeal to students' inherent interests and overcome social division but ended up with a system that removed many of the most uncomfortable underprivileged (chapters 5 and 6). They quickly became much like the organizations that they aimed to replace, and they helped remake many of the very social divisions that they hoped to mend. Given that techno-philanthropism routinely falls far short of reformers' stated ideals, how can it be that cycles of disruptive fixation predictably recur?

BENEFICIARIES OF FAILURE

For James Ferguson (1994), who drew heavily on Foucault's (1977) analysis of prisons in his study of development interventions, the key to understanding the endurance of seemingly ineffective development projects was to focus not on their apparent failures but rather on what these endeavors did manage to accomplish, for whom, and how. By changing the problematic in this way, Ferguson was able to see that while international development projects routinely failed to eradicate poverty, their professed philanthropic aim, they were quite effective at expanding bureaucratic state power. If we similarly ask what perennial cycles of disruptive fixation do achieve, then the enormous amount of money, energy, and affect that are continuously invested into seemingly cutting-edge philanthropic interventions no longer appears as just bad policy or incompetence. When we look at what routine failure accomplishes and for whom, the story becomes more complicated, more interesting, and also more political.

As the vignette at the beginning of this chapter begins to illustrate, a disruptive philanthropic intervention that does not live up to its professed ideals still produces many beneficiaries. In large part because of their involvement in this project, one of the Downtown School's designers landed a prestigious job at one of the largest and most influential philanthropic foundations in the world. Another of the school's designers received millions of dollars in additional funding from foundations and corporate partners, this time to leverage the seemingly unprecedented possibilities of "big data" in game-based learning. Within the broader philanthropic initiative that helped fund the Downtown School, one of the scholars who received the most grant money was hired by one of the world's largest media-technology corporations, only to be later hired as a partner at one of the world's most prestigious design consultancies. Similarly, the program officer for one of the foundations that supported the Downtown School was awarded tens of millions of dollars by that same foundation in order to launch an NGO focused on tech-ed innovations. One of the school's original curriculum designers was tapped to run the middle school, one of the school's founding teachers was headed to graduate school for a PhD, and I got a tenure-track job, in no small part because of the research I conducted at the Downtown School.

These are but a few of the beneficiaries of a "failed" cycle of disruptive fixation, that is, people and groups that benefitted in different ways from a cutting-edge philanthropic intervention that did not come close to realizing its ideals.[1] Taken together, the recurring failures of techno-philanthropism ironically help maintain, and even expand, the industries, research programs, media professionals, and investment opportunities of parties that specialize in diagnosing societal ailments and prescribing seemingly innovative new fixes. For example, cycles of failed educational disruptions have produced and sustained a not-so-small army of experts—in academia, think tanks, consulting firms, NGOs, government agencies, and corporations—whose jobs consist, in part if not in full, in diagnosing what is wrong with education, as well as with prescribing and carrying out seemingly innovative solutions. Similarly, many technology and media companies, as well as many technological experts, have long relied on perpetual rounds of ineffective education reform as a stream of revenue and funding (Buckingham 2007). The lack of success of various cutting-edge philanthropic interventions and movements does not cause these figured worlds to implode; on the contrary, it helps produce conditions for those worlds' ongoing survival and even expansion. One project or movement's inability to finally fix education or development is another project or movement's opportunity. Indeed, it is precisely because a project or movement fails to realize more widely held yearnings and ideals that entrepreneurial reformers can call for new and more ambitious rounds of disruptive philanthropy. Perpetual failures also allow various experts to continuously problematize what went wrong with a given intervention as they help imagine and design alternatives (chapter 2). In this way, figured worlds like education reform and development can perpetuate and expand themselves with a seemingly moral, technocratic, and innovative edge, but they often do so without asking more fundamental questions about whether the means deployed—here education and technology design—can realize the broader social transformations that designers and reformers continually promise.

Those of us who work in higher education are also beneficiaries of the perpetual failure of educational reforms, albeit in ways that are often left unexamined. Not only do US research universities continuously receive large grants by promising to help finally fix education, often in high-tech ways, but they also often entice students and families to pay and borrow hefty sums by promising to deliver the opportunities that K–12 schooling has been unable to deliver. And yet, like high schools before them, colleges and universities are now also finding themselves unable to make good on these promises. Indeed, a likely reason that there is currently a growing fixation with fixing higher education in the United States (Arum and Roksa 2011; Shear 2014) is because many recent college graduates and their families feel that higher educational institutions did not deliver the breadth of promised opportunities (Long 2015; Selingo 2015).

Professional fixers, NGOs, and companies are not the only beneficiaries of perennial cycles of disruptive fixation. As we saw, and despite their understandable frustrations with the competitive educational systems in which they were entangled, many families, especially families who worked in the so-called creative industries but also some families from less-privileged backgrounds, used the Downtown School to gain advantages in those competitive systems. In doing so, these parents also comparatively disadvantaged other families who were also trying to navigate New York City's educational systems but from less advantageous positions. At the most general level, anyone who has gained comparative advantages in educational systems has also benefited from, and thus helped to produce, the seeming failures of those systems. As Varenne and McDermott (1998) astutely observed, the idealization of institutionalized education as a meritocratic race—that is, as a system that should fairly sort people from different backgrounds into the hierarchies of the adult world—ensures the production of educational winners as well as educational losers (Labaree 2010). Once framed in this way, questions of social justice are reduced to questions about whether the playing field is level, and yet, as Bourdieu (1973) and countless other critics of institutionalized education have long argued, privileged families are better equipped to both win these political contests as well as to shape the terrain of struggle (Lareau 2003). Families in relative positions of privilege are by no means guaranteed to reproduce their social standing in their offspring, but they are comparatively well positioned to use educational institutions as a means to both fight for and legitimate their children's ascendancy in inherited and emergent hierarchies.

Failure is also productive in that cycles of disruptive fixation always leave their mark. Cumulatively, cycles of failed intervention not only perpetuate the worlds and industries of reformers, they also extend the reach of those who can profess expertise in these domains as well the modes of governing that those experts, perhaps inadvertently, help install. As Ferguson (1994) pointed out in his study of the development industry, even though development projects routinely fail to combat poverty, their idealized aim, they nevertheless help expand the reach of the bureaucratic state. A similar point could be made about the perennial failure of cutting-edge educational reforms. In a dual process that we could call *educationalization* (Labaree 2008) and *informationalization*, more and more aspects of not just young people's everyday lives, but also the everyday lives of many adults, increasingly fall under the jurisdiction, authority, and practices of those who profess some form of educational or informational expertise. As cutting-edge educational interventions routinely fail to deliver various wished-for outcomes and as more and more demands for social change get delegated to educational and technological experts, a common response is to develop and prescribe, as well as to seek out, more and more seemingly cutting-edge educational remedies. Such an expansion is evident not only in the swelling duration and reach of the school (Patall, Cooper, and Allen 2010), but also in the uneven flourishing of extracurricular, enrichment, and self-help activities (Qvortrup 1994; Halpern 2003; Lareau 2003; Holloway and Pimlott-Wilson 2014), in the burgeoning and class-differentiated market for educational media technologies (Seiter 1993, 2008; Ito 2009), and in the attempts by learning theorists, educational reformers, and media technologists to theorize, design, and connect diverse sites of everyday life into a cohesive educational-informational net (Ito et al. 2013).

EXPERIENCING AND SUSTAINING IDEALISM

Drawing attention to the question of who benefits from the recurring failure of techno-philanthropism can easily lead to the conclusion that cycles of disruptive fixation persist because these diverse beneficiaries somehow conspire to produce mutually beneficial outcomes. According to this more cynical view, diverse beneficiaries of failure know that they are promoting unrealizable solutions, but they collude in propagating outsized hopes because doing so serves their interlocking self-interests. While the figured worlds of education reform and philanthropically oriented technology design undoubtedly include hucksters and cynics, what is more striking is how many participants in these worlds act, with all appearances of sincerity, *as if* their efforts are cutting edge, disruptive, and philanthropic, even as they often help produce regressive consequences.

One of the reasons that they appear able to do so is because failed cycles of disruptive fixation nevertheless help repair and sustain social and political ideals that extend far beyond the figured worlds of professional fixers. Techno-philanthropism exerts the moral and normative forces that it does in large part because it gives concrete instantiation to widely held moral imperatives: to eradicate poverty, to fulfill democratic ideals about equality of opportunity, to forge a united and harmonious polity, and so forth. As such, it is incredibly difficult to challenge techno-philanthropism as an enterprise without also seeming to reject the values and yearnings that legitimize its existence. It is much more tempting to identify problems with specific interventions and movements while keeping faith in the larger enterprises, and hence in the yearnings and values that such enterprises officially represent, intact.

This is a false choice.

Someone can aspire to combat poverty or bridge social divisions without concluding that disruptive educational reforms or development interventions are the best means for bringing about such transformations. But the braiding together of these enterprises with the moral values and longings that sanctify them makes pointed critiques of the former quite difficult, even though they have important political consequences (Ferguson 1994; Easterly 2001, 2006; Fassin 2010). As Ferguson (1994) observed in his study of the development industry, the braiding together of widely held moral ideals with narrowly held technocratic expertise has the effect of depoliticizing political, economic, and social struggles. As we have seen, experts' processes of problematization and rendering technical (Rose 1999; Li 2007) tend to cast issues such as poverty, inequality, and social division in technocratic, and thus seemingly apolitical, terms. It was this tendency to transform more widely held political and moral yearnings into technocratic enterprises that led James Ferguson to famously characterize the world of international development as an "anti-politics machine."

It can be tempting to interpret contemporary techno-philanthropism as another antipolitics machine, as some critical scholars have recently done (Aschoff 2015; McGoey 2015). After all, the wealthy philanthropists who do so much to instigate and support new rounds of disruptive fixation are among the people who have benefitted the most from existing political and economic arrangements. By channeling more widespread concerns with the status quo as well as hopes for substantive change into seemingly apolitical, charitable, and disruptive remedies, techno-philanthropists can evade political outrage while leaving the structural arrangements that benefit them more or less intact. Yet, and unlike Ferguson's account, I think it would be a mistake to characterize contemporary techno-philanthropism as simply another antipolitics machine. For one, debates about both education reform and the social implications of new technologies are often highly public and politicized, much to the chagrin of many of the people who specialize in these professions. In polities that see themselves as liberal-democratic, public debates and struggles over both education reform and the utopian or dystopian role of new technologies in contemporary life provide a sanctioned, personally meaningful, but also mostly structurally unthreatening way for people to affirm their moral ideals and values, including idealizations about democratic citizenship. As the preceding chapters have shown, media industries and entrepreneurial reformers often play a key role in these processes by regularly producing utopian and dystopian accounts about both education and new technologies. As such, the worlds of educators and educational reformers often, and unfairly, catch much of the public and political outrage when broader social ideals remain unmet (Tyack and Cuban 1995). Similarly, understandable concerns with current conditions, as well as anxieties and hopes about the future, are routinely projected onto the latest technological innovations in heated public debates (Buckingham 2000). Given all this public attention and concern, the tremendous money, time, effort, and affect that is recurrently directed into cycles of disruptive fixation do not so much appear as an *anti*politics machine as a politicized buffer zone that helps absorb and fix volatile energies while leaving the sources of those volatilities intact.

While wealthy elites, and privileged groups more generally, undoubtedly benefit from these misplaced forms of hope and concern, and while entrepreneurial reformers and professional media outlets play an outsized role in shaping the terrain of these debates and struggles, it is far too simplistic to suggest that wealthy elites, or any other unified subject, control the strings. In keeping with Ferguson's arguments about the world of development, we cannot look at what failed rounds of disruptive fixation accomplish and then teleologically infer that the resulting effects—the absorption of politically volatile energies, for example—was the plan of some unified actor and thus that all the other actors that enrolled in a cutting-edge philanthropic intervention were somehow conspirators of the state, of capital, or of billionaire technology entrepreneurs, and so forth.

Yet Ferguson's machine imagery is also limited in that, while it rightly decenters accounts that figure reformers and designers as conspirators or cynics, it instead casts them as "cultural dopes" (Hall 1981). Those who do the work of intervening, from the perspective of Ferguson's neo-Foucualdian problematic, appear as cogs in the machine, helping to advance and entrench structures of power, but doing so behind their backs. A puzzle that remains insufficiently addressed by neo-Foucauldian problematics—as well as other problematics that separate the analysis of political-economy from the analysis of situated practices—is how reformers and designers who meet moral calls to improve the world for others manage to produce and maintain their idealism despite having some knowledge of recurring failures, witnessing the ineffectiveness of their own efforts firsthand, and often helping to remake the very ailments that they aim to mend (Li 1999, 2007; Lashaw 2008, 2010). I find it too facile to say that these instrument effects simply happen behind reformers' and designers' backs, just as it is too facile to suggest that such effects are their real, but concealed, intentions.

To build on the insights of Ferguson (1994), Tyack and Cuban (1995), Li (2007), and the many other important works that have examined the cyclical character of philanthropic interventions that routinely fall far short of their idealizations, this book has developed the concept of disruptive fixation. The phrase is meant to draw attention to the interplay between two notions of the term fixation: fixation as tunnel vision—akin to James Scott's (1998) "seeing like a state," as well as Michel Callon's (1998) Goffman-inspired notion of technocratic "framing"—and fixation as attempts to stabilize, or fix, seemingly volatile and unwieldy forces. Taken together, disruptive fixation refers to the cyclical process by which enthusiasm for techno-philanthropism faithfully renews itself even as actual interventions predictably fail to fulfill their professed aims.

Using the case of the Downtown School as an example, a propositional sketch of this cyclical process is as follows: the inability of previous re-formers to finally fix a more structural problem—like poverty or systemic inequality—helps sustain conditions for entrepreneurial reformers, as well as powerful elites more generally, to call for, and sometimes support, new rounds of disruptive fixation. In doing so, these elites often profess that we are in a radically new era as they herald the unprecedented opportuni-ties of recent breakthroughs in technology. Doing so helps convince many people, including themselves, that this time is different (chapter 2). Because these powerful elites do not tend to have deep expertise in the domains they aim to transform, nor the time to try to do so, they recruit and enroll experts. These experts tend to be sympathetic to the philanthropic out-comes that the elites are calling for, but they are also dependent on the support of more powerful outsiders in order to follow up on their insights. This relation of dependency does not determine what experts will design and attempt to implement, but the relationship places significant limits on what experts will imagine and explore.

As these experts respond to entrepreneurial reformers' calls for disruption they problematize what is wrong with the world as they render the world intelligible with, and amenable to, the instruments that they have in hand or are developing (Li 2007). As we saw, it was through these intertwined processes of problematization and rendering technical that fixations—of space (chapter 3), pedagogy (chapter 4), the project's intended beneficiaries (chapter 5), and community participation (chapter 6)—occurred among reformers and designers at the Downtown School. While these fixations helped reformers imagine that they were designing a plausible and novel means for accomplishing hoped for outcomes, they also excluded and distorted much of what they would encounter once they set their projects down in the world. In the words of Michel Callon (1998), their fixations, or in his terminology, their "frames," were "overflown" by the complexities, interrelations, and historical contingencies of the worlds they aimed to transform. Because of this overflowing, a cutting-edge intervention often turns to chaos for reformers once it is launched as factors and forces that were excluded and distorted by their fixations quickly perforate a project and destabilize reformers' carefully crafted plans.

In theory, these moments of overflowing and instability are opportunities when experts might reexamine the limitations of their fixations—they could, for example, attempt to trace the sources of the destabilizing forces in order to better understand the worlds into which they are intervening— and some experts do begin to reexamine the limits of their fixations in these more expansive ways. But the dominant tendency is to engage in a much more pragmatic form of fixation: reformers attempt to quickly stabilize their project by reaching for whatever resources are readily available. In keeping with DiMaggio and Powell's (1983) well-received notion of "mimetic isomorphism," many of the stabilizing resources that are ready-to-hand ironically come from canonical versions of the organizations that reformers aim to disrupt, particularly from the professional communities of which some of the reformers are a part. Yet—and in a curious return to Weber (1978), whom DiMaggio and Powell claimed to have taken us beyond—other stabilizing resources come from outside the worlds of experts and bureaucrats, and particularly from powerful factions of the local community—in this case privileged parents—who offer to help stabilize the project in exchange for enhanced power in the project's governance. While these local elites often espouse commitments to philanthropic outcomes that resonate with reformers' yearnings, they can also exert isomorphic, and even revanchist, pressures on a project, whereas experts to some extent remain forces for change.

At the current historical moment, the pressures that these local elites can exert are likely, and ironically, being amplified by recent attempts to make institutions, particularly state institutions, more responsive to the people they claim to serve, as epitomized in this book by the choice reforms of New York City's public schools. While these reforms appear to have transferred some power away from bureaucrats and toward citizens, they have also empowered their intended beneficiaries in highly uneven ways. At the Downtown School, factions of local elites were simultaneously unsettled and empowered by the choice reforms, and in these conditions they used their power to grab onto and attempt to control the intervention's unique resources. Instead of pushing for openness and heterogeneity, they pushed for the sealing of borders and the tightening of discipline. In this way, a morally sanctified call for disruption was converted into a mechanism that not only locked social processes into prescriptive and regressive forms but that also entrenched more deeply many of the very social ailments that reformers and their backers had hoped to uproot.

One curiosity about a cycle of disruptive fixation is that many of the people who take part in it manage to repair and maintain their idealism, at least for a while. They generally do not become especially cynical or apathetic. At the Downtown School, most designers and reformers continued to act *as if* they were participating in a cutting-edge philanthropic undertaking even as they made the project more and more conventional and increasingly disciplined and purged some of the people they most wanted to help. Many remained passionately committed to the school, and some even proselytized it as an exciting new model of change to other reformers, policymakers, and the media. From an anthropological perspective, the resilience of this idealism—the maintenance of the collectively lived *as if* imaginings that help animate and sanctify a disruptive philanthropic intervention— takes a lot of work. Setbacks, compromises, and contradictions have to be overlooked, rationalized, or forgotten; the creep of disillusionment has to beaten back; hope and optimism have to be repeatedly and collectively rejuvenated.

One way that designers and reformers manage to keep their idealism intact is by framing setbacks as something positive and even empowering. Instead of interpreting setbacks and compromises as indication that their intervention does not have the power to realize its philanthropic promises, reformers often frame unanticipated challenges as opportunities for growth, adjustment, and improvement. In the case of the Downtown School, reformers who had come to the project from the world of technology design not only expected setbacks, but they often also celebrated them. "Fail forward" was, and is, a sort of mantra among the entrepreneurial tech designers involved in the project, as were the ideas of "grit" and resilience among many of the experienced educational reformers, so much so that they treated these dispositions as something to be cultivated in their students. In both cases, maintaining optimism and idealism involved ongoing processes of interpreting indications of failure positively as opportunities for improvement. In doing so, the broader structural, and particularly political-economic, conditions that thwarted the realization of their ideals remained largely unexamined.[2]

Entrepreneurial reformers, technology designers, reform experts, some of the people charged to execute philanthropic interventions, and factions of local elites are also able to mostly maintain their idealisms because many of the stabilizing resources that reformers deploy are canonical and hence unremarkable, especially to experienced reformers and practitioners. For example, experienced educational reformers and educators at the Downtown School tended to classify many of their quasi-Tayloristic practices not as pedagogy but rather as classroom management, the latter of which was seen as a separate precondition for their innovative pedagogy. Novices to these worlds, including myself, learned to make similar distinctions as we became more-experienced reformers and educators (chapter 4). Additionally, a spatialized division of labor often separated the people who called for, supported, and designed the Downtown School from the people who were tasked with executing it on a daily basis. Similarly, local elites, in this case privileged parents, were often spatially removed from the day-to-day workings of the project. As such, canonical practices of discipline and control could remain largely out of sight and out of mind for many of the people who idealized the project, while these same practices became part of the taken-for-granted background of executors' everyday routines.

Designers, reformers, and educators were also able to reconcile tensions in their partnerships with powerful locals in part because such partnerships were legitimated by more general assumptions about the inherently democratic character of community involvement, local participation, or, in the case of schooling, parental involvement. According to the designers' problematizations, these local elites were part of the population that the philanthropic intervention had been designed to benefit. As such, these local elites' involvements in the intervention were sanctioned by discourses that valorized citizen, consumer, community, or local participation in an intervention's design and governance. While reformers and educators were often torn about forging these partnerships, they nevertheless tended to accept them, in part because they did not feel that their project could survive and retain its status as an innovative model of reform without this local political support, and they were probably right (chapter 6).

Finally, more widespread rhetorics about individualism and marketlike consumer choice helped designers, reformers, and local elites disassociate themselves from some the intervention's more divisive effects. These rhetorics allowed responsibility for division to be attributed to the seemingly apolitical preferences of consumers, which in this case were parents choosing schools. For example, most people, including many of the parents of students who left the Downtown School, did not so much challenge the school for helping to remake problematic social divisions as suggest that departing students had not been a "good fit" for the school (chapter 6). When placed in the logic of consumer choice, cultural fit and misfit all too easily depoliticize the ways in which philanthropic interventions can contribute to social division.

Taken-for-grantedness, a spatialized division of labor, and rhetoric about participation and choice can help explain how many of the people who commit themselves to a cutting-edge philanthropic intervention manage to maintain their idealism even as they help remake and even extend many of the processes and relations that they aim to disrupt. But the exposition thus far does not account for how this idealism is repaired and rejuvenated in the face of numerous, and often dramatic, setbacks and compromises. The maintenance of idealism depends not only on practices of overlooking and rationalizing, such as those discussed earlier, but also on the production, documentation, circulation, and ritualistic celebration of practices that appear to fulfill the intervention's innovative and philanthropic idealizations, practices that I have been referring to as sanctioned counterpractices.

At the Downtown School many of these sanctioned counterpractices were stylistic transformations of familiar cultural forms and scripts. For example, reformers instructed teachers to tell students that a paper-and-pencil math test was actually an application to a code-breaking academy. Similarly, they instructed teachers to grade students according to the familiar rubric of five ranked categories, with plusses and minuses for each, but labeled with terms like master and apprentice rather than A, B, C, D, F (chapter 4). Other sanctioned counterpractices, such as the project-based Level Up period at the end of each trimester, were more substantively unconventional as well as less scripted by adults. But these practices were relatively fleeting and carefully contained in circumscribed periods and spaces. In general, sanctioned counterpractices played a relatively minor role in the day-to-day routines of the project, especially when compared to the canonically scripted practices described previously, and their role in daily life diminished as the intervention aged.

Yet sanctioned counterpractices played an especially important role in repairing many people's idealism for the project and hence in keeping the project going. Sanctioned counterpractices were the starring content when designers and reformers ritualistically told stories about the project to themselves and to various supporters and potential allies, including privileged parents, most of whom had little exposure to the project's day-to-day routines. Sanctioned counterpractices were front and center in the school's various showcases, festivals, ceremonies, publicity materials, and conference talks, and they were featured extensively during tours for prospective families, journalists, government officials, academics, designers, and officers from funding agencies. Similarly, when journalists and professional researchers produced accounts about the school, these accounts overwhelmingly focused on and tended to optimistically celebrate the school's sanctioned counterpractices. In many of these accounts, the school's distinctive media technologies were highlighted, as was the agency and creativity of the students. By contrast, the canonically scripted practices discussed previously, as well as the much more mundane and managerial uses of media technologies, were either erased or marginalized in both professionally produced media about the project and in the project's ritualized self-representations. These collective celebrations of sanctioned counterpractices helped recruit and sustain the outside support upon which the intervention depended, and with the help of these allies the project's designers and reformers managed to convince many others that their intervention could and should be emulated. But also, and equally importantly to the survival of the project, the ritualized celebration of sanctioned counterpractices helped many designers, reformers, educators, involved parents, and their supporters experience and repair the collective sense that they were committing themselves, often quite passionately, to an innovative moral enterprise.

The swell of enthusiasm for this particular round of disruptive fixation will eventually recede, and indeed such an ebbing may have already begun. But history also suggests that similar swells of techno-idealism, these invigorated by the seemingly unprecedented philanthropic possibilities of even-newer breakthroughs in media and information technologies, will soon come rushing forth. The cycle is not unlike that of waves repeatedly crashing into a rocky coastline.[3] Each new wave is different, each rushes forth with an impressive confidence and force, and yet each comes to a dramatic halt once it meets the expansive and uneven terrain of the shore. Upon hitting land, the smooth and powerful swell refracts and jumps in countless directions. Eventually the water settles and then recedes, sometimes clashing with smaller currents and eddies that are still rushing forth. For a moment the tumult ceases and the water-soaked shore is calm. But soon another swell, slightly different from the last, returns, only to be rebuffed in a similarly dramatic fashion. Each new swell eventually exhausts its energy and recedes, but these seemingly futile cycles of advance and withdrawal are not without their consequences. Each powerful swell deposits, rearranges, and sometimes sweeps away looser sediments, and over time the cycle cuts deep grooves in even the hardest of rocks.

If there is a constant to this seemingly perpetual cycle, it is the tendency to wish hoped-for outcomes onto recent technological breakthroughs in a way that encourages many people to not only forget that we have tried this before, repeatedly, but also to overlook, simplify, and marginalize whatever cannot be manipulated and controlled with those new means. After ten years and more than $200 million in investments, in 2015 one of the large philanthropic foundations that funded the Downtown School announced that it would no longer prioritize digital media and learning as one of its strategic areas of funding. While not admitting defeat, the president of the foundation declared that it now was time for private companies, government agencies, and other NGOs to support the movement that the foundation had done so much to instigate. With this ending, the president also announced a new beginning, and it is with this new beginning that this book will end. In an essay titled "Time for Change," the president of the foundation optimistically put forward the foundation's ambitious new strategy. They now planned to implement a "solution-driven" philanthropic strategy that would "be bolder and aim higher." They would fund fewer interventions, but the ones that they did fund would be "larger in scale, time-limited in nature, or designed to reach specific objectives." The need for change was urgent, the president of the foundation stressed, and refusing change was "not an option." The essay began:

> Today, people and places around the world, as well as the earth itself, face formidable, complex, and connected problems. At the same time, technological advances and increased connection hold unprecedented promise for the well-being of humanity and society, while creating new and vexing problems.

The president's opening words can be read as a preamble, as well as an epilogue, for disruptive fixation.

APPENDIX

Ethnographic Fixations

Conducting an ethnographic research project inevitably involves fixations that are not unlike some of the fixations that this book has been examining. As conventionally understood, ethnographic fieldwork typically involves researchers locating themselves alongside and within sociocultural processes at particular sites for lengthy periods of time. By doing so, the ethnographers attempt to position themselves alongside and within the historical processes through which other humans and nonhumans make their existence together in conditions that they can only partially control. It involves attempting to develop a better understanding of how differently positioned actors make sense of, participate in, and hence help sustain and change the webs of relations within which they are entangled.

In this sense, and in a more canonically ethnographic vein, much of the empirical work that I conducted for this study occurred by way of my going to a particular place for a lengthy period of time. I moved to New York City from Berkeley, California, in the summer of 2009 and began gathering and producing ethnographic documentation that August. I moved out of New York City in August of 2012 to start my current job in San Diego, California. During my three years in New York, I wrote more than 400,000 words of field notes, most of which describe my experiences as a participant observer in and around the Downtown School, in people's homes, and in online settings. I also generated thousands of pages of interview transcripts and collected myriad digital artifacts. I gathered and assembled this documentation throughout my time in New York, with the majority of this activity taking place during 2009 and 2010, a period when I was funded to conduct fieldwork fulltime.

This close attention to "the local" can be a powerful corrective to the ethnocentrism and positivism that still dominates much of the social sciences, and it can allow for a more nuanced analysis of how social-historical

179

processes work, unfold, and produce unanticipated effects in different places and at different historical moments. But this close attention to local field sites can also entail some of the problematic fixations that this book has been addressing, particularly when ethnographers render the local as a circumscribed space with a particular culture. Such enframing practices, which occur through processes of problematization and rendering technical, imaginatively construct a fixed and comparative geography of other cultures. It is in part because of this fixation that many anthropologists have called upon their fellow ethnographers to reexamine their spatial-cultural assumptions (Gupta and Ferguson 1992, 1997).

While these and similar calls for anthropological self-reflexivity are welcome, the problems of fixation that this book has been examining are more diffuse than the particular fixations that characterize the history of anthropology as a discipline. Among professional academics, fixations are entwined with the intellectual division of labor and its corresponding tendency to develop differentiated realms of expertise, including the expertise of ethnographers who work outside of the discipline of anthropology. In my case, the disciplinary pressures of training in an Information School led me to initially fixate on not just on a particular place and people, but also on the presumed importance of digital media in the lives of those people, a framing that proved quite limiting once I was in the field.

As mentioned in the preface, I began this project with an interest in how school-based peer cultures mediated processes of social reproduction for children growing up in the so-called digital age. To scope my project, I centered my study on the school's first class of seventy-five eleven- and twelve-year-olds. I began fieldwork by trying to place myself, as best I could, alongside these students. While obviously recognized as an adult, I tried to distance myself from educators and other adults in the school: I wore casual clothing, and, with educators' permission, I avoided participating in the canonical practices of school adults, especially practices such as teaching, disciplining, and correcting students. I also initially tried to limit my spatial positioning and movements to those that were available to the students. I sat with the students in class and at lunch, I lined up with them as they moved between classes, and I tried as much as possible to follow the same directives that students routinely received from school adults. Aligning myself next to the students was awkward at first, but after several months many of the students began to treat me as a friend. As our friendships developed, many students also started incorporating me into not just their lives at school, but also their lives online.[1]

One thing that slowly became clear during this stage of fieldwork was that digital media was not nearly as important for the students as I, and the school's designers, had assumed that it would be, neither in nor out of school. Digital media was inextricably part of students' everyday lives, but

very few of the students approximated popular stereotypes about a generation that was engrossed with digital media, and most students had concerns and interests that primarily lay elsewhere. What is more, and despite
the school's public reputation, much of what happened on a daily basis at
the school did not involve students using digital media or playing games.
Moreover, when students did use digital media and play games at school,
the process was often highly scripted by adults, which did not correspond
with the more hopeful idealizations of games and new media as tools that
amplify the agency and power of young people.

A similar pattern emerged as I got to know the reformers, educators,
and many of the parents and family members of the students. After hanging around the school for about six months, I started to invite students,
parents and guardians, and educators to participate in a semistructured
interview. I also conducted a series of show-and-tell-style "media tour"
interviews with fourteen students who were particularly involved in producing media technology.[2] I used these interviews to learn about phenomena that I could not observe directly, including out-of-school routines and
personal histories. These interviews tended to further reinforce my sense
that many people were primarily concerned with matters that did not have
all that much to do with digital media and games, and, what is more, digital
media and games were often of little help as they tried to get a grip on these
matters of concern. Even families who were supportive of the Downtown
School's focus on games and new media seemed to be primarily attracted to
the school for other reasons, and reformers that specialized in game design
and new media often seemed preoccupied dealing with issues for which
their technical expertise was of little help. None of this was good news for
my initial fixations.

As I began to decenter my focus on the role of digital media in the
students' lives, I also began to pay increased attention to the rhetorical
salience that terms like games, design, and digital media seemed to have
among the school's designers, its institutional backers, the press, parents,
and academics such as myself. I began to ask questions about how the polysemous character of terms like games, design, and the digital had shaped
how the school had been imagined and designed in the manner that it had,
how NGOs, philanthropic organizations, and researchers like me were
caught up with these processes, how journalists and media technology corporations took an especially keen interest in digital disruption, and how
political processes were being obscured and worked on by these various
fixations.

As I traced the people and organizations that seemed to take an idealized interest in the school's supposed focus on digital media, games, and
design, I also realized that I needed to develop a more institutional and historical account of what I was observing within and around this particular

project. To develop a better understanding of the historical character of these dynamics, I relied on research by academic historians, newspaper articles, government documents, summaries of legislation, and congressional reports. As I familiarized myself with these works, I increasingly came to see how researchers such as myself, who were often supported by philanthropic foundations like the one that was supporting my work, regularly played a constitutive role in maintaining and shaping what I have been referring to as disruptive fixation. Put differently, I came to see how much of my work since starting graduate school—working on research projects about young people and technology, attending conferences on digital media and learning, meeting with funders and other researchers supported by these funders—as well as much of the work that I have been doing since I became a professor—teaching, writing, giving talks—were and remain part of my field site. In this sense, I came to see that I had already been in "the field" long before I moved to New York City, and I feel that I am still in the field now, albeit in a different location. I suspect the same is true for any ethnographic undertaking, as well as for any scholarly project.

A NOTE ON THE USE OF PSEUDONYMS

In constructing this book I have wrestled with how to protect the anonymity of my research participants in an era when so much material about a field site can be discovered online. In my case, I had the additional challenge of trying to protect anonymity for people who were involved in a project that was especially unique and to some degree famous. As I worked on the project, I came to realize that it would be impossible for me to fully camouflage the identity of the school without also erasing what made the project theoretically and politically important. While I have kept with ethnographic convention and given the school a pseudonym, I am also aware that an enterprising reader could make a strong guess about the school's identity.

Given this possibility, I have put additional effort into trying to protect the anonymity of the persons represented and quoted in the book. My goal has been to construct ambiguity about who did or said what at any given point in the book. The most conventional way that I have attempted to do so is by using pseudonyms for the people involved. But given the school's relative fame, I have also tried to deploy several additional tactics. For one, I purposely use somewhat abstract labels—such as "a creative professional parent" or "one of the school leaders"—in cases where I felt a more concrete designator could lead to unmasking. Similarly, since there were multiple teachers and aids in the school, I have tended to refer to them uniformly as "educators". In terms of the school's designers, principal, and leadership team, I often say "one of the school's designers" or "one of the school's leaders," which, in reality, consisted of about ten people. In some cases I have also switched the gender of pronouns in the hope that doing so will make it more difficult for readers to link a specific quote or description to a specific person. While these abstractions and transformations sacrifice some nuance and rhetorical power, I hope they provide the people represented in this book with a plausible basis for denying that they are the persons represented at a given point in the book.

As for students, all names have been changed and, again, I used descriptions that were fairly generic on many occasions. While I imagine that people who were involved with the school during its first several years will be able to recognize some of the students, I hope my representations of students are sufficiently opaque to mask their identities from readers who know the school only from afar. As for students being unmasked to people who were directly involved with the school, I do not believe I am reporting anything incriminating that is not already known to these insiders. Furthermore, all the students represented in the book will have left or graduated from the Downtown School by the time this book is published. Finally, I have tried to take a cautious approach in how I represent the digital artifacts that people posted online. In particular, I avoid quoting verbatim any materials that students posted online. I do quote several snippets of e-mails by educators and parents, but I attribute them to more generic actors, such as "one of the creative professional parents," and as far as I know these e-mails are not publically searchable.

None of these strategies can guarantee anonymity for the various people that partook in this study, but I do hope they make it difficult for people who were not present for the events described to attribute specific quotes or descriptions of actions to any particular person.

UNRAVELING FIXATIONS

Directing intense attention and curiosity toward the local, the digital, peer cultures, or anything else is not in itself a bad thing, nor are yearnings to help fix or improve worlds that seem broken. While I was nearing completion of a draft of this book, I saw the British artist Tacita Dean give a presentation on her artistic process, and I took special note when Dean repeatedly invoked the term *fixation* to characterize the ways that she had delved into several projects. Dean told, for example, how she had fixated on a photo of Jean Jeinnie, a young girl who stowed away on a ship from Australia to England in 1928, and, on another occasion, how she had fixated on the story of an amateur British sailor, Donald Crowhurst, who entered a contest to circumnavigate the globe in 1968, likely tried to fake circumnavigation, but died, probably by suicide, in the process. What struck me about Dean's self-described fixations was how they led her down such markedly different routes than the fixations that this book has examined. Dean's fixations were intensely attuned to the minutia of the local worlds she encountered, but the focus of her attention and concern constantly moved backward and forward across space and time as various pathways of intersection revealed themselves to her, often in surprising ways. To me, Dean's fixations seemed to unravel, not in a chaotic sense or in the sense of bringing closure to the puzzle that had sparked her initial interest. Rather, they unraveled in the sense of observantly following and documenting interwoven and interlayered processes and themes as they crossed her attentive explorations. Dean's fixations, and hence Dean herself and her works, became more complex, more expansive, more historical, and yet still partial and concrete as she attentively explored the unexpected pathways and relations that unraveled in front of her.

Dean works as an artist and not as a reflexive ethnographer or an activist, and yet the ways in which her fixations unraveled perhaps provide clues for how a critical scholarly or activist practice can be undertaken without resorting to the narrowness of view that so often thwarts such well-intentioned endeavors. Dean's descriptions of her process reminded me that fixations can help produce nonreductive modes of understanding and situated possibilities for political action. By contrast, this book has explored how well-intentioned people became fixated on that which they could foreseeably handle and fix with new technological remedies. In part because of these fixations, many people maintained the best of intentions as they helped tighten the scripts that they aimed to relax and as they helped remake many of the divisions that they hoped to mend.

Notes

Preface

1. I thank Jean Lave for drawing my attention to the prevalence, and politics, of this presumed binary distinction.

Chapter 1: Introduction

1. On the potential for massively open online courses to disrupt education, see Daphne Koller's 2012 TED talk, "What We're Learning from Online Education." http://goo.gl/7nNkWw. On the promise of helping impoverished people from around the world by providing them with laptops, see Nicholas Negroponte's 2006 TED talk, "One Laptop per Child." http://goo.gl/oz6KoS. On the promise of cell phones for economic development, see Jensen (2007). On the emancipatory potential of Internet-enabled peer-production, see Benkler (2006). On the history of optimistic claims about education being ascribed to film, radio, television, and computers, see Cuban (1986, 2001) and Buckingham (2007, 50–74). On the potential for electronic media to bring about a global village, see McLuhan (1962). On the idea that the printing press can bring forth a whole new democratic world, see Thomas Carlyle's *Sartor Resartus* (2000). For a critical assessment of "One Laptop Per Child," see Warschauer and Ames (2010) and Ames (2015). For a critical review of the promises that have been made about the democratizing potential of Internet-enabled peer production, see Kreiss, Finn, and Turner (2010). For a general critique of claims about the democratic potential of new technologies, see Marx (1964), Nye (1994), Mosco (2004) and Morozov (2013).

2. Throughout, and in keeping with ethnographic conventions, I use pseudonyms for all people and organizations that were directly involved in the project. That said, I am aware that the uniqueness of the project makes it impossible to preserve the anonymity of the field site. I discuss this dilemma and my attempts to address it in the appendix.

3. I use the term *philanthropism* rather than *humanitarianism* as the latter has come to be associated with international interventions, whereas the moral sensibility to which I wish to draw attention cuts across domestic and international reform programs. In using the terms *philanthropic* and *philanthropism* I am referring to a moral sensibility that aspires to

promote the well being of others, which includes but is not limited to the work of wealthy philanthropists and philanthropic foundations. The moral sensibility is more generally held and valued.

4. On the endurance of this longing and its tendency to be remade in myths about new technologies, see Mosco (2004, 15–16).

5. Varenne and McDermott (1998) offer a helpful analysis of how the popular metaphor that figures schooling as a race on a level playing field guarantees the production of winners and losers. Also see Labaree (2010).

6. Bourdieu and Passeron's work is unique among these social reproduction theorists in that it introduces the importance of a semiautonomous cultural realm in processes of social reproduction, but like the other reproduction theorists, Bourdieu and Passeron's model treats schools as "black boxes" that reproduce social hierarchies more or less mechanically.

7. It is not surprising that Willis and Ferguson reach similar conclusions about education and development, respectively, as Ferguson cites Willis as one of the main inspirations for his important study.

8. See, in particular, Latour's (1988) critique of treating change as the successful implementation of strategy.

9. Mosco, who uses the notion of myth, rather than lived fiction, reaches similar conclusions: "Myths are not true or false, but living or dead" (2004, 3).

10. I thank Chandra Mukerji (2012, personal correspondence) for drawing my attention to how figured world theory also provides helpful tools for a material theory of politics, as well as Fernando Domínguez Rubio for helping me clarify the distinction between materiality as means and materiality as mediums.

11. Li's inspiration for the phrase *rendering technical* comes from Rose (1999) and Mitchell (2002).

12. Becker's notion has much in common with Li's (2007) notion of trustees. While Becker and Li's notions share much in common, Becker's seems more apt for describing the roles of elites in techno-philanthropism when there is a political crisis of authority. Trustees, as well as Li's notion of *the will to improve*, strike me as more apt for describing the role of elites when established authorities and institutions are fairly stable and secure. The position of the trustee is legitimated in terms of stewardship as well as incremental improvement, whereas moral entrepreneurs' demands are often urgent, fervent, and morally sanctioned. Li also includes bureaucrats and specialists as trustees, whereas I want to make a distinction between those who have the power to call for and support technophilanthropism and those who are tasked to design and execute it.

13. James Ferguson's account of the launch of a particular development project in the Thaba-Tseka district of Lesotho succinctly and evocatively describes this dynamic: "When the project set itself down in Thaba-Tseka it quickly found itself in the position not of a craftsman approaching his raw materials, but more like that of a bread crumb thrown into an ants' nest" (1994, 225).

14. Bourdieu's (1986) notion of *symbolic capital* has influenced my analysis of this dynamic.

Chapter 2: Cycles of Disruptive Fixation

1. Three of these students were born overseas (Ethiopia, Guatemala, and Cambodia) and then adopted by parents in the United States.

2. It is worth noting that while most of these families qualified as privileged compared to the overall population of the United States, let alone the world, in the context of the extreme economic inequality of New York City, there were many local families even more privileged than these families, in some cases, substantially so. In the context of this book I use the terms *privileged* and *less privileged* not as general sociological categories, but rather as relational categories that index the rather large differences in class conditions among the families who attended the Downtown School. In statistical terms, the distribution was bimodal.

3. As quoted in Buckingham (2007, vi). The original quote comes from Papert (1984, 38).

4. Quoted from Duguid (2015, 349).

5. See Corak (2006), Jäntti et al. (2006), Piketty and Saez (2003, 2006), Isaacs et al. (2008), Economic Mobility Project (2011), Hall (2011), Chetty et al. (2014).

6. Florida (2002) builds on ideas about knowledge work, the knowledge economy, and the new economy, all of which extend debates and concerns around the "post-industrial economy," announced by Bell (1973) and related works, such as Porat (1977). One of Florida's main contributions to this tradition was to emphasize the cultural dimensions of knowledge workers. Like Fred Turner's (2006) study of the countercultural roots of cyberculture, Florida emphasized the bohemian aspects of many knowledge workers. For a thorough review of scholarship on the knowledge economy, see Powell and Snellman (2004). For a review of recent scholarly interest in creativity and innovation, see Sawyer (2012). On creating makers, see Wagner (2012).

7. Which is not to suggest that all these local cases are the same or that they are all being caused by the same actors, forces, or processes.

8. On the limits of technological determinism, see Williams (1974), Escobar (1994), and Buckingham (2000). Critics of liberal presuppositions about schooling include Bourdieu and Passeron (1977), Bowles and Gintis (1976), Eckert (1989), Lamont and Lareau (1988), Lareau (2003), Varenne and McDermott (1999), and Willis (1977).

9. On historical rates of inequality, as well as the influence of World Wars I and II on international capitalist competitions see Piketty and Saez (2003) and Piketty (2014).

10. See "Educate to Innovate," on WhiteHouse.gov. http://www.whitehouse.gov/issues/education/k-12/educate-innovate.

11. For example, see Goldin and Katz (2008). See also Langdon et al.'s (2011) report for the US Department of Commerce, Economics and Statistics Administration, titled, "STEM: Good Jobs Now and For the Future."

12. These dynamics have long been studied and analyzed by science and technology studies scholars (Callon 1986; Akrich 1992; Latour 2005).

13. Progressive educational reform comes in many different forms, leading some analysts to suggest that it is a meaningless term. For a history of progressive versus traditionalist reforms, see Tyack and Cuban (1995), Ravitch (2000), and chapter 7 of Labaree (2004).

14. See, for example, the report *A Nation at Risk* (1983), treated by many as a canonical expression of this reactionary moment, which has carried on through reform policies such as No Child Left Behind. For an assessment of how progressive reformers were marginalized over the last several decades, see Hayes (2006).

15. Educational historian Diane Ravitch has famously taken both sides of this issue. Throughout the 1980s, 1990s, and early 2000s, Ravitch advocated for reforms based on test-based accountability and a marketlike choice and competition (Ravitch 2000). More recently, however, Ravitch (2010) has reversed course in the wake of the turn toward high-stakes testing as mandated by No Child Left Behind, a bill she helped bring into being.

16. For a review, see Ravitch and Viteritti, eds. (2000).

17.   For a review of the Children First reforms, see O'Day et al., eds. (2011) and Hill (2011).

18.   For a review see Jennings (2010) and Corcoran and Levin (2011).

19.   NCLB requires schools to make "adequate yearly progress," as measured against state-defined performance targets. Schools that fail to do so gradually lose their local monopoly. First, students are allowed to transfer to other schools and then educators and curricula can be replaced by higher-level bureaucrats; finally, higher-level bureaucrats can close and replace failing schools with alternatives, which could include charters or multiple small schools.

20.   On the wealth gap, see Paul Taylor et al. (2011). On stagnated wage growth, see Drew Desilver, "For most workers, real wages have barely budged for decades," published on October 9, 2014, by the *Pew Research Center.* http://pewrsr.ch/1tEMM7w.

21.   See for example, Lizette Alvarez, "States Listen as Parents Give Rampant Testing an F," in the November 9, 2014, issue of the *New York Times.* http://nyti.ms/1wJ8g8z.

22.   For a summary, see Gonzalez et al. (2010).

23.   These quotes are drawn from a report on the reformers' planning processes.

24.   The digital generation stereotype (Prensky 2001; Palfrey and Gasser 2008) is quite old now and yet it remains remarkably difficult to dislodge.

25.   On the recurring hopes that reformers attach to the new media of an era, see Cuban (1986, 1996, 2001) and Buckingham (2007).

26.   Shaffer (2006) calls these ways of thinking and acting epistemic frames. It is worth noting the emphasis on differences in *epistemic* modes as the basis for defining and distinguishing various communities of practice. Such an emphasis allows this version of techno-philanthropism to resonate with notions like knowledge workers and the creative class as idealized models of work and citizenship for the twenty-first century. It also allows situated theories of learning and knowledge (Haraway 1988; Lave and Wenger 1991) to be domesticated, albeit with good intentions, into the inherited institutional arrangements that these theories criticized.

Chapter 3: Spatial Fixations

1.   For a review of this scholarship, see Sefton-Green (2013).

2.   All these terms are popular in the learning sciences. For diverse examples of learning environments see Sawyer, ed. (2006). My use of these terms is intended as a mention-based reference to this discourse, but I do not use quotes repeatedly for the sake of readability.

3.   One of the ways that I negotiated access to the school was by agreeing to also work as a graduate student researcher on another project funded by the same philanthropic foundation that funded the Downtown School. That project attempted to form a learning network by getting various cultural institutions in New York City—from the Bronx Zoo to the Cooper Hewitt Design Museum to New York Public Library—to coordinate the ways in which they designed and offered programming for youth.

4.   See, for example, controversies over kindergarten access at lower Manhattan's coveted schools in Elissa Gootman, "New York's Coveted Public Schools Face Pupil Jam," *New York Times*, May 8, 2008- http://www.nytimes.com/2008/05/09/nyregion/09schools .html. For evidence that much of this strain on capacity has come from the influx of professionals, see Thompson (2008). Neighborhoods that were facing serious overcapacity problems include: Greenwich Village, the Upper East Side, the Upper West Side,

Brooklyn Heights, DUMBO, Downtown Brooklyn, and parts of Fort Greene. All are neighborhoods with high, and in many cases rapidly increasing, household incomes. The median
household income in Downtown Manhattan, for example, is twice as high as the median
household income in Manhattan as a whole; see Amanda Fung, "Downtown's Population
Boom Seen Rolling On." http://www.crainsnewyork.com/article/20100518/REAL_ESTATE/
100519839.

5.   The Civil Rights Project at UCLA has been tracking school segregation around
the country. See "New York State's Extreme School Segregation: Inequality, Inaction
and a Damaged Future." http://civilrightsproject.ucla.edu/research/k-12-education/
integration-and-diversity/ny-norflet-report-placeholder.

6.   As far as I can tell, there's no clear statement about exactly how this matching process works. Anecdotally, I heard school administrators mention numerous ways in which the
DOE shaped school admissions, looking at factors such as the percentage of students with
learning disabilities, the percentage of students who spoke English as a second language, and
so on. Some professional families complained that the DOE was "dumping" low-performing
students on the Downtown School, but I could find no evidence of such practices. I discuss
this sort of pollution rhetoric in more detail in chapter 6.

7.   One parent told me there were more than 3,000 applicants for one of these
schools. My research on the DOE website suggests that the number of applicants was closer
to 1,200.

8.   I also heard that one selective middle school had a relationship with NYU and
gave priority access to children of NYU professors.

9.   This stereotype about Asian parenting styles was pervasive, and it dovetailed with
Orientalist rhetorics that figure developing countries from Asia, and especially China, as
perhaps technically sophisticated but not innovative and creative like the West, particularly
the United States.

10.   Other scholars have also observed a similar process playing out, suggesting that
the sources of such practices are more structural. See, for example, Posey-Maddox (2014).

11.   While not explored extensively in this study, one unforeseen consequence of the
small school movement is that small schools are often unable to adequately accommodate
students who are legally entitled to accommodations under the Americans with Disabilities
Act. The problem, it seems, is that many small schools do not receive enough funding to
support the various specialists who work with students with different disabilities, and, as
such, parents of children with disabilities often find that they have to seek out schooling options that specialize in working with students who have similar disabilities to those of their
children. Several parents of children with various institutionally diagnosed disabilities chose
to leave the Downtown School after its first year for this reason.

12.   While I was unable to interview families who did not choose the Downtown
School, the school's demographic statistics suggest that the school's emphasis on games
and media production helped attract families with boys at a much higher rate than families
with girls. Indeed several families who did attend the Downtown School suggested that the
school's games and tech focus had been a deterrent to families with girls from their elementary schools.

13.   For a review of sociological scholarship on this topic, see the section on *sieves* in
Stevens, Armstrong, and Arum (2008).

14.   This shift corresponds to a decline in children and young people's independent
access to public space, the greater acceptance of women in paid labor markets, and increased
fears about stranger danger and other perceived threats to and by children and young
people. See Holloway and Pimlott-Wilson (2014) and Jenkins (1998).

15.   Tech-ed reformers and scholars make this school/not-school distinction in
all sorts of ways. Perhaps the most popular way to do so at the time of this study was the

distinction between formal and informal learning. The distinction also tends to map onto the traditional versus progressive distinction in pedagogic commitments, with supporters of progressive pedagogies often conflated with informal learning. For a review of formal versus informal learning see Sefton-Green (2004, 2013). For a criticism of this entrenched distinction see Lave (2011).

16. The term *geeking out* has become shorthand among educational reformers who aim to promote intense and committed engagement with new media technologies. I was a coauthor of the volume (Ito et al. 2010) that introduced the term as a normative goal within the world of education reform.

17. If so, this tendency would be in keeping with the long-standing tradition of gendering play spaces, and, in particular, the tendency of adults to exert more control over play spaces that have been specified for girls rather than boys. See Jenkins (1998) for a discussion of how this dynamic relates to video games.

18. Callon (1998) and Mitchell (2002) observe a similar phenomenon as economists render all of the residual factors that cannot be included in their models as "externalities."

Chapter 4: Pedagogic Fixations

1. Educational game designers refer to this form of "edutainment" as the "chocolate-covered broccoli" approach, a phrase whose origin is frequently attributed to Laurel (2001). What is puzzling is that the designers of the school knew about and even shared this critique of edutainment and yet they also appeared to believe that they were doing something more substantively transformative.

2. I find parallels between this management technique and the "scrum" and "sprint" techniques used in Agile software development. In both cases, managers impose an ambitious temporal constraint on collective tasks, and in doing so they can make the tasks feel urgent and important. As those who have worked in startups know, this feeling of being constantly rushed can be quite intoxicating and can help motivate employees. The original metaphor seems to have been taken from rugby, a highly physical and competitive sport that can evoke a similar rush among players.

3. Each Wednesday afternoon educators, school leaders, some of the school's designers, and often representatives from the school's SSO held a professional development session. While I was not able to observe these meetings, I noticed that all the educators would introduce a new technique at the same time, typically following a professional development session. I got the impression, confirmed in some informal conversations with educators, that professional development sessions were often a mechanism for distributing classroom-management best practices among educators. More experienced educators and school leaders appear to have introduced some best practices, but others appear to have come from the SSO. In subsequent conversations with educators from other schools, I have learned that many of these techniques are quite pervasive in contemporary urban public schools in the United States.

4. When the school moved into its new home, they were able to renovate some of these spaces, but they could not change basic architectural arrangements, such as classrooms.

5. In response to didactic and infantilizing lessons, students would often express solidarity with their peers by doing things like making eye contact and rolling their eyes, or, more confrontationally, by pretending for educators that they were in fact ignorant about the lesson, hence baiting educators to offer even more didactic instruction, a response that could delight other students when the educators took the bait.

6.   Anthropologists and qualitative sociologists have long observed such dynamics in the processes by which persons learn to become members of a social group. See, for example, Geertz (1972) and Weider (1974) as classic examples. Such rites of passage are especially common in tightly knit organizations like fraternities and sororities, boarding school, the military, and the police.

7.   See Stallybrass and White (1986), who drew on Mikhail Bakhtin. See also Taylor (2007), who drew on Victor Turner's (1969) analysis of relations between structure and antistructure in rituals.

8.   Anthropologists and cultural theorists have long drawn attention to the importance of these ritualistic stagings of group self-representation. My interest is in a variant of these stagings in which insiders present themselves as counternormative in moral terms.

9.   For a similar account of the production of effervescence in contemporary software production, see Fred Turner's (2009) analysis of relations between Burning Man and Google. Turner draws in part on Durkheim's famous analysis of the basis of religious feeling but argued that such ritualized practices are central to contemporary models of tech production. As already noted, such models informed the plans for the Downtown School.

10.   The phenomenology of these sorts of experiences has been documented in different disciplines and discourse communities, perhaps most famously in Csikszentmihalyi's (1990) notion of *flow*. The designers of the Downtown School referred to such experiences as "the rise," which has much in common with other notions that have recently become popular among tech-ed reformers, one of which, "geeking out," I helped propagate (see Ito et al. 2010). In the schooling context I see sanctioned counterpractices such as these as akin to the Friday night football games that constitute such an important community ritual at many more conventional American high schools.

11.   David Nye's (1994) historical study of what he calls *the American technological sublime* reaches a similar conclusion about the potential for new technologies to engender feelings of awe and belonging, but Nye focuses on the project of constructing an American national identity. In my case, the subliminal power of new technologies also contributed to reverent feelings of belonging, but with respect to the philanthropic initiative of which they were a part. See also, Leo Marx's (1964) discussion of the technological sublime as well as Vincent Mosco's (2004) analysis of the digital sublime.

Chapter 5: Amenable and Fixable Subjects

1.   Students' emic categories for peer formations varied from more neutral phrases like "a group of friends" or "a group of kids" to more critical terms, such as "pack", "gang," and "clique." I am using clique because it emphasizes the social boundaries produced by friendship groups.

2.   A great deal of scholarship on identity begins with an analysis of the semiotic systems or discursive regimes that produce the subject positions available to persons at a given historical moment. The approach I am advocating begins with social practices and locates the reproduction of discourse, representation, and subject position in people's ongoing practices. Under this framework, practices and semiotic systems are dialectically related in that practices draw on existing semiotic systems as they produce them anew. For a discussion of this relationship, see Lave (1988, 177–80).

3.   One of the ways I started to feel accepted by students was when they started inviting me to participate in these practices.

4. The students who attended the Downtown School are, of course, not representative of students in New York City more broadly since families had to opt into the school. As such, the student body, on average, was likely much more aligned with the school's distinctive focus than would have been the case if families had been randomly assigned to the school.

5. Pokémon, Bakugan, and Naruto are all references to transmedia phenomena—manga (comics), anime (animated television shows), video games, card games, and merchandise—that originated in Japan but now enjoy a transnational fan base, especially among young people.

6. Some students, such as Raka, wished to pick their own pseudonyms, which I have tried to honor, although doing so can create confusions for the reader. In this case, Raka, who was white, chose his pseudonym in reference to the satirist YouTube sensation that was popular among many of the members of his friend group at the time.

7. See also Michel de Certeau's (1984, 24–28) notion of "la perruque."

8. See Willis (1977) for an important rebuttal to structural accounts of social reproduction, all of which, in varying ways, gloss over the contested and, hence, uncertain ways in which people come to occupy positions in hierarchical social divisions. The process is by no means smooth.

Chapter 6: Community Fixations

1. I interpreted much of the put downs and teasing among clique members as status contests where one could win prestige by being able to effectively dish out teasing and put-downs while also appearing not to be affected when others attempted to return them. Clique members also policed each other. For example, when a student went too far and noticeably hurt someone's feelings they would often suggest that they were joking, or other members of the clique would push them to apologize.

2. Never once did I hear privileged parents or reformers suggest that these small acts of nonconformity were perhaps a way for members of nondominant groups to express their resistance to domineering conditions and institutions. See, for example, Scott (1985).

Chapter 7: Conclusion: The Resilience
of Techno-Idealism

1. My thinking in this section benefitted from the notion of *the well-intentioned beneficiary* in Bruce Robbins' (2016) essay "The Logic of the Beneficiary," published in *n+1*. Robbins defines the well-intentioned beneficiary as "the person who knowingly profits from a system she believes to be unjust" (24).

2. For example, at the Downtown School reformers responded to low rates of participation by girls in the school's after-school programs by diversifying their after-school offerings, and, in a related vein, by eventually dropping the tagline "a school for digital kids." All the same, the student body remains nearly seventy percent boys at the time of writing.

3. I thank my colleague Chandra Mukerji for suggesting the tidal metaphor.

Appendix: Ethnographic Fixations

1.   About halfway through the first year, some students started inviting me to be friends on sites like Facebook and YouTube. I had not anticipated these invitations and was initially unsure about whether to accept them. The policy I settled on was that I would accept invitations, but I would not initiate them. I also set limits on how I would engage with their online material. I felt that students were inviting me into their online social worlds much as they had at school, but I did not feel that they had invited me to systematically record and analyze every move they made on sites like Facebook. As such, I tried to interact with the students online much as I would with my other friends on social media: I checked out their profiles when we first connected online, I noticed their updates when they appeared in my news feed, and I would occasionally check their profiles if we had not seen each other in a while.

2.   Interviews with students were approximately forty-five minutes, and interviews with adults ranged from one and one-half hours to six hours, averaging around two hours. Media tour interviews were between one and two hours. Of the seventy-five students who attended the Downtown School in its first year, forty-three students (twenty-four girls and nineteen boys), twenty-two families (eleven of whom had daughters at the school), and five school staff, four of whom were teachers and one of whom was one of the school's founders, agreed to a semistructured interview. In terms of family members, I interviewed nineteen mothers, seven fathers, one grandmother, one aunt, one uncle, and one boyfriend of a student's mother. Additionally, I conducted countless ad hoc interviews with students, parents, educators, and reformers as part of my participant observation work.

REFERENCES

Akrich, Madeleine. 1992. "The De-Scription of Technical Objects." In *Shaping Technology/Building Society: Studies in Sociotechnical Change*, Wiebe Bjiker and John Law, eds. Cambridge, MA: MIT Press, 205–24.

Althusser, Louis. 1971. "Ideology and Ideological State Apparatuses: Notes Toward an Investigation." In *Lenin and Philosophy and Other Essays*. New York: Monthly Review Press, 127–88.

Ames, Morgan G. 2015. "Charismatic Technology." *Proceedings of the 5th Decennial AARHUS Conference*: 109–20.

Anderson, Chris. 2004. "The Long Tail." *Wired Magazine*, October.

Arendt, Hannah. 1961. "The Crisis in Education." In *Between Past and Future: Six Exercises in Political Thought*. New York: The Viking Press, 173–96.

Arum, Richard, and Josipa Roksa. 2011. *Academically Adrift: Limited Learning on College Campuses*. Chicago: The University of Chicago Press.

Aschoff, Nicole. 2015. *The New Prophets of Capital*. New York: Verso.

Becker, Howard S. 1963. *Outsiders: Studies in the Sociology of Deviance*. New York: The Free Press.

———. 1998. *Tricks of the Trade: How to Think about Your Research While You're Doing It*. Chicago: University of Chicago Press.

———. 2008. *Art Worlds*. 25th Anniv. Berkeley: University of California Press.

Bell, Daniel. 1973. *The Coming of Post-Industrial Society: A Venture in Social Forecasting*. New York: Basic Books.

Benkler, Yochai. 2006. *The Wealth of Networks: How Social Production Transforms Markets and Freedom*. New Haven: Yale University Press.

Berger, Bennett M. 2004. *The Survival of a Counterculture: Ideological Work and Everyday Life Among Rural Communards*. London: Transaction Publishers.

Bourdieu, Pierre. 1973. "Cultural Reproduction and Social Reproduction." In *Knowledge, Education, and Cultural Change: Papers in the Sociology of Education*, Richard Brown, ed. London: Tavistock Publications, 71–84.

———. 1977. *Outline of a Theory of Practice*. Cambridge, UK: Cambridge University Press.

————. 1984. *Distinction: A Social Critique of the Judgment of Taste*. Cambridge, MA: Harvard University Press.

————. 1986. "The Forms of Capital." In *Handbook of Theory and Research for the Sociology of Education*, John Richardson, ed. Westport, CT: Greenwood, 241–58.

Bourdieu, Pierre, and Jean-Claude Passeron. 1977. *Reproduction in Education, Society and Culture*. Beverly Hills, CA: SAGE.

Bowker, Geoffrey, and Susan Leigh Star. 1999. *Sorting Things Out: Classification and Its Consequences*. Cambridge, MA: MIT Press.

Bowles, Samuel, and Herbert Gintis. 1976. *Schooling in Capitalist America: Educational Reform and the Contradictions of Economic Life*. New York: Basic Books.

Brown, John Seely, and Paul Duguid. 2000. *The Social Life of Information*. Boston: Harvard Business School Press.

Buckingham, David. 2000. *After the Death of Childhood: Growing Up in the Age of Electronic Media*. Cambridge, UK: Polity Press.

————. 2007. *Beyond Technology*. Malden, MA: Polity Press.

Callon, Michel. 1986. "Some Elements of a Sociology of Translation: Domestication of the Scallops and the Fisherman of St Briuc Bay." In *Power, Action and Belief: A New Sociology of Knowledge?* John Law, ed. London: Routledge & Kegan Paul, 196–223.

————. 1998. "An Essay on Framing and Overflowing: Economic Externalities Revisited by Sociology." *The Sociological Review* 46: 244–69.

Carey, Kevin. 2015. *The End of College: Creating the Future of Learning and the University of Everywhere*. New York: Riverhead Books.

Carlyle, Thomas. 2000. *Sartor Resartus*. Berkeley: University of California Press.

Castells, Manuel. 1996. *The Rise of the Network Society*. Malden, MA: Blackwell Publishing.

Chetty, Raj, Nathaniel Hendren, Patrick Kline, Emmanuel Saez, and Nicholas Turner. 2014. "Is the United States Still a Land of Opportunity? Recent Trends in Intergenerational Mobility." 19844. NBER Working Paper Series. Cambridge, MA.

Christensen, Clayton. 1997. *The Innovators Dilemma: When New Technologies Cause Great Firms to Fail*. Boston: Harvard Business Review Press.

Christensen, Clayton M., Michael B. Horn, and Curtis W. Johnson. 2008. *Disrupting Class: How Disruptive Innovation Will Change the Way the World Learns*. New York: McGraw-Hill.

Chua, Amy. 2011. *Battle Hymn of the Tiger Mother*. New York: Penguin.

Clifford, James, and George Marcus, eds. 1986. *Writing Culture: The Poetics and Politics of Ethnography*. Berkeley: University of California Press.

Coleman, James. 1961. *The Adolescent Society: The Social Life of the Teenager and Its Impact on Education*. New York: Free Press of Glencoe.

Collins, James. 2009. "Social Reproduction in Classrooms and Schools." *Annual Review of Anthropology* 38(1): 33–48.

Committee on Prospering in the Global Economy of the 21st Century. 2005. *Rising Above the Gathering Storm: Energizing and Employing America for a Brighter Economic Future*. Washington, DC: National Academies Press.

Cook, Daniel. 2004. *The Commodification of Childhood: The Children's Clothing Industry and the Rise of the Child Consumer.* Durham, NC: Duke University Press.

Cookson, Peter. 1994. *School Choice: The Struggle for the Soul of American Education.* New Haven, CT: Yale University Press.

Corak, Miles. 2006. "Do Poor Children Become Poor Adults? Lessons from a Cross Country Comparison of Generational Earnings Mobility." 1993. IZA Discussion Paper. Bonn, Germany.

Corcoran, Sean P., and Henry M. Levin. 2011. "School Choice and Competition in New York City Schools." In *Education Reform in New York City: Ambitious Change in the Nation's Most Complex School System*, Jennifer A. O'Day, Catherine S. Bitter, and Louis M. Gomez. eds. Cambridge, MA: Harvard Education Press.

Corsaro, William. 2005. *The Sociology of Childhood*, 2d ed, Thousand Oaks, CA: Pine Forge Press.

Corsaro, William A., and Donna Eder. 1990. "Children's Peer Cultures." *Annual Reviews in Sociology* 16(1): 197–220.

Csikszentmihalyi, Mihaly. 1990. *Flow: The Psychology of Optimal Experience.* New York: Harper Collins.

Cuban, Larry. 1986. *Teachers and Machines: The Classroom Use of Technology Since 1920.* New York: Teachers College Press.

———. 1996. "Techno-Reformers and Classroom Teachers." *Education Week.*

———. 2001. *Oversold and Underused: Computers in the Classroom.* Cambridge, MA: Harvard University Press.

Cucchiara, Maia Bloomfield. 2013. *Marketing Schools, Marketing Cities: Who Wins and Who Loses when Schools Become Urban Amenities.* Chicago: University of Chicago Press.

Davis, Mike. 1990. *City of Quartz: Excavating the Future in Los Angeles.* New York: Verso.

de Certeau, Michel. 1984. *The Practice of Everyday Life.* Berkeley: University of California Press.

Deleuze, Gilles. 1992. "Postscript on the Societies of Control." *October* 59: 3–7.

DiMaggio, Paul J., and Walter W. Powell. 1983. "The Iron Cage Revisited: Institutional Isomorphism and Collective Rationality in Organizational Fields." *American Sociological Review* 48(2): 147–60.

Dourish, Paul. 2007. "Seeing Like an Interface." In *Proc. Australian Computer-Human Interaction Conference OzCHI*, 1–8. Adelaide, Australia.

Dreyfus, Hubert. 1991. *Being-in-the-World: A Commentary on Heidegger's Being and Time, Division I.* Cambridge, MA: MIT Press.

Duguid, Paul. 2008. "Community of Practice Then and Now." In *Community, Economic Creativity, and Organization*, Ash Amin and Joanne Roberts, eds. New York: Oxford University Press, 1–10.

———. 2015. "The Ageing of Information: From Particular to Particulate." *Journal of the History of Ideas* 76(3): 347–68.

Easterly, William. 2001. *The Elusive Quest for Growth: Economists' Adventures and Misadventures in the Tropics.* Cambridge, MA: MIT Press.

———. 2006. *The White Man's Burden: Why the West's Efforts to Aid the Rest Have Done So Much Ill and So Little Good*. New York: Oxford University Press.

Eckert, Penelope. 1989. *Jocks and Burnouts: Social Categories and Identity in the High School*. New York: Teachers College Press.

Eckert, Penelope, and Sally McConnell-Ginet. 1995. "Constructing Meaning, Constructing Selves: Snapshots of Language, Gender and Class from Belten High." In *Gender Articulated: Arrangements of Language and the Socially Constructed Self*, Kira Hall and Mary Buchholtz, eds. New York: Routledge, 469–507.

Economic Mobility Project. 2011. "Economic Mobility and the American Dream— Where Do We Stand in the Wake of the Great Recession?" Washington, DC.

Escobar, Arturo. 1994. "Welcome to Cyberia: Notes on the Anthropology of Cyberculture." *Current Anthropology* 35(3): 211–31.

———. 1995. *Encountering Development: The Making and Unmaking of the Third World*. Princeton, NJ: Princeton University Press.

Fassin, Didier. 2010. "Noli Me Tangere: The Moral Untouchability of Humanitarianism." In *Forces of Compassion: Humanitarianism Between Ethics and Politics*. Santa Fe, NM: School for Advanced Research Press, 35–52.

Ferguson, Ann Arnett. 2001. *Bad Boys: Public Schools in the Making of Black Masculinity*. Ann Arbor, MI: University of Michigan Press.

Ferguson, James. 1994. *The Anti-Politics Machine: "Development," Depoliticization, and Bureaucratic Power in Lesotho*. Minneapolis: The University of Minnesota Press.

Florida, Richard. 2002. *The Rise of the Creative Class: And How It's Transforming Work, Leisure, Community and Everyday Life*. New York: Basic Books.

Foucault, Michel. 1977. *Discipline and Punish: The Birth of the Prison*, 1st Amer. ed. New York: Pantheon Books.

Fung, Amanda. 2010. "Downtown's Population Boom Seen Rolling On." *Crain's New York*. http://www.crainsnewyork.com/article/20100518/ REAL_ESTATE/100519839.

Gee, James Paul. 2003. *What Video Games Have to Teach Us About Learning and Literacy: Revised and Updated Edition*. New York: Palgrave Macmillan.

———. 2008. "Learning and Games." In *The Ecology of Games: Connecting Youth, Games, and Learning*, Katie Salen, ed. The John D. and Catherine T. MacArthur Foundation Series on Digital Media and Learning. Cambridge, MA: MIT Press, 21–40.

Geertz, Clifford. 1972. "Deep Play: Notes on the Balinese Cockfight." *Daedalus* 10(1): 1–37.

Goldin, Claudia, and Lawrence F. Katz. 2008. "The Race between Education and Technology: The Evolution of U.S. Educational Wage Differentials, 1890 to 2005.". Cambridge, MA: Harvard University Press.

Gonzalez, Heather B, John F. Sargent Jr., and Patricia Moloney Figliola. 2010. "America COMPETES Reauthorization Act of 2010 (H.R. 5116) and the America COMPETES Act (P.L. 110–69): Selected Policy Issues." 7–5700. Washington, DC.

Gootman, Elissa. 2008. "New York's Coveted Public Schools Face Pupil Jam." *New York Times*.

Graham, Stephen, and Simon Marvin. 2001. *Splintering Urbanism: Networked Infra-structures, Technological Mobilities and the Urban Condition*. New York: Routledge.

Gupta, Akhil, and James Ferguson. 1992. "Beyond 'Culture': Space, Identity, and the Politics of Difference." *Cultural Anthropology* 7(1): 6–23.

———. 1997. "Discipline and Practice: 'The Field' as Site, Method, and Location in Anthropology." In *Anthropological Locations: Boundaries and Grounds of a Field Science*, Akhil Gupta and James Ferguson, eds. Berkeley: University of California Press, 1–46.

Hall, Stuart. 1981. "Notes on Deconstructing the Popular." In *People's History and Socialist Theory*, Raphael Samuel, ed, London: Routledge & Kegan Paul, 227–40.

———. 1987. "Gramsci and Us." *Marxism Today* June.

———. 2011. "The Neoliberal Revolution." *Soundings* 48(1): 9–28.

Halpern, Robert. *2003. Making Play Work: The Promise of After-School Programs for Low-Income Children*. New York: Teachers College Press.

Haraway, Donna. 1988. "Situated Knowledges: The Science Question in Femi-nism and the Privilege of Partial Perspective." *Feminist Studies:* 575–99.

Hart, Gillian. 2004. "Geography and Development: Critical Ethnographies." *Progress in Human Geography* 28: 91–100.

———. 2009. "D/developments after the Meltdown." *Antipode* 41 (S1): 117–41.

Hassrick, Elizabeth Mcghee, and Barbara Schneider. 2009. "Parent Surveillance in Schools: A Question of Social Class." *American Journal of Education* 115: 195–225.

Hayes, William. 2006. *The Progressive Education Movement: Is It Still a Factor in Today's Schools?* Lanham, MD: Rowman & Littlefield Education.

Hill, Paul T. 2011. "Leadership and Governance in New York City School Reform." In *Education Reform in New York City: Ambitious Change in the Nation's Most Complex School System*, Jennifer A. O'Day, Catherine S. Bitter, and Louis M. Gomez, eds. Cambridge, MA: Harvard Education Press, 17–32.

Hirschman, Albert O. 1970. *Exit, Voice, and Loyalty: Responses to Decline in Firms, Organizations, and States*. Cambridge, MA: Harvard University Press.

Holland, Dorothy, William Lachicotte, Debra Skinner, and Carole Cain. 1998. *Iden-tity and Agency in Cultural Worlds*. Cambridge, MA: Harvard University Press.

Holland, Dorothy, and Jean Lave. 2001. "History in Person: An Introduction." In *History in Person: Enduring Struggles, Contentious Practice, Intimate Identi-ties*, Dorothy Holland and Jean Lave, eds. Santa Fe, NM: School of American Research Press, 3–33.

———. 2009. "Social Practice Theory and the Historical Production of Persons." *Actio: An International Journal of Human Activity Theory* (2): 1–15.

Holloway, Sarah L., and Helena Pimlott-Wilson. 2014. "Enriching Children, Institutionalizing Childhood? Geographies of Play, Extracurricular Activities, and Parenting in England." *Annals of the Association of American Geographers* 104(3): 613–27.

Ingold, Tim. 2011. *Being Alive: Essays on Movement, Knowledge and Description*. New York: Routledge.

Irani, Lilly. 2015. "Hackathons and the Making of Entrepreneurial Citizenship." *Science, Technology & Human Values* 40(5): 799–824.

Isaacs, Julia B, Isabel V Sawhill, and Ron Haskins. 2008. *Getting Ahead or Losing Ground: Economic Mobility in America*. Washington, DC: Brookings.

Ito, Mizuko. 2008. "Introduction." In *Networked Publics*, Kazys Varnelis, ed. Cambridge, MA: MIT Press, 1–14.

———. 2009. *Engineering Play: A Cultural History of Children's Software*. Cambridge, MA: MIT Press.

Ito, Mizuko, Sonja Baumer, Matteo Bittanti, Danah Boyd, Rachel Cody, Becky Herr-Stephenson, Heather A. Horst, et al. 2010. *Hanging Out, Messing Around, and Geeking Out: Kids Living and Learning with New Media*. Cambridge, MA: MIT Press.

Ito, Mizuko, Kris Gutiérrez, Sonia Livingstone, Bill Penuel, Jean Rhodes, Katie Salen, Juliet Schor, Julian Sefton-Green, and S. Craig Watkins. 2013. *Connected Learning: An Agenda for Research and Design*. Irvine, CA: Digital Media and Learning Research Hub.

James, Allison, Chris Jenks, and Alan Prout. 1998. *Theorizing Childhood*. New York: Teachers College Press.

Jäntti, Markus, Knut Røed, Robin Naylor, Anders Björklund, Bernt Bratsberg, Raaum Oddbjørn, Eva Österbacka, and Tor Eriksson. 2006. "American Exceptionalism in a New Light: A Comparison of Intergenerational Earnings Mobility in the Nordic Countries, the United Kingdom and the United States." 1938. IZA Discussion Paper. Bonn, Germany.

Jenkins, Henry. 1998. "Complete Freedom of Movement: Video Games as Gendered Play Spaces." In *From Barbie to Mortal Kombat: Gender and Computer Games*, Justine Castell and Henry Jenkins, eds. Cambridge, MA: MIT Press, 330–63.

Jenkins, Henry, Katie Clinton, Ravi Purushotma, Alice J. Robinson, and Margaret Weigel. 2006. *Confronting the Challenges of Participatory Culture: Media Education for the 21st Century*. Chicago: The John D. and Catherine T. MacArthur Foundation.

Jennings, Jennifer L. 2010. "School Choice or Schools' Choice? Managing in an Era of Accountability." *Sociology of Education* 83(3): 227–47.

Jensen, Robert. 2007. "The Digital Provide: Information (Technology), Market Performance, and Welfare in the South Indian Fisheries Sector." *The Journal of Quarterly Economics* 122(3): 879–924.

Kelty, Christopher. 2013. "From Participation to Power." In *The Participatory Cultures Handbook*, Aaron Delwiche and Jacobs Henderson, eds. New York: Routledge, 22–32.

Koller, Daphne. 2012. "What We're Learning from Online Education." *TEDGlobal* 2012. http://www.ted.com/talks/daphne_koller_what_we_re_learning_from_online_education?language=en.

Kreiss, Daniel, Megan Finn, and Fred Turner. 2011. "The Limits of Peer Production: Some Reminders from Max Weber for the Network Society." *New Media & Society* 13(2): 243–59.

Kucsera, John, and Gary Orfield. 2014. *New York State's Extreme School Segregation: Inequality, Inaction and a Damaged Future*. Los Angeles: The Civil Rights Project at UCLA.

Labaree, David F. 2004. *The Trouble with Ed Schools*. New Haven, CT: Yale University Press.

———. 2008. "The Winning Ways of a Losing Strategy: Educationalizing Social Problems in the United States." *Educational Theory* 58(4): 447–460.

———. 2010. *Someone Has to Fail: The Zero-Sum Game of Public Schooling*. Cambridge, MA: Harvard University Press.

Lamont, Michele, and Annette Lareau. 1988. "Cultural Capital: Allusions, Gaps and Glissandos in Recent Theoretical Developments." *Sociological Theory* 6(2): 153–68.

Langdon, David, George McKittrick, David Beede, Beethika Khan, and Mark Doms. 2011. "STEM: Good Jobs Now and for the Future." ESA Issue Brief 03–11 Washington, DC: US Department of Commerce.

Lareau, Annette. 1987. "Social Class Differences in Family-School Relationships: The Importance of Cultural Capital." *Sociology of Education* 60(2): 73–85.

———. 2003. *Unequal Childhoods: Class, Race, and Family Life*. Berkeley: University of California Press.

Lareau, Annette, and Kimberly Goyette, eds. 2014. *Choosing Homes, Choosing Schools*. New York: Russell Sage Foundation.

Lareau, Annette, and Vanessa Lopes Muñoz. 2012. "'You're Not Going to Call the Shots': Structural Conflicts between the Principal and the PTO at a Suburban Public Elementary School." *Sociology of Education* 85(3): 201–18.

Lashaw, Amanda. 2008. "Experiencing Imminent Justice: The Presence of Hope in a Movement for Equitable Schooling." *Space and Culture* 11(2): 109–24.

———. 2010. "The Radical Promise of Reformist Zeal: What Makes 'Inquiry for Equity' Plausible?" *Anthropology & Education Quarterly* 41(4): 323–40.

Latour, Bruno. 1987. *Science in Action: How to Follow Scientists and Engineers through Society*. Cambridge, MA: Harvard University Press.

———. 1988. *The Pasteurization of France*. Cambridge, MA: Harvard University Press.

———. 2005. *Reassembling the Social: An Introduction to Actor-Network-Theory*. New York: Oxford University Press.

Laurel, Brenda. 2001. *Utopian Entrepreneur*. Cambridge, MA: MIT Press.

Lave, Jean. 1988. *Cognition in Practice: Mind, Mathematics and Culture in Everyday Life*. New York: Cambridge University Press.

———. 2008. "Epilogue: Situated Learning and Changing Practice." In *Community, Economic Creativity, and Organization*, Ash Amin and Joanne Roberts, eds. New York: Oxford University Press. 283–94.

———. 2011. *Apprenticeship in Critical Ethnographic Practice*. Chicago: University of Chicago Press.

Lave, Jean, and Etienne Wenger. 1991. *Situated Learning: Legitimate Peripheral Participation*. Cambridge, UK: Cambridge University Press.

Lefebvre, Henri. 1991. *The Production of Space*. Donald Nicholson-Smith, trans. Oxford, UK: Blackwell.

Lessig, Lawrence. 2007. "How Creativity Is Being Strangled by the Law." In *The Annual TED Conference*. Monterey, CA.

———. 2008. *Remix: Making Art and Commerce Thrive in the Hybrid Economy*. London: Penguin.

Lewis, Amanda E. 2003. *Race in the Schoolyard: Negotiating the Color Line in Classrooms and Communities*. New Brunswick, NJ: Rutgers University Press.

Li, Tania Murray. 1999. "Compromising Power: Development, Culture, and Rule in Indonesia." *Cultural Anthropology* 14(3): 295–322.

———. 2007. *The Will to Improve: Governmentality, Development, and the Practice of Politics*. Durham, NC: Duke University Press.

Lindtner, Silvia. 2014. "Hackerspaces and the Internet of Things in China: How Makers Are Reinventing Industrial Production, Innovation, and the Self." *Journal of China Information* 28(2): 145–67.

Lindtner, Silvia, Garnet Hertz, and Paul Dourish. 2014. "Emerging Sites of HCI Innovation: Hackerspaces, Hardware Startups & Incubators." In *Proc. ACM Conf. Human Factors in Computing Systems CHI'14*. Toronto, 439–48.

Long, Heather. 2015. "Is College Worth It? Goldman Sachs Says Maybe Not." *CNN Money*. http://money.cnn.com/2015/12/09/news/economy/college-not-worth-it-goldman/index.html.

Marx, Leo. 1964. *The Machine in the Garden: Technology and the Pastoral Ideal in America*. New York: Oxford University Press.

McLuhan, Marshall. 1962. *The Gutenberg Galaxy*. Toronto: University of Toronto Press.

McGoey, Linsey. 2015. *No Such Thing as a Free Gift: The Gates Foundation and the Price of Philanthropy*. London: Verso.

Mehta, Jal. 2013. *The Allure of Order: High Hopes, Dashed Expectations, and the Troubled Quest to Remake American Schooling*. New York: Oxford University Press.

Mitchell, Timothy. 2002. *Rule of Experts: Egypt, Techno-Politics, Modernity*. Berkeley: University of California Press.

Morozov, Evgeny. 2013. *To Save Everything Click Here: The Folly of Technological Solutionism*. New York: PublicAffairs.

Mosco, Vincent. 2004. *The Digital Sublime: Myth, Power, and Cyberspace*. Cambridge, MA: MIT Press.

Mukerji, Chandra. 1989. *A Fragile Power: Scientists and the State*. Princeton, NJ: Princeton University Press.

———. 2012. "Space and Political Pedagogy at the Gardens of Versailles." *Public Culture* 24(3): 509–34.

National Commission on Excellence in Education. 1983. *A Nation at Risk: The Imperative for Educational Reform*. Washington DC: United States Department of Education.

Neff, Gina. 2012. *Venture Labor: Work and the Burden of Risk in Innovative Industries*. Cambridge, MA: MIT Press.

Negroponte, Nicholas. 2006. "One Laptop per Child." *TED2006*. http://www.ted.com/talks/nicholas_negroponte_on_one_laptop_per_child?language=en.

Nelson, Margaret K. 2010. *Parenting Out of Control: Anxious Parents in Uncertain Times*. New York: NYU Press.

Norman, Donald. 1988. *The Psychology of Everyday Things*. New York: Basic Books.

Norman, Donald, and Stephen Draper, eds. 1986. *User Centered System Design: New Perspectives on Human-Computer Interaction*. Hillsdale, NJ: Erlbaum.

Nye, David E. 1994. *American Technological Sublime*. Cambridge, MA: MIT Press.

Ochs, Elinor, and Tamar Kremer-Sadlik, eds. 2013. *Fast-Forward Family: Home, Work, and Relationships in Middle-Class America*. Berkeley: University of California Press.

O'Day, Jennifer A., Catherine S. Bitter, and Luis M. Gomez, eds. 2011. *Education Reform in New York City: Ambitious Change in the Nation's Most Complex School System*. Cambridge, MA: Harvard Education Press.

Ogbu, John U. 1987. "Variability in Minority School Performance: A Problem in Search of an Explanation." *Anthropology & Education Quarterly* 18(4): 312–34.

Orr, Julian E. 1996. *Talking About Machines: An Ethnography of a Modern Job*. Ithaca, NY: Cornell University Press.

Palfrey, John, and Urs Gasser. 2008. *Born Digital: Understanding the First Generation of Digital Natives*. New York: Basic Books.

Papert, Seymour. 1984. "Trying to Predict the Future." *Popular Computing* (October).

———. 1993. *The Children's Machine: Rethinking School in the Age of the Computer*. New York: Basic Books.

Pascoe, C. J. 2007. *Dude, You're a Fag: Masculinity and Sexuality in High School*. Berkeley: University of California Press.

Patall, Erika A., Harris Cooper, and Ashley B. Allen. 2010. "Extending the School Day or School Year: A Systematic Review of Research (1985–2009)." *Review of Educational Research* 80(3): 401–36.

Piketty, Thomas. 2014. *Capital in the Twenty-First Century*. Cambridge, MA: Harvard University Press.

Piketty, Thomas, and Emmanuel Saez. 2003. "Income Inequality in the United States, 1913–1998." *The Quarterly Journal of Economics* 118(1): 1–39.

———. 2006. "The Evolution of Top Incomes: A Historical and International Perspective." *American Economic Review* 96(2): 200–5.

Porat, Marc. 1977. *The Information Economy: Definition and Measurement*, Washington DC: Office of Telecommunications, US Department of Commerce.

Posey, Linn. 2012. "Middle- and Upper-Middle-Class Parent Action for Urban Public Schools: Promise or Paradox?" *Teachers College Record* 114(1): 122–64.

Posey-Maddox, Linn. 2014. *When Middle-Class Parents Choose Urban Schools: Class, Race, and the Challenge of Equity in Public Education*. Chicago: University of Chicago Press.

Powell, Walter W., and Kaisa Snellman. 2004. "The Knowledge Economy." *Annual Review of Sociology* 30: 199–220.

Prensky, Marc. 2001. "Digital Natives, Digital Immigrants." *On the Horizon* 9(5): 1–6.

Qvortrup, Jens. 1994. "Childhood Matters: An Introduction." In *Childhood Matters: Social Theory, Practice and Politics*, Jens Qvortrup, Marjatta Bardy, Giovanni B. Sgritta, and Helmut Wintersberger, eds. Aldershot, UK: Avebury, 1–24.

Ravitch, Diane. 2000. *Left Back: A Century of Failed School Reforms*. New York: Simon & Schuster.

———. 2010. *The Death and Life of the Great American School System: How Testing and Choice Are Undermining Education*. New York: Basic Books.

Ravitch, Diane, and Joseph P. Viteritti, ed. 2000. *City Schools: Lessons from New York*. Baltimore, MD: The John Hopkins University Press.

Resnick, Mitchel, John Maloney, Andres Monroy-Hernandez, Natalie Rusk, Evelyn Eastmond, Karen Brennan, Amon Millner, et al. 2009. "Scratch: Programming for All." *Communications of the ACM* 52(11): 60–67.

Robbins, Bruce. 2016. "The Logic of the Beneficiary." *n + 1* (24): 21–30.

Rose, Nikolas. 1999. *Powers of Freedom: Reframing Political Thought*. New York: Cambridge University Press.

Ross, Andrew. 2003. *No Collar: The Humane Workplace and Its Hidden Costs*. Philadelphia: Temple University Press.

Sabel, Charles F. 2005. "Globalisation, New Public Services, Local Democracy: What's the Connection?" In *Local Governance and the Drivers of Growth*. Trento, Italy: OECD Centre for Entrepreneurship, SMEs and Local Development, 111–31.

Said, Edward. 1978. *Orientalism*. New York: Random House.

Sandholtz, Judith Haymore, Cathy Ringstaff, and David Dwyer. 1997. *Teaching with Technology: Creating Student-Centered Classrooms*. New York: Teachers College Press.

Sassen, Saskia. 2001. *The Global City: New York, London, Tokyo*, 2d ed. Princeton, NJ: Princeton University Press.

Sawyer, R. Keith. 2012. *Explaining Creativity: The Science of Human Innovation*, 2d ed. New York: Oxford University Press.

Sawyer, R. Keith, ed. 2006. *The Cambridge Handbook of the Learning Sciences*. New York: Cambridge University Press.

Scott, James C. 1985. *Weapons of the Weak: Everyday Forms of Peasant Resistance*. New Haven, CT: Yale University Press.

———. 1998. *Seeing Like a State: How Certain Schemes to Improve the Human Condition Have Failed*. New Haven, CT: Yale University Press.

Sefton-Green, Julian. 2004. *Literature Review in Informal Learning with Technology Outside School*. Bristol, UK: Futurelab.

———. 2013. *Learning at Not-School: A Review of Study, Theory, and Advocacy for Education in Non-Formal Settings*. Cambridge, MA: MIT Press.

Seiter, Ellen. 1993. *Sold Separately: Parents & Children in Consumer Culture*. New Brunswick, NJ: Rutgers University Press.

———. 2008. "Practicing at Home: Computers, Pianos, and Cultural Capital." In *Digital Youth, Innovation, and the Unexpected*, Tara McPherson, ed. Cambridge, MA: MIT Press, 27–52.

Selingo, Jeffrey J. 2015. "Is College Worth the Cost? Many Recent Graduates Don't Think So." *The Washington Post*, September 30.

Sennett, Richard. 2006. *The Culture of the New Capitalism*. New Haven, CT: Yale University Press.

Shaffer, David Williamson. 2006. *How Computer Games Help Children Learn*. New York: Palgrave Macmillan.

Shaffer, David Williamson, Kurt R Squire, and James P Gee. 2005. "Video Games and the Future of Learning." *Phi Delta Kappan* 87(2): 104–11.

Shear, Michael. 2014. "Colleges Rattled as Obama Seeks Rating System." *The New York Times*, May 25.

Shirky, Clay. 2008. *Here Comes Everybody: The Power of Organizing without Organizations*. New York: Penguin Press.

Sims, Christo. 2012. "The Cutting Edge of Fun: Making Work Play at the New American School." PhD diss., University of California, Berkeley.

———. 2014a. "From Differentiated Use to Differentiating Practices: Negotiating Legitimate Participation and the Production of Privileged Identities." *Information, Communication & Society* 17(6): 670–82.

———. 2014b. "Video Game Culture, Contentious Masculinities, and Reproducing Racialized Social Class Divisions in Middle School." *Signs: Journal of Women in Culture and Society* 39(4): 848–57.

Snellman, K., J. M. Silva, C. B. Frederick, and R. D. Putnam. 2014. "The Engagement Gap: Social Mobility and Extracurricular Participation among American Youth." *The ANNALS of the American Academy of Political and Social Science* 657(1): 194–207.

Stallybrass, Peter, and Allon White. 1986. *The Politics and Poetics of Transgression*. Ithaca, NY: Cornell University Press.

Stevens, Mitchell L., Elizabeth A. Armstrong, and Richard Arum. 2008. "Sieve, Incubator, Temple, Hub: Empirical and Theoretical Advances in the Sociology of Higher Education." *Annual Review of Sociology* 34 (1): 127–51.

Strauss, Anselm. 1978. "A Social World Perspective." *Studies in Symbolic Interaction* 1: 119–28.

———. 1982. "Social Worlds and Legitimation Processes." *Studies in Symbolic Interaction* 4: 171–90.

———. 1984. "Social Worlds and Their Segmentation Processes." *Studies in Symbolic Interaction* 5: 123–39.

Suchman, Lucy. 2006. *Human-Machine Reconfigurations: Plans and Situated Actions*. 2d ed. New York: Cambridge University Press.

———. 2011. "Anthropological Relocations and the Limits of Design." *Annual Review of Anthropology* 40(1): 1–18.

Takhteyev, Yuri. 2012. *Coding Places: Software Practice in a South American City*. Cambridge, MA: MIT Press.

Taylor, Charles. 2007. *A Secular Age*. Cambridge, MA: Harvard University Press.

Taylor, Paul, Rakesh Kochhar, Richard Fry, and Gab Velasco. 2011. *Wealth Gaps Rise to Record Highs Between Whites, Blacks and Hispanics*. Washington, DC: Pew Research Center.

Thompson, E. P. 1967. "Time, Work-Discipline, and Industrial Capitalism." *Past and Present* 38: 56–97.

Thompson, William C. 2008. *Growing Pains: Reforming Department of Education Capital Planning to Keep Pace with New York City's Residential Construction*. New York: Office of the New York City Comptroller

Thorne, Barrie. 1993. *Gender Play: Girls and Boys in School*. New Brunswick, NJ: Rutgers University Press.

———. 2009. "'Childhood': Changing and Dissonant Meanings." *The International Journal of Learning and Media* 1(1): 1–9.

Tsing, Anna. 2005. *Friction: An Ethnography of Global Connection*. Princeton, NJ: Princeton University Press.

Turner, Fred. 2006. *From Counterculture to Cyberculture: Stewart Brand, the Whole Earth Network, and the Rise of Digital Utopianism*. Chicago: University of Chicago Press.

———. 2009. "Burning Man at Google: A Cultural Infrastructure for New Media Production." *New Media and Society* 11(1 & 2): 73–94.

Turner, Victor. 1969. *The Ritual Process: Structure and Anti-Structure*. Ithaca, NY: Cornell University Press.

Tyack, David B. 1974. *The One Best System: A History of American Urban Education*. Cambridge, MA: Harvard University Press.

Tyack, David B., and Larry Cuban. 1995. *Tinkering Toward Utopia: A Century of Public School Reform*. Cambridge, MA: Harvard University Press.

Varenne, Hervé, and Ray McDermott. 1998. *Successful Failure: The School America Builds*. New York: Westview Press.

Wagner, Tony. 2012. *Creating Innovators: The Making of Young People Who Will Change the World*. New York: Scribner.

Wajcman, Judy. 2007. "From Women and Technology to Gendered Technoscience." *Information, Communication & Society* 10(3): 287–98.

———. 2009. "Feminist Theories of Technology." *Cambridge Journal of Economics* 34(1): 143–52.

Warschauer, Mark, and Morgan Ames. 2010. "Can One Laptop Per Child Save the World's Poor?" *Journal of International Affairs* 64(1): 33–51.

Weber, Max. 1978. *Economy and Society: An Outline of Interpretive Sociology*. Berkeley: University of California Press.

Weider, D.L. 1974. *Language and Social Reality: The Case of Telling the Convict Code*. The Hague: Mouton.

Williams, Raymond. 1974. *Television: Technology and Cultural Form*. New York: Routledge.

Willis, Paul. 1977. *Learning to Labor: How Working Class Kids Get Working Class Jobs*. New York: Columbia University Press.

Zelizer, Viviana. 1985. *Pricing the Priceless Child: The Changing Social Value of Children*. New York: Basic Books.

INDEX
